Acheson and Empire

Acheson
and
Empire

*The British Accent in
American Foreign Policy*

John T. McNay

University of Missouri Press
Columbia and London

Library of Congress Cataloging-in-Publication Data

McNay, John T., 1957–
    p. cm.
    Includes bibliographical references (p.   ) and index.
    ISBN 0-8262-1344-8 (alk. paper)
    1. Acheson, Dean, 1893–1971. 2. Acheson, Dean, 1893–1971—Influence.
3. Acheson, Dean, 1893–1971—Political and social views. 4. Statesmen—
United States—Biography. 5. United States—Foreign relations—1945–1953.
6. United States—Foreign relations—1945–1953—Decision making. 7. United
States—Foreign relations—Great Britain. 8. Great Britain—Foreign relations—
United States. 9. Great Britain—Foreign relations—1945– 10. Imperialism—
History—20th century. I. Title.
E748.A15 M34 2001
327.73'0092—dc21
[B]   2001027550

Text design: Stephanie Foley
Jacket design: Vickie Kersey DuBois
Typesetter: BOOKCOMP, Inc.
Printer and binder: The Maple-Vail Book Manufacturing Group
Typefaces: Palatino and Stone Serif

For my mother
Mary "Sass" McEacheran McNay, 1920–1977

Contents

Acknowledgments

This book is the culmination of a great deal of work that began when I first entered graduate school at the University of Montana in 1990. There, at the University of Hawaii, and at Temple University, I have incurred countless personal and professional debts too numerous to mention in detail.

The person most responsible for my finishing this project, however, is Richard H. Immerman of Temple University. His unflagging support, steady encouragement, and infectious enthusiasm have meant a great deal to me personally and were essential to my progress. I have learned much from him. In addition to the great respect I have for him as a scholar, I also consider him a good friend.

A special notice should also be paid to the other distinguished historians who assisted me during my graduate career and have helped me since embarking on my career. Their investment of time and expertise has challenged my thinking and pushed me to produce better historical work. They include Russell F. Weigley, David Alan Rosenberg, James Hilty, Michael Mayer, Robert McGlone, Gary Hess, and Robert Jervis. Retired professor Idus Newby of the University of Hawaii deserves a special note of thanks for donating his time and considerable editing skills toward improving the final manuscript. I also appreciate the personal time and advice that Ambassador Mike Mansfield and Ambassador George McGhee offered to me. Needless to say, all these people have contributed to the virtues of this work but are not responsible for any shortcomings it may contain. Ambassador McGhee, in particular, disagrees with this study's conclusions.

My colleagues at Raymond Walters College of the University of Cincinnati have been uniformly supportive and understanding of my efforts, and I appreciate that very much. I continue to benefit by the support and encouragement of my former colleagues at Shippensburg and Cheyney Universities. I also appreciate the criticisms offered by the members of the Philadelphia International History Group.

Funding for this project derived from several sources including the History Department and Graduate School at Temple University, the Harry S. Truman Library Institute in Independence, Missouri, and the Center for the Study of Force and Diplomacy at Temple.

The professional and helpful staffs at the National Archives in Washington, D.C., the Public Record Office in England, and the Yale University Archives all contributed to the completion of this project. The staff at the Truman Library in particular lived up to their reputation in hospitality and expertise. The assistance of the Temple University Libraries and the University of Cincinnati Libraries, particularly the very helpful staff at Raymond Walters College, benefited me a great deal.

I am grateful to friends too numerous to mention for their support, advice, and willingness to talk about Dean Acheson. Their patience with my obsession, particularly in our evening sessions after our monthly James A. Barnes Club meetings in Philadelphia, has been appreciated.

The staff at the University of Missouri Press, in addition to being skilled and professional, has been supportive and enthusiastic about this project, and I particularly appreciate the help of Maurice Manring who has overseen the transformation of manuscript into book. Further, I also appreciate the careful critiques of the manuscript made by the press's chosen professional reviewers.

In an odd sort of way, a grandfather whom I never met has had a significant influence on this book. Thomas McNay was a British subject who served for twelve years in the army, mainly during the reign of Queen Victoria. As a loyal "Tommie," he served the Crown in distant parts of the empire and was wounded during an engagement in the Boer War in South Africa. As I have considered Acheson's motivations in dealing with the imperial world, my own connections to that world have not been far from my mind.

Finally, none of this could have been possible without the love and support of my family, especially my parents, Mr. and Mrs. John T. McNay Sr. No one, however, would have found more pleasure in the publication of this work than my mother, the late Mary "Sass" McEacheran McNay. It is to her that this book is dedicated.

Acheson and Empire

Introduction

∞

Some of the recent trends in historical writing downplay the importance of individuals and ideas and stress instead the role of impersonal forces in history. Although that ordering of priorities has its justifications, this study will argue to the contrary of it. The fact that Dean Gooderham Acheson, rather than someone else, was secretary of state in the Truman administration mattered a great deal in the diplomatic history of that administration and in the international relations of the allied powers and their adversaries in the late 1940s and early 1950s.

Individuals make choices, and U.S. foreign policy did, in fact, change when Acheson entered and left high office. Human agency is an especially key factor in foreign policy making. Diplomacy, in the final analysis, is neither accidental nor impersonal; if it were, individuals would be absolved of responsibility for the policies they make. Although constraints on individual policy makers are often formidable, their decisions are never altogether predetermined. As two historians of American diplomacy have stated in another context, "Decisions were taken by fallible, flesh-and-blood human beings who faced real choices and who cannot be dismissed as mere chips on the tide of history."[1]

Historians as well as social scientists have recently given increased attention to the psychological dimensions of decision makers and decision making. Richard H. Immerman and many others have studied the impact of personality on policy. "Cognitive psychologists uniformly agree that once we have formed a belief we are reluctant to discard or even qualify it," Immerman has written. "New evidence will be interpreted to conform to our prior beliefs: If it is consistent with them, it will be accepted; if inconsistent or ambiguous, it will be discredited or ignored. This tendency is most pronounced when the belief is deeply felt and deeply held." Psychological theory can thus help us explain how and why decision makers decide as they do by providing, among other things, "clues for locating

1. Fred I. Greenstein and Richard H. Immerman, "What Did Eisenhower Tell Kennedy about Indochina? The Politics of Misperception," 587.

errors in perception and judgment." Memory theory is similarly useful. Individual memory is a lens through which experience is filtered and interpreted. "Autobiographical memory provides our sense of continuity and personal identity," Robert E. McGlone, a historian of memory, has written. "Memory is the compass of our actions."[2]

Together these sets of theory inform this study of aspects of the foreign policy of Dean Acheson, aspects that are especially illuminated by a worldview deeply rooted in Acheson's personal history. The study began as an inquiry into the issue of Irish neutrality in World War II and the cold war. I wanted specifically to understand why Eire rejected the U.S. invitation to become a charter member of the North Atlantic Treaty Organization (NATO). Was there a deeper reason than the logic of geography for the invitation itself, and for the published explanation that the Irish government could not join as long as Britain, a leading NATO signatory, occupied Ulster? Further, was the Irish request that the United States approach Britain about ending the occupation a meaningful diplomatic initiative, and was it given fair consideration by the United States?

The swift finality of the American rejection of the Irish initiative seemed hard to justify. The abrupt slamming of the door on the Irish after only a cursory discussion suggested that something more than the careful weighing of U.S. interests was involved. Pondering the matter, I looked into what Secy. of State Dean Acheson had had to say about it. Discovering that Acheson's personal and family roots were among Ulster Protestants, I wondered what, if any, influence that fact had had on his rejection of the Irish initiative. The seeds of this study were sown.

The study seeks to place aspects of Acheson's foreign policy in the context of his personal history. Its central argument is that as secretary of state Acheson adhered to a worldview that not only grew out of his Ulster heritage but also encouraged him to see international relations generally, and U.S. policy specifically, in terms derived from traditional British-style imperialism. This study tests that argument through an analysis of the triangular relationships among the United States, Great Britain, and each of four nations—Ireland, India, Iran, and Egypt—trying to escape British imperial control or influence during Acheson's tenure as secretary of state.

It contends that the widely accepted view that Acheson was a foreign policy realist is misleading and must be modified to take into account the influence of an "imperial paradigm" that gave many of his policy

2. Immerman, "Psychology," 161; McGlone, "John Brown's Family and Harper's Ferry," 52. See also Michael Kammen, *The Mystic Chords of Memory: The Transformation of Tradition in American Culture* and *In the Past Lane: Historical Perspectives on American Culture,* and Patrick Hutton, *History as an Art of Memory.*

decisions an "unrealist" rather than a realist character. Historians have overlooked this important element of Acheson's diplomacy, I believe, because they have overstressed the continuity of U.S. policy during the cold war era, and have fallen prey to Acheson's success in masking his imperial paradigm behind a veil of realist rhetoric.

An analysis of Anglo-American relations with the four nations just named will, I believe, substantiate these interpretations. Despite Ireland's minor role in cold war diplomacy, the story of its relationship with Britain in the Acheson years contains the keys to understanding Acheson's world-view and thus his diplomacy. Ireland is the most representative example of British imperialism, the island empire's first and last colony. There, the British first learned their imperial practices and attitudes, and it is there, in the postimperial world, the British have had the most difficulty extricating themselves. India was nearly as important in the British imperial experi-ence and in its role in Acheson's imperial vision, but for entirely different reasons. India's strategic and economic importance to the British made it the "jewel in the British crown," and Acheson's steadfast support of British policy there not only risked U.S. interests but also illustrated the lengths to which Acheson was willing to go with his imperial views.

The parallel record of Acheson's diplomacy involving two states in the Islamic world, Iran and Egypt, illustrates additional similar aspects of his imperial concerns. In Iran, a growing nationalist movement during the early cold war years sought to wrest the country and its oil resources from British control and influence. Although Acheson urged the intransigent British to compromise with the nationalists, his reluctance to challenge the British on fundamental imperial matters froze U.S. policy toward Iran in indecision. His objective in urging compromise was to maintain British control of the oil fields, a purpose that poisoned American relations with an important Islamic state, as a similar stance toward Egypt undermined American relations with—and interests in—another part of the Islamic world. In the face of ardent Egyptian nationalism, Acheson again urged the British to compromise, but only in ways that would maintain their control of Suez. His diligent support of the British and French in the Suez crisis in 1956, when he was no longer secretary of state, shows the extent of Acheson's commitment to imperialist, as opposed to realist, objectives. At the end of his life, Acheson was still advocating white imperial-style rule in other parts of Britain's imperial domain, this time in Rhodesia and South Africa, in order, he said, to preserve Western access to strategically important minerals in those states.

These aspects of Acheson's diplomacy, which I will document and analyze in this study, suggest that Acheson was not the realist he claimed to be or that most historians have said he was. On the contrary, on many issues that cried out for realistic approaches, Acheson practiced a diplomacy that incorporated a nostalgic, romantic admiration for empire. That this was the case, and that historians have overlooked it, suggests that in international politics, some idealisms may be more easily passed off as "realistic" than others. That may be especially true when the policies those idealisms propose coincide with the wishes or imperatives of self-professed "realists," whether in the foreign policy establishment or in academia, and the ease of doing so may be one of the consequences of the "swinging door" many individuals use in moving back and forth between the two arenas. In any case, realist historians and other students of cold war diplomacy have been able to divert criticism from policies they approve by touting the realism they ascribe to those policies. It may be time to reevaluate the powerful concept of realism by testing it against the actualities of the policies statesmen and historians have applied it to.

As secretary of state, Acheson unflaggingly supported the former imperial powers, especially Great Britain, in policy matters with colonialist implications. Realist historians, as well as nonrealists who label Acheson a realist, have argued that close alliance with Britain was essential to the success of U.S. foreign policy in the cold war, whatever the cost. Anglo-American unity, they maintain, was necessary to counter the Soviet threat. There is much to be said for that view, but at some point the view itself must be weighed against U.S. interests in the postcolonial world that began to emerge in 1948 in the wake of Indian independence. When he became secretary of state in 1949, Acheson supported British policies to such an extent that many people in that world increasingly perceived the United States as little better than a front for British interests. Nationalists and anticolonialists around the world, including those in Ireland, India, Iran, Egypt, and elsewhere, petitioned the Truman-Acheson administration for help in resisting Britain and other imperial nations only to have their petitions resisted or rejected in the interest of shoring up imperial power. This not only contributed to the nonaligned movement among "third world" states, which was often critical of, and even hostile to, U.S. interests, but also generated and sustained a lingering bitterness toward the United States. In addition, by misleading the British about the potential long-term assistance inherent in a close Anglo-American alliance, London was encouraged to devote its increasingly precious resources to situations that were to a large extent unsalvageable.

These consequences were hardly intentional on Acheson's part; he was not consciously sacrificing U.S. interests to British prerogative. On the contrary, he was certain that what he did served not only American interests but the larger interests of Western civilization as well. Acheson was equally sure that U.S. and British interests in the cold war world were the same, a fact that explains the unprecedentedly close relationship he enjoyed with the British ambassador in Washington, Sir Oliver Franks. Acheson and Franks met regularly and privately at each other's homes. Franks became an unofficial member of the U.S. policy-making group, and, in Acheson's words, issues involving the United Kingdom were treated as if they were domestic matters. In this atmosphere, differences between American and British interests blurred, with some consequences to U.S. interests.

The kind of neoimperialism these circumstances permitted and encouraged separated Acheson from foreign policy realists. As demonstrated below, some of Acheson's basic policies are irreconcilable with realism. Michael Joseph Smith has noted that realism as a philosophy is notoriously difficult to pin down. However, all realists agree on the need to "accept and understand the world as it is" rather than as they would like it to be and insist that "this understanding provides the foundation" for their realist ideas and policies.[3] That is not a formulation that covers Acheson's policy toward the colonial world, where he shunned the nationalist movements then sweeping that world. Like it or not, Washington would eventually have to deal with those nationalist movements on terms it could not always control.

In an important study of the realists, Joel Rosenthal has singled out Acheson as the only one of the so-called realists who did not change his beliefs over the years, and this inflexibility was inconsistent with one of the cardinal principles Hans Morgenthau ascribed to realism. According to Morgenthau, "The realist saw the world as fluid, dynamic, and constantly changing. Time and place, as well as culture and context, were [thus] vitally important factors in the consideration of any problem."[4] Of course, Acheson did change some views—on the war in Vietnam, for example, but even on this disastrous issue the change was grudging and reluctant after years of resisting the facts of the situation.

3. Smith, *Realist Thought from Weber to Kissinger*, 1. Other important works on realism include several by George F. Kennan, including *American Diplomacy, 1900-1950, Russia and the West under Lenin and Stalin,* and *On Dealing with the Communist World.* See also Hans J. Morgenthau, *Politics among Nations: The Struggle for Power and Peace, Vietnam and the United States,* and *In Defense of the National Interest: A Critical Examination of American Foreign Policy;* Kenneth W. Thompson, *Political Realism and the Crisis of World Politics;* Niccolo Machiavelli, *The Prince and His Discourses* (New York: Modern Library, 1950); and Henry Kissinger, *A World Restored: Metternich, Castlereagh, and the Problems of Peace, 1812-1822,* and *Diplomacy.*
    4. Rosenthal, *The Righteous Realists*, 5.

Acheson's support for outmoded imperial relationships, like his reluctance to adapt to changing circumstances, grew out of his unrealistic universalism, his belief that the United States must craft a single foreign policy
for the whole world. This belief encouraged him to support imperial-
style relationships. Just as he would rightly attack those he believed to
be idealists for trying to impose their views on the world, Acheson, too,
tried to impose universal views on the world. Rather than the "pragmatic
realist" described by James Chace and other historians of Acheson's foreign policy, Acheson tried to put in place an ideologically based policy
in the colonial world based on preservation of imperial control during
his tenure of office. Acheson shared a Eurocentric viewpoint common to
realists, but he went beyond other realists in his efforts to preserve the old
system of empire. It is for this that I believe he is more aptly described as
a romantic imperialist.

The Truman Doctrine was the most striking of Acheson's departures
from realism. The doctrine was, of course, the product of joint endeavors,
but Acheson claimed it as his own and promoted it in sweeping, unrealistic
terms. After setting the process for the Truman Doctrine in motion, Acheson carefully pushed it toward completion. It was Acheson who asked
to speak at an important meeting with congressional leaders when he
believed Secy. of State George Marshall had not presented the argument
for aiding Greece and Turkey strenuously enough. "In desperation I whis-
pered to [Marshall] a request to speak. *This was my crisis,*" he wrote later.
"For a week I had nurtured it. These congressmen had no conception
of what challenged them; it was my task to bring it home."[5] Granted his
request to speak, Acheson outlined a scenario of world affairs rooted in his
personal views of imperial mission. The United States had a duty to defend
Western civilization against the Russian menace, just as Rome had once
defended civilization against barbarism. Not since Rome and Carthage
had the world been so divided, he argued, apparently forgetting for the
moment that he had used the same metaphor only two years earlier in
1945, though at that time it had been the Islamic world that played the role
of the barbarians. This kind of apocalyptic imagery was characteristic of
Acheson's thinking, and it appeared regularly in his writing and speaking.
The conceptions reflected deeply held beliefs stemming in large part from
his Ulster heritage.

---

5. Acheson, *Present at the Creation: My Years in the State Department,* 219. The most
thorough account of those event-packed days is Joseph M. Jones, *The Fifteen Weeks.* Although
Jones, who was a participant, is careful to recount that many people were involved at various
stages in the development of the Truman Doctrine, a careful reading will show Acheson
always guiding the process at crucial points.

In later years, Acheson defended his use of extreme imagery as necessary to convince legislators and the public that the policies he advocated were essential to the national interest. This was rationalization after the fact. Certainly, Acheson's apocalyptic images had some effect on isolationists, Asia-firsters, and budgetary conservatives, but Acheson was a man of principle who chose his words—and his metaphors—carefully. His talk of clashes between civilization and barbarism stemmed not from political expediency but from a worldview that encouraged that kind of thinking.

George Kennan was among the first to point out the problems realists saw in the Truman Doctrine. The language of the doctrine, Kennan later explained in his memoirs, "placed our aid to Greece in the framework of a universal policy rather than in that of a specific decision addressed to a specific set of circumstances."[6] This universalism expressed Acheson's idealism, and Kennan was not the only realist to be disturbed by it.

Morgenthau, the intellectual father of realism, also saw at once that the language of the Truman Doctrine violated the realist principles he espoused, and he expressed his concern. The problem for Morgenthau, as Michael Joseph Smith has pointed out, was the doctrine's sentimentalism. "The Truman Doctrine," Morgenthau wrote, "transformed a concrete interest of the United States in a geographically defined part of the world into a moral principle of worldwide validity, to be applied regardless of the limits of American interest and power." The language of the doctrine, Morgenthau also noted, failed to discriminate between "what is desirable and what is possible." Morgenthau knew that Acheson was responsible for the unrealistic nature of this and other policies of the Truman administration, but he did not know that fact was rooted in Acheson's romantic worldview. According to Smith, Morgenthau was troubled that Acheson seemed to accept the "realistic requirements of American foreign policy," but was nonetheless responsible for policies that were often sentimental or idealistic.[7] Still, Morgenthau admired Acheson as a statesman and was willing to excuse his lapses from what Morgenthau considered wise policy. He even praised the speech that Acheson made in 1950 to the National Press Club that supposedly omitted South Korea from the U.S. "defense perimeter," an omission that some believe may have influenced North Korea's decision to invade. Instead, Morgenthau praised the omission because he believed it "cut down—at least in

---

6. Kennan, *Memoirs, 1925-1950*, 320.
7. Smith, *Realist Thought*, 148, 117, 149. See also Morgenthau, *Politics among Nations*, 121.

words—the Truman Doctrine to the size of the national interest of the United States."[8]

The label of "realist" is useful to only a limited extent with regard to Acheson's policies toward Europe. When he ventured from Europe's shores, a nostalgic romance with empire colored his policies in a manner that did not serve U.S. interests. Some writers have been confused by his tactical choices in occasionally not siding with British policies. In fact, when the British were not living up to what Acheson conceived as their imperial obligations, he often strongly opposed their policies. This did not alter his overall strategic plan to maintain if not enhance imperial systems of control in the former colonial world. For example, he urged compromise on the British in Egypt and Iran not because he saw the justice of the arguments against Britain. Not at all. Rather, he saw compromise as the way to continue the British imperial presence in states where it was under fire. Preservation of the imperial power was the objective; compromise was the means.

Still, the complexity of Acheson's thinking has made him endlessly interesting to study. Despite his professed admiration for nineteenth-century diplomats, the statesman Acheson most admired was Cardinal Richelieu, the seventeenth-century architect of French power under Louis XIII. There are striking parallels between Acheson and Richelieu as stewards of their respective nations' foreign policies that warrant consideration for what they tell us about Acheson. Each man depended on the loyalty of his superior to maintain his position of power and influence under great criticism, and in turn demonstrated great devotion to his superior. Each was a power behind the scenes because his superior deferred to his judgment in the area or areas of his responsibility and prerogative. And given Acheson's Ulster heritage, he surely approved Richelieu's decision to turn away from Catholic Spain and pursue greater glory for France.

Acheson sought to live a life governed by honorable principles. Although some of these concepts led to his imperial paradigm, other principles led to his controversial but courageous defense of Alger Hiss. Whether in retrospect Hiss was innocent is irrelevant to the principled stand Acheson took. Maintaining that each person must judge the case by

8. It seems highly unlikely that Acheson was really trying to restrict the doctrine or that he was responsible for encouraging the North Korean attack. He was only repeating what Gen. Douglas MacArthur and others had been saying for some time. Further, it was not Acheson's purpose to change any policy through the address. As he himself wrote, he did not expect to be accused of "political innovation" in the speech (*Present at the Creation*, 355-58). James Matray supported this view in an address made at the annual conference of the Society of Historians of American Foreign Relations in Toronto, June 22-24, 2000.

his or her personal standards and principles, Acheson said: "For me there is very little doubt about those standards or those principles. I think they were stated for us a very long time ago. They were stated on the Mount of Olives and if you are interested in seeing them you will find them in the 25th Chapter of the Gospel according to St. Matthew beginning with verse 34." But Acheson was not done there. He later expanded on the point:

> There were also personal reasons for stating my attitude. One must be true to the things by which one lives. The counsels of discretion and cowardice are appealing. The safe course is to avoid situations which are disagreeable and dangerous. Such a course might get one by the issue of the moment, but it has bitter and evil consequences. In the long days and years which stretch beyond that moment of decision, one must live with one's self; and the consequences of living with a decision which one knows has sprung from timidity and cowardice go to the roots of one's life. It is not merely a question of peace of mind, although that is vital; it is a matter of integrity of character.[9]

Acheson went on to argue that the way he dealt with the Hiss situation "represented a tradition in which I had been bred going back beyond the limits of memory." Although the context differs, it is especially important to this study that Acheson himself recognized that the traditions he reflected were more than those of his personal experience. They were inherited understandings handed down through generations from Ulster, his ancestral home.

Regarding race relations, Acheson supported civil rights. He successfully petitioned the Maryland governor in 1963 for the lives of three young black men who had been sentenced to death for raping a white woman. Acheson argued that white men would not have faced the same punishment. Further, Acheson in retirement defended black protesters to Harry Truman and urged the former president to keep his less tolerant views to himself. There is much to admire in Dean Acheson, particularly today when honorable conduct by our public servants seems a rare commodity.

The most recent biography, *Acheson: The Secretary of State Who Created the American World*, by James Chace, is a finely written and informative contribution to Acheson studies, but it does not critically examine Acheson's record as secretary of state. And, in Frances Fukuyama's words, it does not "provide us with significantly clearer insight into the inner man."[10] Two

---

9. Acheson, *Present at the Creation*, 360-61.
10. Fukuyama, "A Moral Compass to the World," *New York Times Book Review*, Aug. 23, 1998, p. 6. See also Evan Thomas's review in the *Washington Monthly* (June 1998): 40-42.

earlier studies of Acheson's tenure as secretary of state, which appeared in the 1970s, are similarly limited. Both works, one by Gaddis Smith and the other by David S. McLellan, are warmly complimentary of Acheson and his policies, and both emphasize Acheson's role in mobilizing the Western powers against the Soviet threat. In these matters, the two studies are representative of the voluminous literature that explores all or parts of Acheson's role in the early cold war toward Europe.[11]

In another study, Douglas Brinkley deals primarily with Acheson's life after he left public office and taps sources that were not previously used, particularly Acheson's personal papers at Yale University.[12] Brinkley brings a largely uncritical eye to Acheson's work. His focus is on how Acheson attempted to remain in the policy-making arena after he left office rather than what Acheson believed and the nature of his diplomatic design.

Despite these studies' considerable value, and other broader surveys of the cold war, none of them attempts to link the Acheson who grew up a child of empire and champion of his beloved "Tommies," waited on by Irish servants in a Church of England rectory with the old man who supported the continuation of white minority rule in British Africa. The purpose of this study is to make that linkage clear.

Although I would not agree with the harsh language, it was this anachronistic attachment to empire that led the iconoclastic journalist I. F. Stone in June 1949 to contend, "What speaks through Acheson is no longer the free American spirit but something old, wrinkled, crafty and cruel, which stinks from centuries of corruption."[13] Stone's language is extreme as well as colorful. Yet, there is a kernel of truth to what he wrote. Moreover, the observation is evidence of Stone being, once again, ahead of his time in identifying the limitations of men in high office.

Thomas contends that Chace's study provides no new perspectives. What is needed for Acheson, he says, is a writer "who is willing to explore his subject's complicated psyche."

11. Perhaps the classic realist portrayal of Acheson is Norman A. Graebner, "Dean Acheson." Other biographical approaches include G. Smith, *Dean Acheson*, and McLellan, *Dean Acheson: The State Department Years*. More recent is John Lamberton Harper, *American Visions of Europe: Franklin D. Roosevelt, George F. Kennan, and Dean G. Acheson*. Harper emphasizes Acheson's Victorian qualities, but ignores his Irish Protestant background and its imperial implications.

12. Brinkley, *Dean Acheson: The Cold War Years, 1953–1971*. See also Brinkley, ed., *Dean Acheson and the Making of U.S. Foreign Policy*. These works focus more on what Acheson did than why he did it or the consequences. They also have a Eurocentric approach that slights the colonial world.

13. Stone, *The Truman Era*, 77.

1

Champion of Empire

∞

Nobody ever loses the stamp which the age of
youthful impressions has imposed on him.
—OTTO VON BISMARCK

In the twilight of the Victorian era, the British imperial government found itself engaged in a bloody struggle against insurgents in South Africa. In the Boer War, as the effort to put down the insurgency came to be known, settler farmers of German-Dutch ancestry battled British troops to a standoff, only to have the full force of the empire brought down on them in the spring of 1902. British forces did what was necessary to gain victory, including burning villages, herding people into concentration camps, and committing other forms of ruthlessness. The victory won the empire few admirers internationally, but one of those few was a boy in Middletown, Connecticut, Dean Gooderham Acheson, son of the local Episcopal priest. The boy had nothing but sympathy for the British and their empire, as he fondly recalled years later.

The nine-year-old Acheson's espousal of the British cause in the Boer War earned him the scorn of "erstwhile friends" in largely Irish Catholic Middletown. "Our appealing Tommies, Kipling's absent-minded beggars," Acheson recalled, were seen in pro-Boer Middletown as "bullies bent on crushing the sacred flame of liberty, as in Ireland, and starving women and children in 'concentration' camps."[1] This ill treatment at the hands of neighbors shattered Acheson's "innocent and eclectic enjoyment

---

1. Acheson, *Morning and Noon*, 11-12. The use of "Tommies" to refer to typical private soldiers in the British army has its origins in a story in the *Illustrated London News*, July 7, 1883. The story told of the return from India of Pvt. Tommy Atkins. In 1892, Rudyard Kipling generalized the term in his popular poem "Tommy," which contains the line: "God Bless you Tommy Atkins, We're all the world to you" (*Oxford English Dictionary*, vol. 18, 2d ed., pp. 213-14).

of nationalism," and the episode had an enduring impact on the impressionable boy. For one thing, it was *British* imperialism (which he labeled "nationalism") that inspired him and blended readily into his American identity. Acheson had theretofore had no experience "of public disapproval, the loneliness of a small minority, of how fierce nationalism [that is, the nationalism of his Irish Catholic neighbors] could be when aroused." The nationalisms he confronted as secretary of state were not expressions of the benign, preservative patriotism he read into the British actions in the Boer War, but manifestations of the "fierce," threatening assertiveness he encountered from his Irish Catholic neighbors and associated with the Boers. This episode was thus formative in the most fundamental sense. *Contempt* would be the best word to describe Acheson's opinion of the indigenous nationalist movements with which he had to deal as secretary of state in the colonial world.

The imperial vision that later contoured Acheson's foreign policy was thus rooted in early life experiences that gave him personal reasons for celebrating British imperialism. His lifelong allegiance to the empire explains his unprecedented relationship as secretary of state with British ambassador Sir Oliver Franks. Gaddis Smith, one of Acheson's biographers, has characterized that relationship as "the key to [Acheson's] handling of Anglo-American relations." Acheson's appointment books show that he saw Franks officially more often than he saw all other ambassadors together. He also saw him unofficially; the two men met regularly and informally in each other's homes. "We met alone, usually at his residence or mine, at the end of the day before or after dinner," Acheson later recalled. "No one was informed even of the fact of the meeting. We discussed situations already emerging or likely to do so, the attitudes that various peoples in both countries would be likely to take, what courses of action were possible and their merits, the chief problems that could arise." When it served their purposes, Franks and Acheson worked out unified strategies for approaching their respective governments on issues of mutual concern. The relationship eventually reached a point at which, in Acheson's words, "we thought of these relations and their management as part of domestic affairs." Paul H. Nitze, one of Acheson's closest aides in the State Department, later commented on this intimate relationship. "Dean Acheson and I had the highest confidence in [Franks's] character, intelligence and wisdom," Nitze recalled. "He considered him very much a member of our policy group."[2]

2. Smith, *Dean Acheson*, 144-45; Acheson, *Present at the Creation*, 423-24; Nitze to the author, Sept. 22, 1992. I have found useful Michael Hopkins's perceptive work on the Acheson-

What was it about Acheson that prompted him to identify so closely with the British ambassador to consider Anglo-American relations "domestic affairs," as if Britain were the forty-ninth state or the United States a part of the empire? Clearly, U.S. and British interests did not always coincide. Biographers and others have noted Acheson's Anglophilia and emphasized its influence on his foreign policy, but their explanations for it typically go little further than comments on his "British" demeanor and dress. They note his father's English birth and rise through the Episcopal priesthood to a bishopric. However, they ignore, or are unaware of, Acheson's Ulster heritage and his personal heritage in Britain's age-old "Irish problem."

Dean Acheson was born on April 11, 1893, in the rectory of Holy Trinity Episcopal Church in the small Connecticut community of Middletown. His parents, Edward and Eleanor Gooderham Acheson, were British subjects. Edward Acheson was an Episcopal priest, and Eleanor Gooderham was a Canadian whose family had made a fortune in the distillery business. Because of the wealth of the Gooderhams, the Achesons lived substantially beyond the means of a provincial minister's salary.[3]

From his early days, Dean Acheson was conscious of his ethnic heritage, and as an adult molded it to suit the identity he fashioned for himself. In an autobiographical work, *Morning and Noon,* Acheson omitted the fact of his father's English birth, and describes him instead as "the son of an Ulster-born, Scotch-Irish, professional British soldier" who had "a south-Irish mother from Cork, descendant of English settlers brought there by Henry II to live 'within the pale.'" The "dominant influence in the rectory" in which Dean Acheson grew up was thus "a British subject, with deep affection for Ireland, where he had spent long periods with his mother's people." This "affection" was molded by the context in which it developed, a context not unlike that of settler outposts in other parts of the British Empire. The affection was thus not for a free and independent Ireland but for the British suzerainty there. How this translated in the impressionable Acheson into attitudes toward the Catholic Irish is unclear. "After all, natives were natives," George Orwell once wrote of British attitudes toward the people of Burma, "interesting no doubt, but finally

---

Franks relationship presented as "Special Allies? Dean Acheson and Oliver Franks," at the Society of Historians and American Foreign Relations Conference at Toronto, June 22-25, 2000.

3. It is important to recognize the links between the Anglican/Episcopal church and empire. As one historian has noted, "When all is said, the nearest thing the Empire had to a religion of its own . . . was the rite of the Anglican Church, diffused in such mysterious ways across the World" (James Morris, *Heaven's Command: An Imperial Progress,* 334).

only a 'subject' people, an inferior people."[4] Acheson never candidly voiced such specific views toward the Irish masses or any other people, but in dealing with "native" nationalisms in high office, his actions seemed to reflect the kind of thinking Orwell described.

The loyalties of Acheson's mother were clear, too. Eleanor Gooderham Acheson, who had enormous influence on her son, was a devoted imperialist. "My mother's enthusiasm for the Empire and the Monarchy was not diluted by a corrupting contact with Canadian nationalism," Acheson later wrote. On the contrary, her enthusiasm "was renewed from the very headwaters when she went to boarding school in England."[5]

Acheson's exposure to imperialism and to concomitant views toward colonial peoples thus continued through his formative years. The rectory in Middletown employed two domestic servants, both Irish Catholics, and their presence must have ratified for young Dean the views his parents encouraged. Acheson remembered with fondness and easy familiarity Cazzie, the family cook, and her niece Maggie, the housemaid. Both women had poor command of English, and the "green" Maggie, just out of Ireland, amused the Acheson children by her inability to read well.

Still, "nationality was not a divisive notion" in the Acheson household. The United States was best in young Acheson's reckoning, though England and Canada "were very good too." Ireland, on the other hand, "half idyll and half-myth, of Cazzie's tales was so entrancing that no wonder she always cried over having left it." The Irish Acheson remembered from his formative years were perceived as romantic, foolish, and given to misrepresenting the truth, perceptions that may have influenced his judgment on Irish issues in later years. On Saint Patrick's Day, to humor Cazzie, Acheson's father would hang on the flagpole "a great green flag with a golden harp on it," and "all the local Irishmen would go by the house to take their hats off to it." As they did so, Acheson and his sister stood on the porch and shouted nonsensical phrases ending with "Erin go bragh," Gaelic for "Ireland forever." "Whatever our hearers thought it meant," Acheson wrote of this slogan of Irish nationalism, "it was to us the end of an incantation which we had to recite in unison before my father would produce from behind his back presents which he had brought us." Acheson's account suggests the slogan was meaningless to him but probably irrelevant to the Irish of Middletown as well, whose allegiance to Ireland, he suggests, was shallow and ephemeral. The important thing

---

4. Acheson, *Morning and Noon*, 9-10; Orwell, *Burmese Days*, 118.
5. Acheson, *Morning and Noon*, 10.

about the Saint Patrick's Day celebrations to young Acheson had been the green peppermint cookies that were their reward. The queen's birthday, in contrast, was a profoundly respectful occasion in the Acheson household, and young Acheson grasped the respectfulness. On that day, "the Union Jack flew from the flagpole," Acheson recalled, "and at dinner we were given a few drops of diluted claret with which we stood solemnly while my father said, 'The Queen,' at which we all said, 'The Queen,' too, and drank our claret."[6]

"All that I know I learned at my mother's knee and other low joints," a journalist quoted Acheson as saying to "a stranger in striped pants" who, at a diplomatic function, praised Acheson's achievements. Although no doubt said in jest, this old joke nonetheless makes the point that Acheson learned much of his perceptions of the world at home.[7] In another family memoir, *Acheson Country*, Dean Acheson's son David emphasizes the influence of these early experiences on his father's worldview. According to David, when his father was overly exuberant or angry, he was said by the family to be showing his "wild Ulster side," a phrase also frequently applied to Dean Acheson's father. David Acheson noted too his family's ancient links to Edinburgh, Scotland, where Achesons as early as the sixteenth century had a country place, called Gosford House, outside the city and two houses on the Royal Mile that runs between Edinburgh Castle and Holyrood Palace, the royal family's official residence in Scotland. One of the latter houses still bears the Acheson family crest. "That Acheson lineage is uncertain in its connection with our family," David Acheson wrote of the Edinburgh Achesons, but the family tradition maintained that one of its members, Sir Archibald Acheson, had helped James VI of Scotland secure the throne of England as James I, for which James rewarded him with "a considerable part of County Armagh in Ulster" and the title of earl of Gosford.[8]

Though the bloodline was undocumented, Dean Acheson grew up in a family whose tradition associated him with the British aristocracy, with service to the Crown, and the Ulster Protestant ascendancy. "Our immediate branch of the family, after many centuries in Scotland, migrated to Ulster in the time of James I," Acheson wrote in 1950. "My grandfather, Alexander Acheson, went into the British Army shortly before the

6. Ibid., 10-12. Acheson does not translate the phrase "Erin go bragh."
7. From profile of Acheson by Joseph Hamburger, "Dean Acheson," *New Yorker*, Nov. 12, 1949.
8. David C. Acheson, *Acheson Country: A Memoir*, 29-30.

Crimean War and was stationed at the arsenal in Woolwich, England, at the time of my father's birth."[9] According to David Acheson, Alexander Acheson had been "a non-commissioned officer in the Royal Artillery, [and] fought with the Heavy Brigade at Balaclava in the Crimean War." The records of this service have been lost, but family tradition had it that Alexander was from County Armagh.

The most influential of Dean Acheson's forebears on his imperial thinking was his father, Edward Campion Acheson. Edward Acheson was born at Aldershot in Kent, England, in 1857, while his father, Alexander, was stationed at the Woolwich Arsenal near there. According to David Acheson, in the 1870s, Edward migrated to Canada, where he attended Queen's College and Wycliffe Theological Seminary in Toronto, taking time out to serve in the army during the Metis Rebellion in 1883. In that conflict, Edward's unit, the Queen's Own Rifles, was ambushed at Cut Knife Creek, and from the ensuing fracas, in David Acheson's words, "Edward emerged a national hero." According to an early historian of the rebellion, as the Queen's Own Rifles withdrew from a firefight, Edward Acheson and another soldier, Private Lloyd, undertook, under enemy fire, to recover the body of a slain comrade. In a "remarkable exhibition of heroism" during which Lloyd was seriously wounded, Acheson accomplished the recovery. "The enemy were at a moderately close range," wrote the historian of the incident, "and firing incessantly."[10]

This incident and Edward Acheson's heroism fit readily into the family tradition of the Achesons' place in the British imperial order. Settled chiefly in northern Manitoba along the Red and Assiniboine Rivers, the Metis were rough and ready frontier people who blended poorly into the rest of Protestant British Canada.[11] Ethnically part-Indian and part-European, culturally French, religiously Roman Catholic, the Metis spoke a patois that melded French, English, and native languages. Most white Canadians considered them rustic savages. The leader of the Red River Expedition in 1870, which preceded Acheson's arrival, was Col. Garnet Wolsey, an Anglo-Irishman who blamed the rebellion on Catholic priests who "openly preached from their altars resistance to the Canadian government." Even the flags the rebels carried, Wolsey maintained, "had been

9. Acheson to Mrs. R. A. Pritchard, Dec. 22, 1950, Dean Gooderham Acheson Papers, box 24, folder 307, Sterling Memorial Library, Yale University. Hereafter the entire Acheson collection at Yale will be referred to as the Acheson Papers.

10. C. P. Mulvaney, *The History of the Northwest Rebellion of 1883*, 169-71, cited in D. C. Acheson, *Acheson Country*, 31-33.

11. This is, of course, a problem faced today by the Quebecois.

made by nuns."[12] Surely, their Ulster Protestant heritage influenced the Achesons' reading of this incident, including Edward's role in it.

Dean Acheson's personal history was thus rooted in Protestant Ulster and in the historic struggle of the English and Scottish settlers to maintain control over the Catholic majority there and in the rest of Ireland. The very doggedness and durability of the Catholic Irish struggle for independence encouraged the Protestant settlers to regard the Irish as barbarous and uncivilized, whereas the impoverishment and cultural decay caused by English policy encouraged them to see the "natives" as backward and degraded. The result among Ulster Protestants was the sense of a civilization under siege, a sense that emerges again and again in Dean Acheson's words and thought. Long before Acheson's birth, this image had become an integral part of the Ulster Protestant worldview. Acheson once wrote that he supported a code of international conduct "based on the perceptions of what was decent and civilized."[13] His own perception of what that meant was filtered through his and his family's Ulster heritage.

The Irish historian Patrick Buckland has described the sense of imperial identity of Protestant settlers in Ulster in terms that seem applicable to Acheson and his heritage. "They resembled colonists in other parts of the world, such as Algeria or Rhodesia," Buckland wrote, "where settlers formed a compact and dominant minority determined in the face of local nationalisms to preserve their ascendancy, traditions, and feeling of community." Their own sense of nationalism was "hazy," Buckland continued; they were unable to regard themselves as altogether British, but they were certain of their separateness from the Irish. That was "why they identified so strongly with the Empire."[14]

Karl S. Bottigheimer, another historian of Ireland, has used the prism of Ulster Unionism—the view that Northern Ireland must remain a part of the United Kingdom, whatever the cost—in a way that enables one to see some of a worldview based upon it. To Ulster Unionists, according to Bottigheimer, the absorption of Ulster into Catholic-dominated Ireland would be "a lamentable step backward, a surrender of power and prestige to lawless and uncivilized Celts." Even Home Rule within the United Kingdom, a step far short of Irish independence, to the Unionists would have "meant turning the clock back by centuries," reversing the historic centralization of the British Isles under English leadership, and abandon-

---

12. Byron Farwell, *Queen Victoria's Little Wars*. For more on the rebellion, see Morris, *Heaven's Command*.

13. Acheson, *Morning and Noon*, 18. Also cited in Chace, *Acheson: The Secretary of State Who Created the American World*, 19.

14. Buckland, *A History of Northern Ireland*, 6.

ing the Ulster Protestants to "barbarous domination" by Irish Catholics. "In this Manichean view of the world as a ceaseless struggle between goodness and evil," Bottigheimer wrote, "Home Rule would amount to a triumph of Satan. Hence the passionate resistance of the Ulster Protestants and some of their brethren in England and Scotland."[15]

In a more recent study, two Irish writers, John McGarry, a Protestant, and Brendan O'Leary, a Catholic, reiterate these views. McGarry and O'Leary locate the wellspring of Ulster Unionism in "a profound contempt for Irish nationalism and Catholicism." As a result, Unionists proclaim "the merits of being part of a great imperial power as opposed to a small independent neutral nation," assume "British culture to be the acme of civilization and Irish culture to be the converse," assert "Protestantism to be incontestably superior to Catholicism," regard "Britain as the epicenter of genuine liberty, democracy and justice by contrast with benighted Ireland," and take "opposition to British institutions as a sign of ineffable backwardness, amorality, immorality, or cultural immaturity."[16]

These attributes of Ulster Unionism seem fatally compromised today, but as Karl Bottigheimer argued persuasively, Unionism was "a gospel of compelling force" around the turn of the twentieth century when Dean Acheson first encountered it. In the world of the young Acheson, the tenets of Ulster Unionism as well as the more expansive principles that under-girded English domination of Ireland resonated. Nothing in Acheson's education, first at Groton, which modeled itself on English public (that is, private) schools, and then at Yale, encouraged him to question those tenets. When twelve-year-old Dean entered Groton in 1905, he entered a society that reinforced his sense of social privilege and superiority. Near Boston, Groton had been founded by the celebrated Endicott Peabody, who sought to educate his charges for leadership and public service, and toward that end sought to inspire in them an aristocratic sense of noblesse oblige. The school's motto was *Cui Servivre Est Regnare,* "To Serve Him Is to Rule." Peabody softened the implications of this *regnare* (to rule) by emphasizing those of *servivre* (to serve); under his leadership, though, Groton prepared its students less for college than for positions of power and influence. This "temple of muscular Christianity," as it was popularly known, educated many of the future leaders of the foreign policy establishment of Acheson's generation, among them Franklin Roosevelt, Joseph C. Grew, Averell

15. Bottigheimer, *Ireland and the Irish,* 220-21. See also Morris, *Heaven's Command,* 162; R. F. Foster, *Modern Ireland, 1600-1972;* James G. Leyburn, *The Scotch-Irish: A Social History;* Bernard Porter, *The Lion's Share: A Short History of British Imperialism, 1850-1983;* Jonathan Bardon, *A History of Ulster;* and John Ranelagh, *A Short History of Ireland.*
16. McGarry and O'Leary, *Explaining Northern Ireland: Broken Images,* 121.

Harriman, and Sumner Welles, as well as Acheson, all of whom enrolled in the first decade of the twentieth century. They learned there, among other things, to conform to the ways of their position in the world and to appreciate the elevated nature as well as something of the responsibilities of that position. To one mother who pleaded with Peabody not to expel her errant son because he was a "very unusual" boy, Peabody responded, "Groton, madam, is no place for the unusual boy." "We knew that we moved in a world apart," one graduate later wrote of his experience at the school, "and always, of course, in a world above."[17]

Acheson learned these things well, for they reinforced what he had already absorbed at home. "The whole history of mankind," he wrote in 1950, "is full of instances where civilized people have been threatened by the onrush of masses who would overcome them by sheer numbers. So long as these civilizations have been virile, so long as they have used all their powers of mind and organization and production they have been more than equal to this threat."[18] This mushy formulation seems more akin to the social Darwinism of William Graham Sumner than to Peabody's noblesse oblige; nonetheless, the earliest surviving statement of the formulation is a poem Acheson wrote at Groton in 1906. Titled "The Combat," the poem relates the story of a contingent of Roman soldiers led by a consul named Horatius who encounters a band of barbarians on one of the bridges into ancient Rome. While a band played "The Star-Spangled Banner," discipline among the Romans broke down—the steadfastness of the soldiers and loyalty to their commander failed—because of which the soldiers are routed, Horatius is abandoned, the bridge is lost, and the barbarians pour into the city.[19]

A second poem, "Great Caesar," written about 1908, echoed these sentiments. In the opening stanza, Caesar, the conquering hero, lies basking in the glory of his conquests:

> A smile was on his sunburnt face
> He heard the name of "Caesar" spoke
> With awe and praise by every race
> He heard it ring from every tongue

17. Benjamin Welles, *Sumner Welles: FDR's Global Strategist*, 11-14. See also Chace, *Acheson*, 23-24. For more on Welles, see Irwin Gellman, *Secret Affairs: Franklin Roosevelt, Cordell Hull, Sumner Welles*; and Frank Graff, *Strategy of Involvement: A Diplomatic Biography of Sumner Welles, 1933-1943*.

18. Acheson Papers, box 47, folder 16. This paragraph is part of several pages of notes dictated by Acheson for possible use in speeches. The paragraph is crossed out and labeled "omit," but Acheson used the concept it expresses in many speeches.

19. The poetry is found in the Acheson Papers, box 46, folder 1.

From Gaul's fair plains to
Asia's strand.

Thus distracted by reverie, Caesar drops his vigilance, and a troop of Gallic barbarians surprises him. This time, however, there is no failure of loyalty among his soldiers, who, outnumbered, battle the barbarians to a standoff. Seeing his men hard-pressed, Caesar charges to their rescue, but has to be rescued by soldiers who ride to his side. Believing the rescuing soldiers are reinforcements, the Gauls flee, and Caesar is victorious:

And so his thoughts were not all dreams
His name was cried both far and wide
His honor sung in every town
His prowess praised on every side.

Acheson based these bits of juvenilia on "The Lays of Rome," by Thomas Babington Macaulay, one of the great men of Victorian letters—and imperialism. The example suggests the extent to which Acheson, and other schoolboys of his class and place, was drilled in Victorian, and thus imperialist, literature. Macaulay wrote "The Lays of Rome" while he was an imperial functionary in India in the 1830s. As president of the General Committee of Public Instruction in Calcutta, Macaulay had overseen the reordering of Indian education in the Raj to bring it in line with imperial needs. Borrowing phraseology earlier applied to another imperial reformer, one of his biographers has remarked that Macaulay's educational reforms "infused Oriental despotism [with] the spirit of British freedom." In India, the biographer added, Macaulay made a "constant study" of how to elevate the intellectual and moral character of Indians who fell under the purview of the school system he reformed.[20] That was the kind of reforming endeavor Acheson appreciated.

The subject matter of Acheson's poems reveals the classical content of his education. "I gained great pleasure and knowledge of English from the study of Greek," Acheson told a youth studying Latin in 1964, describing his own experience as a student, and "some, but less, of both from Latin. Greek really teaches one style and precision in expression. . . . Caesar, Virgil, Cicero, I found heavy; the Latin poets better. But Homer, Xenophon, Thucydides, the New Testament and, especially, the dramatists, have to be read in Greek to be appreciated."[21]

---

20. Jane Millgate, *Macaulay,* 64. See also Owen Dudley Edwards, *Macaulay,* and G. R. Potter, *Macaulay.*
21. Acheson to Gary A. Chilcott, Mar. 17, 1964, Acheson Papers, box 5, folder 57.

Endicott Peabody had been reluctant to admit Acheson to Groton, and while there Acheson had been an indifferent scholar and a bit of a rebel. Some historians have used these facts to suggest that Groton had little effect on Acheson the man. However, Acheson left Groton admiring and respecting Peabody, and had a lifelong involvement in Groton affairs. More tellingly, he sent his son David there, and gave every indication that his own education had lasting effects on his ideas and values. The love of the classics and of classical history nurtured there stayed with him, and he was always eager to draw parallels between the status and ultimate fate of the United States and ancient Rome. He often repeated Gibbonesque themes of empires declining and falling to barbarians—if not to Christians. Lyndon B. Johnson "seems to me to be almost fanatically preoccupied with Asia, particularly Southeast Asia, and particularly Vietnam," Acheson wrote in 1968, long after he left high office. "All questions, domestic and foreign, seem to have been subordinated to this all-absorbing peripheral war on the very outskirts of Empire. It is the kind of thing one reads about in Gibbon."[22]

Acheson was an avid reader, from the classics to Gibbon, and particularly of nineteenth-century British history and literature. He inherited his father's library, which was rich in British history and biography, including works by and about men he especially admired, such as Palmerston and Disraeli. In retirement, he enjoyed R. F. Delderfield's *God Is an Englishman*, and several books by G. M. Young, particularly *The Victorian Age*, a sympathetic portrait of the era. He recommended Alan Moorehead's uncritical study of British imperialism in Africa, *The White Nile*, as "an excellent book" and "a good introduction to Africa."[23] This praise of Moorehead's work is instructive for what it reveals of Acheson's mind-set. Moorehead's Africa was a world of European explorers bringing the blessings of imperial civilization to backward peoples. Mildly rebuking the racist views of explorers he otherwise admired, Moorehead finds "amusing" Richard Burton's remarks that Africans "seem to belong to one of those childish races which, never rising to man's estate, fall like worn-out links from the great chain of animated nature." Moorehead also quotes matter-of-factly such remarks of Burton's that "Eastern and Central intertropical Africa lacks antiquarian interest, . . . has few traditions, no annals, and no ruins," "contains not a single or ornamental work of art, a canal, or a dam," and "is, and ever has been, beyond the narrow bounds of civilization."

22. Acheson Papers, box 8, folder 107.
23. Acheson to Edward Burling, Feb. 2, 1953, Acheson Papers, box 4, folder 53; Acheson to James Robinson, Acheson Papers, box 24, folder 307.

As if to minimize the myopia of these attitudes, Moorehead added, "In fairness it has to be recognized that Burton was not a great shooter or killer of Africans." Moreover, Burton probably felt "more disgust than dislike" toward Africans, whom he believed lived in a "crude wilderness, where there was nothing to satisfy the requirements of a fastidious and sophisticated mind."[24]

In the same vein, Moorehead glorified Charles Gordon and described his ill-fated stand at Khartoum as a heroic moment in imperial history. Critical of the inadequate aid given to Gordon, Moorehead believed that a similar lack of resolve led Britain to the debacle at Suez in 1956. "The British invasion of Egypt in 1882," Moorehead wrote of the aftermath of Gordon's death, "bears a depressing resemblance to the abortive Anglo-French campaign on the Suez Canal in 1956, except that the earlier adventure was handled so much more efficiently and was successfully carried through."[25] Acheson has similarly argued that once the Anglo-French attack at Suez was launched, the United States had an obligation to make certain the British and French prevailed. He was therefore harshly critical of the Eisenhower administration's action in forcing the British and French to cease the attack and withdraw their forces.

Acheson studied history chiefly through biography, and seems to have sought in the biographies of great statesmen models for his own conduct in high office. He considered Plutarch's *Lives* flawed because Plutarch sacrificed factuality to moral instruction. Good biography, Acheson insisted, must put "a man in his historical setting and deal with the mutual effect [of the setting and the man] on one another." His favorite biographies included Sir John Neale's *Queen Elizabeth,* C. V. Wedgwood's *Charles I,* Winston Churchill's *Marlborough,* and David Cecil's *Lord Melbourne,* as well as Lytton Strachey's *Elizabeth and Essex* and *Eminent Victorians.* He also admired Page Smith's *John Adams,* Carl Sandburg's *Lincoln,* and Dumas Malone's *Jefferson.* What the subjects of these biographies had in common that appealed to Acheson was perhaps the breadth of their visions of England or America (or Anglo-America), the boldness with which they pursued their vision, and the success they achieved or the steadfastness of their adherence to principle in the face of defeat. Here as elsewhere, Acheson identified with winners, though, occasionally, with principled losers such as Charles I or "Chinese" Gordon.

After Groton, Acheson attended Yale, where his social success exceeded his academic achievement. Elected to Scroll and Key rather than the more

24. Moorehead, *The White Nile,* 32-34.
25. Ibid., 179-96, 199-213.

prestigious Skull and Bones, he nonetheless belonged to the elite world he deemed his proper place. His graduating classmates voted him the fifth "wittiest" and tenth "sportiest" of their numbers, and the prediction of his future in the class yearbook derived no doubt from the image he fashioned of himself: "Dean Acheson as missionary in British East Guatemala." Ironically or not, the editor of the yearbook added, "Who could ever conceive of Dean as a missionary either in or out of Guatemala?"[26]

The Yale experience not only strengthened Acheson's sense of social class but also reinforced his Anglo-American identity. Much of the Yale campus resembled an English aristocratic estate, and Acheson participated in the quintessentially English sport, rowing. The coach of the rowing team was Averell Harriman, son of Union Pacific railroad magnate E. H. Harriman and himself a Groton graduate. One of the highlights of Acheson's rowing career was a trip with Harriman to England in January 1912, ostensibly to study the methods of the Oxford rowing team. There, Acheson attended the Grand Challenge Cup race at Henley, reveled in the atmosphere of Oxford, and returned to Yale more sure than ever of the reality of Anglo-America.

Acheson graduated from Yale in 1916 and immediately enrolled at Harvard Law. There, he first became serious about his studies. "Excellence counted," he discovered; "a sloppy try wasn't enough."[27] At Harvard Law, Acheson fell under the influence of Prof. Felix Frankfurter, who helped him "discover the breadth of the human intellect." He later recalled:

> This was a tremendous discovery, the discovery of the power of thought. Not only did I become aware of this wonderful mechanism, the brain, but I became aware of an unlimited mass of material that was lying about the world waiting to be stuffed into the brain. It was just one step further to the philosophic approach to matters—to learning that you need not make up your mind in advance, that there is no set solution to a problem, and that decisions are the result of analyzing the facts, of tussling and grappling with them.[28]

It is worth noting that in this statement of his intellectual awakening Acheson remarked that an understanding of the world must be undergirded philosophically, that decisions should not be made in a vacuum

---

26. *The History of the Class of 1915*, vol. 1 (New Haven: Yale University, 1915), quoted in G. Smith, *Dean Acheson*, 5.
27. Walter Isaacson and Evan Thomas, *The Wise Men: Six Friends and the World They Made: Acheson, Bohlen, Harriman, Kennan, Lovett, McCloy*, 87.
28. Hamburger, "Dean Acheson."

or choices exercised arbitrarily. This insight informed his understanding of his own worldview, and remained with him throughout his career in foreign policy.

Acheson graduated fifth in his Harvard Law class, and Frankfurter recommended him to Justice Louis D. Brandeis as a law clerk. With Brandeis, Acheson began another relationship that had an enduring effect on his life. The two men became personal and intellectual friends. Through Brandeis, Acheson met other members of the Supreme Court, including Oliver Wendell Holmes; these three men, Frankfurter, Brandeis, and Holmes, constituted a triumvirate of advisers he consulted for decades.

Each of the three men influenced Acheson in his own way. Personally, Acheson was closest to Frankfurter, and after he became secretary of state, he and Frankfurter, now himself a justice on the Supreme Court, routinely walked to work together from Georgetown. The two made a striking pair, the tall and lean secretary of state and the shorter, stocky justice striding side by side, followed by Frankfurter's limousine when rain threatened. If the testimony of both men can be believed, they never talked politics. "We just talk," Frankfurter once said. As this suggests, Frankfurter's influence on the younger man was more inspirational than intellectual, serving chiefly, perhaps, to reinforce the views Acheson had when he first encountered Frankfurter.

Acheson, by contrast, held Oliver Wendell Holmes in awe. "I felt he had all knowledge in his head," said Acheson, who in his early years in Washington paid monthly calls on Holmes. Acheson admired Holmes as one of the great thinkers in American legal history, and was especially enamored of his concept of legal realism. Yet, Holmes seems to have functioned more as an idol Acheson admired than an intellect to be followed. That was the role of Brandeis, whose intellectual influence on Acheson was pervasive. During the two years that he worked as his law clerk, Acheson was impressed by Brandeis's willingness to appeal to transcendent moral principles in calculating the meaning of the law, a practice Acheson's own background and temperament encouraged and validated. Acheson later attested to the importance of Brandeis's influence by devoting an entire chapter in one of his autobiographical works to his experience as Brandeis's law clerk. He was "a man of impressive influence on all who came near him," Acheson wrote of Brandeis, crediting him with the character of an Old Testament prophet for his devotion to moral absolutes. At Brandeis's funeral in 1942, Acheson said of his apprenticeship, "These were years during which we were with the Justice and saw in action his burning faith that the verities to which men had clung through the ages were verities; that evil could never be good; that falsehood was not truth, not even if all the ingenuity of science reiterated it in waves that encircled the earth."[29]

By the time he said these words, Acheson was working his way into the upper levels of the foreign policy establishment. It is worth noting, therefore, that these words are not those of a realist. They are, however, consistent with a worldview rooted in Acheson's personal history. Acheson believed in universal truths, truths that grew out of his heritage and experience and had by 1941 matured into a comprehensive worldview.

By this time, too, Acheson had polished his personal style. Even at Yale he had been known for being well dressed, and thereafter his self-fashioning included meticulous attention to dress and appearance. As one writer put it, "His sartorial equipment stops just short of undue elegance," consisting almost invariably of pin-striped gray or blue suits, "ties with commanding, colorful diagonals," and "gray or black Homburgs." Equally important was the distinctive, well-clipped mustache that came to be as characteristic of Acheson's persona as Ike's smile, FDR's cigarette holder, and Churchill's cigar were of the personae of those men. "In the morning light, his big reddish-gray mustache is an object of remarkable distinction," one writer remarked while Acheson was secretary of state. "It has a personality of its own, and people who have happened by and seen Acheson emerge [from his home] in the morning have often experienced the disquieting illusion that two entities are on their way to work, the Secretary and the Secretary's mustache."[30]

Acheson was enormously proud as well as self-conscious of his mustache. It was, in the words of Philip Hamburger, "a major link to his past," a means of identifying with his father, the imperial war hero, who had worn "a Guardsman's mustache, thick and imperious, with a disdainful droop." Acheson first grew the mustache at Yale, "partly in defiance and partly out of respect for his father," and partly no doubt as an expression of who he believed he was and wanted to be. The mustache was even said to bristle when he showed his "Ulster streak."[31]

After World War I, Acheson joined the prestigious Washington law firm of Covington and Burling, where he prospered during a long association. His skills were showcased early, in 1922, when he assisted in a case before

29. Gary J. Aichele, *Oliver Wendell Holmes Jr.: Soldier, Scholar, Judge*, 152-66; Acheson, *Morning and Noon*, 102-3. In another context, Acheson argues that Brandeis is not interested in any "universal plumb plans." This should not be seen as appealing to a realistic approach (cited in G. Smith, *Dean Acheson*, 8-9). Rather, it simply reflects the belief shared by both men that most people lack the intelligence to change the world for the better.

30. Hamburger, "Dean Acheson," pt. 1, 38-40.

31. Ibid.

the World Court at The Hague involving Norwegian claims against the U.S. government for property seized during World War I. His thorough research and brilliant presentations in the trial became characteristic marks of his work as a lawyer.[32] Acheson, however, was always more interested in government—and power—than in law. In the Democratic administration that came to Washington in 1933, he became undersecretary of the Treasury, though he had hoped to be named to the higher-profile position of solicitor general. At Treasury, he had more than the usual responsibility of an undersecretary because of the failing health of Secy. William H. Woodin, but after eight months Acheson resigned because of differences of opinion with President Franklin D. Roosevelt over the latter's gold purchase plan. Acheson regarded the plan as unconstitutional. He returned to private law practice, but maintained his interest in politics, supporting Roosevelt's reelection in 1936 and 1940. In 1941, he returned to the administration as assistant secretary of state concerned chiefly with economic affairs, a position he held through the war. In 1945, he resigned the position but immediately thereafter succeeded Joseph C. Grew as undersecretary in the department. In the latter position he entered the highest level of foreign policy formulation and implementation.

To understand Acheson's role at that level, it is necessary to comprehend the worldview that informed his thinking about policy. To all matters involving imperial nations and colonial peoples, Acheson brought the Ulsterman's respect for established political forms and contempt for anyone who challenged these forms, especially subject peoples who resisted imperial domination. In high office, Acheson voiced these views only privately in correspondence or in carefully coded diplomatic language. "India rather appals [*sic*] me," he wrote in retirement to his friend Sir Patrick Devlin, who was then working to maintain white minority rule in Rhodesia. "One of my other prejudices is Indians. I know I ought to like them, and, indeed, have liked some. But by and large they and their country give me the creeps."[33]

Acheson's attitude toward "things [C]eltic" was likewise "rather low." "Should we go to Scotland? We have never been there," he wrote Devlin while he and his wife were contemplating a vacation. "So far Ireland seems to have absorbed all of Alice's enthusiasm for things [C]eltic; and mine is rather low." Whenever Acheson spoke or wrote of his family's generations in Ulster, he was careful to distinguish his ancestors from

---

32. The firm became known as Covington, Burling, and Rublee in 1921. For a good summary of the case, see Chace, *Acheson*, 52-56.
33. Acheson to Devlin, Mar. 18, 1959, Acheson Papers, box 7, folder 96.

the Catholic Celts. "My paternal grandparents came on one side from Scots transplanted to Ulster in 1603; on the other from English people transplanted to the pale by Henry II," he once wrote. "They never had a high opinion of the Celtic Irish." In differentiating his ancestors from the Celtic Irish, Acheson was representative of the Scotch-Irish in America. According to their historian, James Leyburn, the Scotch-Irish did not mind being called Irish "unless by that they were confused with the Catholic Irish."[34]

Given their long experience first with imperialism and then big-power exploitation, Latin Americans also fared poorly on Acheson's pecking order of peoples. In the early days of the Truman administration, according to an informant of journalist Drew Pearson, Acheson told jokes and "made sneering remarks in meetings about Latin Americans. Since the Latins, he said, were going to be with us anyway, why bother to help them? His jokes were repeated afterward at lunch. If the Latins had heard them, it would have been disastrous."[35]

Asked in 1962 to speak to a group of Asian and African diplomats, Acheson asked his longtime secretary, Barbara Evans, to consult the State Department on what he should talk about. After the consultation, Evans, who understood his contempt for many people in the colonial world, wrote Acheson, "Anything you have to say to junior and middle grade African and Asian career diplomats would be acceptable, regardless of whether it is in the curriculum or not. (I am quite sure [the State Department adviser] would withdraw his blanket approval if you said some of the things you would like to say to junior and middle grade African and Asian diplomats.)" Evans, after working closely with Acheson for years, was clearly aware of his feelings regarding the Asian and African nations. Such views gained Acheson friends among imperialists and white settler officials. One such friend was H. L. T. Taswell, the South African ambassador to the United States. "While your speeches always contain pungent and interesting remarks," Taswell wrote Acheson about one of his recent talks, "I was particularly amused by your simile: 'Like a cannon loose in an 18th Century ship of the line during heavy weather, the principle of egalitarianism can wreak considerable havoc to the crew without harm to the enemy.'" For years Acheson carried on a friendly correspondence

34. Acheson to Devlin, July 4, 1961, Acheson Papers, box 8, folder 97; Acheson to the Rev. Gerard Ferguson, Carrickmacross, County Monaghan, Ireland, undated but most likely early Apr. 1971, Acheson Papers, box 10, folder 127; Leyburn, *The Scotch-Irish*, 142-43.
35. Pearson, *Diaries, 1949-1959*, 10. Pearson's informant was his longtime friend George Bowden, a Chicago lawyer active in the Democratic Party. During World War II, Bowden had worked with Bill Donovan in the OSS.

with Sir Roy Welensky, prime minister of the white minority government of Rhodesia, referring in one of his letters to Britain's opposition to Welensky's government as "a mad policy" of the "demented" prime minister, Harold Wilson.[36]

Out of office, Acheson supported continued European domination of Africa. Not only did he defend white minority rule in Rhodesia and South Africa, but he also supported continued Portuguese control of Angola. "No sensible person can believe that African peoples can find their way toward a stabilized and civilized life without the help of the Europeans who know them best," Acheson wrote a Portuguese friend in 1961. Consistently critical of European nations that failed his test of beneficent imperialism, Acheson added: "The tragedy of the Congo is that due in large part to Belgium's own fault many Congolese lost faith in the Belgians."[37]

These attitudes should not be equated with hardened racism. Acheson was not as bigoted as were, say, the worst defenders of white supremacy in South Africa or the American South. He was instead a paternalist of the sort he understood Victorian imperialists to have been. Acheson supported the civil rights legislation Congress passed in the 1950s and 1960s and in his retirement years urged Truman to suppress his less tolerant attitudes toward African American protests. This and many other things suggest that Acheson's worldview incorporated not the kind of racism that historically characterized white treatment of blacks in the United States but the kind of social and political hierarchism that traditionally rationalized British imperialism, especially among men who viewed it at a distance. In 1963, to illustrate, Acheson urged Maryland governor J. Millard Tawes to commute the death sentences of three black youths recently convicted of raping a white girl. In similar cases involving white men, he pointed out, the death penalty was not imposed, raising "real doubt about the equality of justice." Commutation of the sentences "would be in the interest of our neighborhood and the relations of those who live there and are, in the main, successfully working out the problems of our common life. A sense of unequal treatment will inject new poison into that life and make heroes out of criminal offenders." When Tawes commuted the youths' sentences to life, Acheson praised him for doing

36. Evans to Acheson, undated, Acheson Papers, box 41, folder 38; Taswell to Acheson, Aug. 12, 1970, Acheson Papers, box 30, folder 385; Acheson to Welensky, July 11, 1968, Acheson Papers, box 33, folder 430.
37. Acheson to Pedro Pereira, Mar. 27, 1961, Acheson Papers, box 24, folder 311.

so.[38] The praise was consistent with his attitudes concerning European imperialism.

Acheson's Victorian concepts, including those related to British imperialism, played a large role in the way he understood the twentieth century. Given his personal heritage of Ulster and Ireland, it is a mistake for students of his foreign policy to ignore or discount these things. When Acheson spoke at a strategy seminar at the National War College in 1959, he was clearly, though perhaps inadvertently, describing his own Victorian worldview:

> One of the great troubles is that we don't see what is around us; we don't see it at all, because we look through eyes which we have inherited from our grandparents and great-grandparents.
>
> Our conceptions are 19th Century conceptions. We do not see the world in which we live. We see some other world. We live almost in the way which proves Bishop [George] Berkeley's conceptions that reality is subjective. . . .
>
> We look at the world through the conceptions and through the life of the 19th Century.[39]

In 1962, Acheson said much the same thing at the Truman Library: "We are nineteenth century people. Our minds are our great-great-grandmothers' and fathers' minds. We aren't twentieth century people. Our ideas are inherited ideas."[40]

Acheson made these remarks in an effort to make sense of the postwar world for his audiences, but the statements reflect a personal struggle to understand himself. Acheson often used examples from the nineteenth century to understand or explain circumstances in his own time. He believed, despite himself, that the political and social order he imagined Victorianism to have been resonated in the middle of the twentieth century. Without regard to the vast differences between the time periods, he could not help but believe that the system that prevailed in the earlier, simpler era offered an ideal for statesmen in his own day. "The idea of a world-wide consensus moved by Progress and Perfectibility toward peace, the rule of law and abolition of even the means of force," he wrote

38. Acheson to Tawes, May 21, 1963, Acheson Papers, box 30, folder 385. For more on Acheson's Victorian mind-set, see Harper, *American Visions.*

39. Acheson, National Strategy Seminar, National War College, Washington, D.C., July 21, 1959, Acheson Papers, series 3, box 50, folder 45.

40. Acheson, address at the Harry S. Truman Library Institute for National and International Affairs, Independence, Mo., Mar. 31, 1962, Acheson Papers, box 51, folder 54.

in 1961, looking back nostalgically to "the one world" he believed existed in the Victorian era. That idea, he continued, speaking of his own day, "persists like plants without roots which draw their nourishment from the air." International disorder had turned the idea into "a cruel hoax" in his own day; the old idea of a worldwide consensus had been displaced by "an unbridgeable conflict" between two sides in a new bipolar world Acheson himself had confronted in office.[41]

When Dean Acheson conceptualized the nation's foreign policy, it was in terms of imposing order on a disordered world. Foreign policy, he argued in 1954, should be at once unitary and global, as much a matter of strategy, security, and economics as of politics and diplomacy. "Do we cut the pattern according to the cloth," he asked himself on this subject, "or do we cut the cloth according to the pattern?" "The first requirement," he answered, "is that there must be a pattern." "Foreign policy in the East and in Western Europe cannot be separated," he said on another occasion, with the Korean War in mind. "We must have a single foreign policy for both sides of the world."[42]

This Achesonian ideal of "a single foreign policy," of "one world" as it were, contradicted the basic precept of realism. It grew out of Acheson's own experience and worldview, and his endorsement of it is a measure of the romanticism that characterized his approach to foreign policy. He derived the "one-world" ideal from his understanding of the nineteenth-century Pax Britannica, which had, unfortunately, he believed, been replaced by the two worlds he had to deal with as secretary of state. One of those worlds, led by the Soviet Union, was "revolutionary and hostile to every conception of constitutional order." Because of Soviet power, "there cannot be for many, many years, perhaps several generations, the sort of world that the nineteenth century was, and out of which have come most of our ideas" of how the world should be.[43] To restore that "sort of world" was the ideal to which Acheson committed U.S. foreign policy, despite the imperialism and Eurocentrism that had characterized it and the necessity he faced in the State Department of dealing with a postimperial world in which non-Europeans, such as Chinese on the world level and Indians, Iranians, Egyptians, and others on regional levels, were primary players

41. Acheson, "Fifty Years After," 4-5.
42. Acheson, "The Responsibility for Decision in Foreign Policy," 1-12; Memorandum of Conversation, Records of the Policy Planning Staff, 250/46/29/02-03/05, box 17. British officials present were Ambassador Sir Oliver Franks and from the Foreign Office, Sir Roger Makins and Robert Scott.
43. Acheson, address at the Harry S. Truman Library Institute for National and International Affairs, Acheson Papers, box 51, folder 54.

in international affairs. The failure to grasp the imperatives of this sea change for the receding fortunes of Britain and France and for the rising power of the United States as the superpower of the Western alliance in the cold war world is the source of the tragedy of Acheson's stewardship of U.S. foreign policy.

In his own manner and with his own understandings, Acheson recognized this. He understood that the day of nineteenth-century imperialism had passed. Yet, the niceties he thought had defined the imperial order and the relationships he thought had characterized it had, he believed, been admirable and efficacious forces in sustaining the harmonies that characterized the old order, and were thus worth the effort necessary to resuscitate them in the new order. That was why the actions of the Eisenhower administration against the British and French during the Suez crisis of 1956 so incensed him. When the Soviets or their proxies meddled in matters that concerned the Western powers and their client states, they did so without respect for the rule of law, and the Western powers had the right, and the obligation, under the rules of international conduct to do what was necessary to preserve order and protect their interests. This logic enabled Acheson to see Britain and France as injured parties in the Suez crisis, and to justify what they tried to do. It is foolish, he wrote in 1961 of the response of the Eisenhower administration to British and French aggression at Suez, "to condemn as wicked that kind of power which manifests itself in the launching of military force across the frontier of another state" while condoning the action of the state—Egypt in this case—that provoked it.[44]

Loyalty to allies, especially to the British but also to other Western imperial powers, was one of the basic concepts of Acheson's foreign policy. "Loyalty to allies is something which is fundamental to any decent people," he said in 1964. "I have often said that I do not think you can get much help on the substance of foreign policy from moral principles. I do think you can get help in behavior toward foreign countries from moral principles. And one moral principle is that loyalty is better than disloyalty." He also believed "that help to people who are struggling and who need help should be truly designed to benefit them."[45] In the abstract, such statements are difficult to contest, but abstractions do violence to the pragmatism prized by realists. To realists, loyalty is less valued than flexibility and what one might call ad hoc–ness in the pursuit of carefully

---

44. Acheson, "Fifty Years After," 4-5.
45. Acheson, speech to the Arkansas Bar Association, July 4, 1964, Acheson Papers, box 52, folder 62.

delineated interests. The *content* of the principles of Acheson's foreign policy and the *actualities* of his "behavior toward foreign countries" in the colonial and postcolonial worlds were, as this study demonstrates, anything but realist.

Acheson's lingering attachment to a romanticized vision of the "one world" of the nineteenth century, a world presided over by the European imperial powers, is one demonstration of that fact. To "the young, white, American male, life beckoned invitingly," Acheson told the Arkansas Bar Association of that world in 1964. "The hazards of which he was hardly aware, lay chiefly in sub-microscopic organisms which cut off life, in alcohol, and in the lottery of marriage. But these were traps for others. For him success and position were almost certainly the rewards of hard work, a modicum of virtue and discretion, and a little luck."[46]

As steward of U.S. foreign policy, Acheson saw himself as part of a historical continuum that went back to that bygone world. "What we do," Acheson wrote after he left office, "is as much a part of history as what our predecessors did." This historical sense, this consciousness of "the forces of history," encouraged Acheson to see the bipolar world that emerged after World War II, and that he confronted in high office, in more or less Manichaean and apocalyptic terms. "I think that the situation we are faced with in the world today has only been equaled once before, that I know of, in the history of the world," he told the Maryland Historical Society in late 1945. "That was the situation which occurred at the time of the Mohammedan conquests in the Mediterranean" during the Middle Ages. The "Roman world [had been] split into two," and the conquests "cut off practically all of the Eastern Empire and left [Christian] Byzantium alone." "All of the Eastern Mediterranean, all of North Africa and Spain were taken out of the Roman world. The Mediterranean itself ceased to be what it had been." As the Moors moved northward into "the Frankish Kingdom, towns dispersed because trade dispersed, and Europe was thrown back upon land and labor. . . . It took a thousand years to struggle painfully back."[47]

Acheson believed this situation was not unlike the one he perceived in the postwar world. Without American and British involvement and leadership, a new Dark Age threatened to descend on Europe. "New robber barons could exploit the situation of Europe more effectively than in the Dark Ages through using new ideas of organization such as fascism,"

46. Ibid.
47. Acheson to Edward Burling, undated but probably written in 1961, Acheson Papers, box 4, folder 53; Acheson Papers, box 46, folder 7.

he argued. He said of the situation then, in 1945, "improved tools of barbarism are at the disposal of the chieftain who would rule the isolated communities of the New Dark Ages," and should such a chieftain triumph, "it would take hundreds and hundreds of years of painful effort to regain worthwhile things in our civilization of free ideas, of liberty, and of the ability to live a little bit above the limits of mere subsistence."[48]

Two years later, Acheson pushed the precedents for this life-and-death struggle between civilization and barbarism back to the classical period, a conceptualization he borrowed from his late Victorian roots. "No such polarization of power as now exists in the world has existed since the time of ancient history," he told the American Society of Newspaper Editors in the spring of 1947 in defense of Truman Doctrine aid to Greece and Turkey. "Not since the period of Athens and Sparta and Rome and Carthage have there been only two great powers in the world." The same "challenging problem" existed in 1947 that existed in those earlier epic struggles between democracy and totalitarianism. In 1947 as then in a bipolar world, a great democratic power, "laying its stress upon the worth of the individual, the preservation of individual rights and individual enterprise, upon the belief that the state exists for the individual," was arrayed against "a police state exercising rigid control and discipline over the individual and operating on the principle that the individual is the servant and creature of the state."[49]

In reaching for a vision to guide him through this epic struggle, Acheson looked back to the romanticized understanding he had of the Victorian world order, an understanding rooted not in cold war realism but in British imperialism and the Protestant ascendancy in Ulster. "The 19th Century was most unusual," he told an audience at the National War College in 1961.

> There was the greatest absence of international war, inter-tribal war which has ever taken place in human history. [There] was probably in parts of the world greater economic movement than in all the prior history of man put together, including discovery of the wheel [and] the industrial revolution. . . . There was probably a greater freedom of movement and thought, goods and capital, than had ever taken place before or which perhaps takes place now. The world, in a curious way, partly by domination, partly by other means, seemed to be one world. This was all brought about, I venture to say, through the Concert of Europe, through the six great empires, European empires, whose

48. Acheson Papers, box 46, folder 7.
49. Acheson Papers, box 47, folder 11.

domination or control stretched over almost the entire globe. Not that
they controlled every part of it but their influence did.

Despite the problems with historical accuracies in this statement concerning, for example, the incidence of warfare and the number of "great"
European empires, the statement itself opens a revealing window onto
Acheson's thinking about world order, including the role of European
imperialism in fashioning and maintaining order in the world. The world
in the nineteenth century, he said in an equally revealing statement at the
University of Virginia in 1966, was characterized by

> more of an international order than at any time since or for more
> than a millennium before. . . . The Peace of Vienna brought about a
> durable concert of the great empires of Europe. Their colonial pos-
> sessions spread authority and sanction for order almost everywhere;
> and where their writs did not run their frigates and gunboats navi-
> gated. . . . The result was in large measure the maintenance of peace,
> security of person and property, respect for the obligation of contract,
> and greater economic development than in the whole period since the
> invention of sail and wheel.[50]

Acheson was eager to associate the United States with this tradition of
beneficent European power. He was highly critical of Charles de Gaulle
and others who would dissociate Europe from the United States. "Such a
notion, in my view, is the grossest error," he wrote in 1965. "The United
States is a European power. It is impossible for us to have 'extravagant concern for European affairs'—or for Europeans to have extravagant concern
with our affairs—because theirs and ours . . . are common concerns. . . .
We are irrevocably a European power." The Atlantic Ocean joined rather
than separated Europe and the United States in his creative geography,
just as the Mississippi River joined rather than separated New Orleans
and Memphis.[51]

History likewise joined the United States and Europe, not only in
conventionally cultural ways and in the recent experiences of World War II
and the cold war, but in the imperial "adventure" as well. The two decades
spanning the turn of the twentieth century, he told a National War College
audience in 1946, "was the period when the destiny of the United States,
the shadow of it, was thrown across the world, . . . a period when great
people went to the Philippines and took up there the task of leading the

50. Acheson Papers, box 53, folder 71.
51. Acheson, "Isolationists Are Stupid."

Filipinos to civilization and on to freedom. Cuba, Porto Rico [*sic*]—all sorts of problems were easy to take on because the manifest destiny of the United States would take us anywhere. It was a period of expansion, of big thinking, a period of adventure."[52] The historical amnesia this statement suggests concerning what might be called the downside of American imperialism was also an aspect of Acheson's mind-set.

Yet, Acheson was aware of that downside, as is frequently evident in his ruminations on the world order. "Of course, it will be said that I am talking the language of imperialism or colonialism or both," he told an audience at Cambridge University in 1957, "and that a policy of maintaining strength and unity at the center of the free world, as of first importance, will antagonize Asian and African peoples who, if we look at the future, should weigh more heavily with us than Europe." Critics who focus too exclusively on that part of the equation, he suggested, are shortsighted, and their shortsightedness causes unnecessary problems in U.S. and Western relations with "dependent peoples, newly come to manage their own affairs and those who aspire to do the same." If the experience of those peoples with America's European allies had sometimes been bitter, as he acknowledged that it had, they should in reacting to that fact contemplate the fate of other peoples whose experience had been with "imperialism in the Russian style."[53]

Undermined by World War I and effectively destroyed by World War II, the age of European imperialism had been "perhaps the most universal and impressive which this globe will see." Guiding the course of events in that world, the "great" empires of Europe had crafted "a balance of power and a truly wise order or system. . . . This created the peace, this made possible the economic progress, this made possible the 'one world.' "[54]

The purpose of this overview is to delineate the chief aspects of Acheson's mind-set that relate to the subject of this study, not to critique this picture of the Victorian world, which was central to that mind-set. However, because of the wide gap between that picture and the actualities of the Victorian world, a few comments on it are in order. All of us remember history selectively and pick from its vast store of facts, events, and understandings things that resonate for our being and purposes. What we reject or omit will be varied, for the selections will have policy implications. This was certainly true for Acheson's highly selective understanding of what he regarded as the golden age of international relations, an age for

52. Acheson Papers, box 46, folder 10.
53. Ibid.
54. Acheson, speech at Truman Library, Acheson Papers, box 51, folder 54.

him in which a few great statesmen in a few imperial capitals guided the world through what Acheson imagined as an era of peace, progress, and prosperity for the general benefit of mankind. That imagined world reflected his own time, place, and perspective, all of which encouraged him to see what he saw and miss what he missed.

Take, for example, the matter of peace. How could a man of Acheson's intelligence describe as even relatively peaceful the three or four generations from, say, the Congress of Vienna to the Boer War? To list only a few of the largest episodes that belie that description, one might point to the Mexican War, the Civil War, the perennial wars against the Plains Indians, the Spanish-American War, and the Filipino insurrection involving the United States; such major episodes in the British Empire as the Indian Mutiny and the Zulu and Boer Wars; the endless "incidents" across the European colonial world that went undignified by the label of "war"; and the Crimean and Franco-Prussian wars in Europe itself. For a man like Acheson, though, the era included no war that threatened the imperial system itself, and thus no war that interrupted "peace" as did World Wars I and II or that threatened peace as did the cold war. Any war, however "small," destroys or displaces someone's world, but none of the wars of the Victorian era threatened to destroy what Acheson considered more important, the Victorian world order itself. Yet, as one historian has noted, there was never a year in the long reign of Queen Victoria when British soldiers did not fight someone somewhere in the world, in what Rudyard Kipling called Britain's "savage wars of peace."[55]

A second reason for Acheson's myopic understanding of the Victorian world order was his inability to understand, to say nothing of empathize with, the peoples subjected to the European imperium, whether the Irish in Europe itself; the Indians, Arabs, Iranians, and others in civilizations advanced even by the standards of the most demanding Eurocentrist; or the peoples of smaller, often insular cultures, many of whom suffered catastrophically from the imperial incursion. Acheson seems to have had an inability, literally an incapacity, to comprehend the experiences of such peoples with imperialism, and thus their reactions to the continued presence of British (and other) imperialists while he was secretary of state. "There is an idea, I think a wholly wrong idea, abroad that people who have been oppressed throw off their aggressors and assume control of their own affairs. This, I think, is not true at all," Acheson said at the National War College in 1963. As the result of a failure of will among imperialists, "power [has] fallen from their feeble hands." He continued,

---

55. Quoted in Farwell, *Queen Victoria's Little Wars*, 1.

"It is obvious that colonialism is coming to an end, not because it is wicked, not because the powers in Africa or South Asia or East Asia, are going to seize their independence, but because nobody else has either the strength or the desire to continue to exercise colonial control." Anti-imperialism is thus "merely an attitude of the mind, and not a very sensible one at that. . . . Colonialism ended not because the colonial peoples became able to govern themselves and not because they had the strength to gain their own independence, but because rule fell from the enfeebled hands of the imperial powers of Europe and left the dependent people, unable to govern themselves, and in a most precarious and difficult situation."[56]

Independence for colonial peoples was thus not something that grew out of the emergence of the peoples themselves but something indigenous agitators demanded for selfish and shortsighted purposes. "For almost 50 years, the fires of revolution have been sweeping through Asia," Acheson told the National Press Club in 1950. "These fires had been smoldering slowly for centuries—and might have gone on smoldering—who knows how long?—if the idea of progress had not come, like a wind to fan them. The wind of progress blew from the west, and it brought to ever increasing numbers of people the bewitching idea that life could be better." It was this desire for the kind of material well-being associated with the West, and not political maturation, that encouraged "revolution" in the colonial world. "To millions in Asia," revolution "suggests simply food in their stomachs and a roof to crawl under out of the rain." Westerners who sympathized with the aspirations toward these goals framed their sympathies in ethical maxims that had the effect of disrupting the formulation of responsible foreign policy. "One of the most invoked and delusive of these maxims is the so-called principle of self-determination," Acheson said at the University of Massachusetts in 1964. This "moralistic" principle "is not merely no help to wise policy decisions, it can be a positive menace to them."[57]

In conclusion, then, Acheson's worldview was rooted in an imperial paradigm of how the world ought to be organized. Faced with the problem of realism versus idealism in U.S. foreign policy, Acheson opted to ridicule his critics and adhere to a nineteenth-century view of the situation— an outdated view that suggested the possibility that the United States could lose its European allies if it failed to support them in the colonial world. Although Acheson did not recognize it, this breakup of coalitions

56. Acheson Papers, box 51, folder 57; Acheson, address to the Arkansas Bar Association, July 4, 1964, Acheson Papers, box 52, folder 62.
57. Acheson Papers, box 47, folder 15; Acheson Papers, box 52, folder 62.

had also been plausible in the nineteenth century when relatively equal European powers jockeyed for position. However, Acheson's implication that in the bipolar post–World War II era the British or the French or other Western nations would cooperate in the breakdown of the NATO alliance because of a lack of U.S. support in the colonial world seems far-fetched. Not only do the aftermaths of the crises at Dien Bien Phu and Suez serve as evidence against this position, but so does the crisis over the French decision to create an independent military force in the 1960s. Further, it is also important to acknowledge that one of French president Charles de Gaulle's main problems with the North Atlantic Treaty Organization was the too cozy relationship between the "Anglo-Saxon powers," a partnership Acheson championed. Ironically, while arguing for unity between North America and Western Europe, Acheson's stress on the special relationship with Britain and its imperial connections contributed not only to problems in the colonial world but also to the greatest schism experienced by the alliance.

As one historian has written of Acheson's stewardship of U.S. foreign policy, his approach to cold war diplomacy "involved the twofold process of exploiting the [Soviet] threat in order to overcome the threat and to reconstitute the chaotic and demoralized Western state system."[58] That he extended that effort into the colonial world is a crucial but inadequately analyzed dimension of Achesonian diplomacy.

58. McLellan, *Dean Acheson*, 172.

2

The Special Relationship

∞

The "special relationship" with Britain was the central feature of Dean Acheson's foreign policy design. In separating that relationship from the larger one with Europe, in which context it was certainly valuable, and defining it to include the tottering British Empire, Acheson tied policy to a series of problematic enterprises. Given the imperial paradigm that dominated his mind-set, Acheson could never see the colonized peoples as autonomous historical agents or as potential allies in the bipolarized world he confronted as secretary of state. Britain and the states emerging, or trying to emerge, from imperial domination all suffered from Acheson's formulation of the special relationship: the one encouraged to hold on to the empire, the others discouraged from seeing the United States as an ally in their efforts to realize legitimate aspirations. The inevitable results were disappointment in Britain and resentment of the United States in the colonial world.

Yet, the specifics of the special relationship during Acheson's tenure in high office are relatively poorly documented. Despite its centrality to his foreign policy, Acheson said little and wrote even less about the relationship. The reason for this apparent anomaly is that Acheson considered the relationship too important to submit to political or partisan scrutiny and potentially too controversial to have its specifics or its implications spelled out for critics in or out of policy-making circles. He therefore kept silent about the partnership, even as he drew the two nations into tighter alliance in distant parts of the world. When members of his staff joined a Foreign Office group to craft a policy paper on the relationship for a London conference in 1950, an angry Acheson had all copies of the paper burned, and gave the Americans responsible for it "a thorough dressing down for their naivete." Writing about the Anglo-American relationship, he said, was "stupidity." "In the hands of troublemakers," he later wrote of the burned paper, "it could stir up no end of hullabaloo." Commenting on the incident years later, Acheson said, "Nothing ever seemed to me truer" than that the special relationship existed; likewise, "nothing has ever seemed to me more dangerous than talking about it, and certainly writing it down." He continued, "Over and over again there comes up this question of our special relationship with the British. It exists; it seems to me to be at the very heart of what we must do to try and hold the world together, but it seems to me to be more and more something you must know and never speak about."[1]

To avoid the mistake of believing that Acheson's Anglophilia was undistinctive among other American diplomats, one should listen carefully to British diplomat Sir Roger Makins, deputy undersecretary of state for foreign affairs from 1948 to 1952, later ambassador to Washington, and one of the most pro-American of British statesmen. "All through that period there was latent in many American minds—this feeling about colonialism—and how it was something quite contrary to American ideas and couldn't be supported," Makins later recalled of the Acheson era. "One often had the feeling that some Americans always saw a budding George Washington in every dissident or revolutionary movement. So there was undoubtedly that feeling. I think it would be difficult to gauge the precise effect it had, but that it was there I have no doubt whatsoever."[2]

The historian Warren Kimball and others have argued that when Franklin D. Roosevelt faced public opposition to his efforts to help the Allies and prepare the nation for entry into World War II, he turned to indirect methods of persuasion and manipulation to achieve his purpose. Acheson faced a parallel situation in moving the United States toward closer alliance with Britain. Like Roosevelt, Acheson faced political opposition and indifference; important elements of the American public and of the Truman administration resisted the kind of alliance with Britain he believed necessary for the security of both nations. Despite the resistance, Acheson clung steadfastly to his purposes, "always pulling policy," as Kimball said of Roosevelt and his advisers, in his direction "whenever the noise of other forces dies down."[3] Many of those purposes ran counter to administration policy, but Acheson's pursuit of them began even before he became secretary of state.

Acheson early demonstrated his commitment to policies favorable to Britain and its imperial interests while he was undersecretary of state. On

1. Acheson, *Present at the Creation*, 387-88; Lawrence S. Kaplan, "Dean Acheson and the Atlantic Community," in *Making U.S. Foreign Policy*, ed. Brinkley, 28-54.

2. Sir Roger Makins, Oral History, 8-10.

3. Kimball, *The Juggler: Franklin Roosevelt as Wartime Statesman*, 8. See also Robert Dallek, *Franklin D. Roosevelt and American Foreign Policy*.

January 20, 1947, Sir James Balfour of the British Embassy in Washington wrote to Neville Butler at the American desk in the Foreign Office that Cornelius Van H. Engert of the State Department was, at Acheson's direction, preparing a paper reviewing Anglo-American relations and pointing out areas in need of improvement. Engert, who knew Butler well, dropped by the British Embassy to talk informally about his report. "Engert," Balfour told Butler of their conversation, "said that, as one who was eager to do everything possible for the cause of Anglo-American relations, he had come to enquire whether there were any particular British desiderata which we might wish to bring to his confidential notice for the purpose of assisting him in presenting a balanced appreciation." According to Balfour, Engert asked if there was anything Balfour might "wish to bring to his special attention" off the record, and whether he would also put in writing "problems of a common interest in the security and economic field." Engert, who was preparing this paper "on a purely personal basis" at Acheson's direction, would, Balfour added, "respect our confidence if we decided to take advantage of this generous offer."[4]

This was not the first time Acheson had used Engert to further British interests. In the preceding autumn, as Balfour noted, Engert had used "background material which we gave him in a private talk about His Majesty's Government's position in the Middle East at a time when he was preparing, at Acheson's invitation [again], a paper on the strategic importance of that area to the United States." Engert, Balfour told Butler, "has been good enough to let us see this top secret paper which he told me had been entirely approved by the State Department who had shown it to the White House." Balfour sent on a copy of the paper to the Foreign Office, which appreciated Engert's cooperation but found it potentially troubling. "Mr. Engert is the most Anglophile member of the whole American foreign service," Wilson Young, an official there, wrote in sending Balfour's telegram to the prime minister, "to the point indeed of doing himself a disservice and of reducing the value which we might otherwise expect to obtain from such a friendly colleague."[5]

With Butler's assistance, Balfour promptly supplied the written report to Engert, who studied it with "great care" and "was filled with gratitude at this prompt answer to his request." Engert "asked me," Balfour told Butler, "to let you know how very deeply he appreciated the effort of yourself and others concerned in preparing what he rightly described as

4. Balfour to Butler, Jan. 20, 1947, Records of the Foreign Office, 60998/AN252/1/45, telegram 369, Public Record Office, Kew, England (hereafter cited as PRO).

5. Ibid.; Wilson Young to Prime Minister's Private Secretary, undated but probably about Jan. 25, 1947, Records of the Foreign Office, 60998/AN252/1/45, PRO.

'a masterly summary of your attitude.' " Engert also assured Balfour of his "utmost discrimination" in using the report. "Engert," Balfour added, "was particularly delighted by the phrase, which he said was the core of his own attitude to Anglo-American relations, that 'any decline in the position and prestige of the British Commonwealth will damage the common cause.' "[6]

Acheson shared this view of the Commonwealth. His choice of the Anglophile Engert to assess Anglo-American relations and recommend policy "improvements" shows how eager he was for the report, intended for Secy. of State George C. Marshall, to promote the special relationship. When it arrived in Marshall's hands, Acheson could independently endorse its findings and thus enhance its impact. This is just one example of many in the future in which Acheson encouraged the British to believe that it was possible that long-term U.S. policy could be established to support the empire. William L. Clayton, then assistant secretary for economic affairs, was among those in the State Department who recognized the shortsightedness of this. "The trouble with the British," Clayton wrote Undersecy. Robert Lovett in 1948, "is that they are hanging on by their eyelashes to the hope that somehow or other, with our help, they will be able to preserve the British Empire and their leadership of it." Instead of trying to save the empire, Clayton argued that Britain should, in its own interest, work to tie itself more closely to Western Europe. "Britain not only fails to do this but by her attitude is actually discouraging others," Clayton continued. "She refuses to take any step which might upset the preferential pattern of the Empire bloc." A frustrated Clayton concluded, "I think if we make it very clear to the British that, with complete cooperation on their part, we can possibly save them but that we cannot save their position as leader of the Empire bloc and do not intend to try, we will begin to see results in our herculean efforts to pull Europe out of the hole."[7]

The policy Clayton urged upon Lovett would, among other things, have turned the British toward free trade rather than imperial preference, but Acheson would have none of that. Joseph D. Coppock, an adviser on international trade policy from 1945 to 1953, for example, later remembered that "Acheson wasn't very much interested in economic issues." Acheson had been deeply involved in the Bretton-Woods talks and was certainly "conversant" with the issues. "But," Coppock maintained, "he did not give any particular attention to economic matters."

6. Balfour to Butler, Jan. 31, 1947, Records of the Foreign Office, 60998/AN252/1/45, PRO.

7. Clayton to Lovett, Sept. 17, 1948, Records of the Policy Planning Staff, RG 59, box 27, National Archives.

Coppock added that he was not alone in his belief. "Many people in the economic offices felt that Acheson tended to neglect the economic work," he recalled. As one of the architects of the Hoover Commission recommendations on government reorganization, Acheson had been, in Coppock's reckoning, largely responsible for changes that "decimated the economic offices" of the State Department. Leroy Stinebower, another State Department economist, shed further light on Acheson's views as they related to Britain's imperial trade. Contrary to Acheson's purposes, Stinebower said, the "voice of the Department as a whole was basically interested in a freely working trade economy, and trying to work for it pretty well up to the time I left [in March 1952]." However, free trade "didn't have the warm support of Mr. Acheson when he became Secretary of State." Stinebower said he preferred not to say that Acheson "sabotaged" free trade. "He just wasn't interested in it," he said, "and it suffered from the disinterest of the Secretary more than it did from open hostility." The result was a movement away from the established American support for free trade. Acheson stood in sharp contrast to the free traders, such as Cordell Hull and Will Clayton. Acheson "really didn't believe one bit" about this free-trade approach, Stinebower said, adding that Acheson "was terribly disinterested" in the many bilateral and trilateral trade talks then going on. "I can remember Dean saying, 'Oh, heck with it. Trade isn't important. Money is the important thing to make the international economy work the way you want it to work."[8] This stance, of course, favored British imperial interests. London at midcentury was still a center for international money lending, and much of its international power and influence benefited from that fact. Acheson would do nothing to jeopardize that power and influence.

Evidence of Dean Acheson's assumptions about the financial value of the British Empire in international affairs can be seen long before he became secretary of state. During his brief tenure at the Treasury in 1933, someone in the British Embassy in Washington made a shrewd evaluation of Acheson and noted his imperial sympathies. According to the evaluation, Acheson was a rising young lawyer who had already made such a good name for himself in legal circles that the Roosevelt administration had considered him for the position of solicitor general. "He has not much money and has no experience in finance," the author of the evaluation concluded, noting Acheson's close association with Justice Louis Brandeis, and "he probably owes his appointment [at Treasury] to the fact that he is a close personal friend of Mr. Lewis Douglas [later

8. Coppock, Oral History, 126-27; Stinebower, Oral History, 37-38, 12-14.

Acheson's ambassador to London], the director of the budget." Still, Acheson was "an intelligent, energetic and humorous man," and "well known to the Embassy, with whom he has always been on friendly terms."[9]

Acheson's admiration for Britain and its role in the world explains, at least in part, the stance he took during the controversy over currency reform in the early months of the Roosevelt administration. Roosevelt's reforms included abandonment of the gold standard and manipulation of the value of the dollar in order to inflate the depressed economy, both of which Acheson opposed and over which he resigned from the Treasury. Roosevelt's goal was to increase the purchase price of gold, which would then, he believed, cause prices to increase. Increased prices would help small farmers and producers across the country. Acheson's position in the controversy grew out of his conservative views on economic matters, which meant among other things that they coincided with the thinking— and the interests—of British financial and imperial circles. Britain, which had itself been forced to remove the pound from the gold standard from 1919 to 1925, opposed the removal of the gold base for currencies used in international trade because the use of that base functioned to enhance the value of the pound sterling and the centrality of British finance in the international economy. It also, coincidentally, helped prop up the empire. The British fears that Roosevelt's manipulations of the value of the dollar would adversely affect the international financial structure from which London benefited were valid. Further, as historian David Reynolds has observed, the gold standard had much to do with maintaining the image, if not the reality, of London as the imperial financial center.[10]

Acheson and others sympathized with British concerns in these matters not simply because of the British sentiments but also because they believed that Roosevelt's currency manipulations would be dangerous. In a radio address on world trade in 1945, Acheson looked back on the 1920s and 1930s as a period in which nations resorted to unsound monetary strategies, including Roosevelt's gold purchase plan to solve short-term problems at the expense of long-term financial stability. "Eventually, the gold standard collapsed in all but a very few countries," Acheson remarked, "and was replaced by a confused patchwork of currencies and exchange controls that played havoc with foreign trade." Yet, Roosevelt was focused on the domestic market and had been converted to the views of economist George F. Warren that prices would simply rise by

9. Records of Leading Personalities in the U.S.A., May 30, 1933, PRO.
10. Reynolds, *Britannia Overruled: British Policy and World Power in the Twentieth Century,* 105-6.

increasing the purchase price of gold. The program was rejected by most of Roosevelt's monetary advisers; undaunted, he went ahead with his plans but eventually appointed a committee to evaluate the situation. Dubbed the New York Group, its members included Acheson, the governor of the Federal Reserve, the director of the budget, and a pair of academic economists. The group rejected the theory behind Roosevelt's plan. It opposed unilateral monetary policy and entered a strong plea for international cooperation. As a first step, the committee, on which Acheson clearly played a powerful role, recommended that Britain's cooperation be enlisted. Roosevelt rejected the committee's recommendation and went ahead with the program in November 1933. Prices were not affected, but exchange rates fluctuated widely and government bond prices dipped sharply. In January, Roosevelt adopted a more permanent program with devaluation of the dollar but a fixed gold price. In the end, Roosevelt's attempt to do something for the farmers won him their strong support despite the lack of concrete price gains.[11]

In retrospect, Acheson's stance on currency reform seems unduly rigid from an economic standpoint and indifferent to the plight of most Americans during the depth of the Great Depression, the problem Roosevelt was trying to address. His stance was not sinister; he was not the calculated tool of international—or imperial—financiers selfishly defined. Acheson's convictions were instead those of the "hard money" orthodoxy that Roosevelt's Keynesian economics was in the process of displacing. Certainly, those convictions grew in part from, and expressed the interests of, the social and economic class with which Acheson identified himself. His own economic success did nothing to sensitize him to the social consequences of currency deflation during depressed times. In the context of this study, though, Acheson's role in the gold purchase imbroglio seems best understood as an illustration of his intellectual rigidity, his readiness to stand steadfastly to principles rooted in his mind in moral verities without regard to pragmatic considerations. This was in fact one of the taproots of the unrealism that later characterized his foreign policy, and it suggests that his support for Britain and the empire in that policy was rooted in intellectual convictions deeper in his personality than his admiration for Britain or the empire alone.

Acheson resigned from the Treasury over this dispute and returned to his private legal career in November 1933. Yet, Roosevelt could not let a

---

11. Acheson, "Building the Peace," NBC Radio, Mar. 10, 1945, Acheson Papers, box 46, folder 6. Much of my discussion of the gold program is derived from Elmus Wicker, "Roosevelt's 1933 Monetary Experiment," 864-79.

man so capable as Acheson sit out the fast-approaching war; he appointed him to the State Department in February 1941. This time when the two men encountered legal problems preventing aid to the British, Acheson was there to lend Roosevelt a hand and, in turn, help the British imperial cause again. Certainly, no later than World War II and perhaps as early as 1933, he became convinced that the maintenance of the international order Britain had presided over from the early nineteenth century to World War I and in which the empire—and the United States—had flourished depended on the United States assuming the role and shouldering the responsibilities Britain had once exercised. The formulations of that order in Acheson's mind made the interests of Britain and the United States more or less identical.

Before and during World War II, this formulation led Acheson to give systematic attention to the economic dimensions of international problems that caused the decline of Britain and the rise of the United States. He thus supported U.S. aid to Britain from Roosevelt's Lend-Lease Act of 1941 to the Marshall Plan of 1947 and thereafter. This turn in his thinking tied together economic development and effective foreign policy. Acheson maintained that America's own development was based on imperial investment from abroad. "It is the method of expanding production, employment and consumption," he said of imperial investment in 1941, "which can benefit both the country furnishing it and the country receiving it."[12] Acheson argued that this process could once again be repeated with the United States as the imperial driving force. "Because of our preponderant economic and financial strength," he declared in 1944, "we are in a position to assume leadership in the promotion of the necessary international economic policies and we have an obligation to do so." In the postwar world, American economic and financial prowess could preserve a world order consonant with the special interests of the imperial order. "In large part," Acheson continued, "this is a problem of opening the channels of international capital movements and reviving the flow of foreign investment." Such an opening would function by providing an immediate "market for United States products and, by developing foreign countries, increasing the purchasing power of the

12. In January 1941, Acheson replied to a writer who had expressed his support for Acheson's legal position that there was nothing unconstitutional about the destroyers-for-bases deal of 1940. "I regard it as high praise that you found nothing Jesuitical in my arguments. Notes like yours . . . encourage me a great deal, coming as they do with others urging me to return to England where the writers believe that I properly belong" (letter to Rufus J. Trimble, Jan. 14, 1941, Acheson Papers, box 30, folder 389).

peoples of those countries for foreign products, including those of the United States."[13]

A careful reading of Acheson's opinions shows a connection between his nostalgic imperial worldview and his policy choices. "Britain, which once had the training and capabilities to manage a world system, no longer has the ability," Acheson argued in the series of lectures he published as *Power and Diplomacy*. "The United States, which has the material capability, lacks the experience and the discipline needed for responsible management." This statement implied that through a special relationship with the British, the old world system could be resurrected. "As I have suggested," Acheson wrote nostalgically, "in the nineteenth century an international system of sorts not only kept the peace for a century but also provided highly successful working arrangements."[14]

Policies attuned to these shifting circumstances could preserve the old "British" order in a new "American" one. Investment and development had fueled the old order and enabled it to achieve a great, "if unevenly distributed," rise in living standards. This was the result of "the export of capital, primarily by Great Britain," at levels far exceeding those of current or prospective levels of U.S. foreign investment. In fact, to reach levels the British had once achieved, American investment would have to be increased by a factor of thirty, which Acheson estimated would be the equivalent of two new Marshall Plans each year for a number of years, a level he recognized as politically unfeasible. What was feasible and necessary, Acheson believed, was "a system for the export of capital, much greater than our present hand-to-mouth efforts." He continued, "The system has been destroyed which expanded the power of Western Europe and permitted industrial development"; he added, "one to replace it will be devised, managed, and largely (but not wholly) financed by the United States."[15]

To appreciate the meaning of these proposals, it is necessary to remind ourselves of the imperial nature of the old world order Acheson defended nostalgically as well as the new one he envisaged hopefully. The new system would, like the old one, benefit lenders and investors more than recipients, at least if Acheson realized his hope of preserving the existing political order in the colonial world. That was, of course, the fly in the

13. Acheson, statement to the Special House of Representatives Committee on postwar economic policy, Nov. 30, 1944, Acheson Papers, box 46, folder 5.

14. Acheson, *Power and Diplomacy*, 6.

15. Ibid., 18-20. Acheson cited to support his opinion A. K. Cairncross, *Home and Foreign Investment, 1870-1913*.

ointment of Acheson's entire design, and by ignoring it and its implications for U.S. policy—or, rather, failing to address those things with
the realism they called for—Acheson's hope was a romantic dream of a
bygone world.

Before he became secretary of state in 1949, Acheson served as a member
of the Hoover Commission that President Truman had appointed to
recommend plans for a major reorganization of the federal government
to adapt the bureaucratic structure to new responsibilities and functions
that the New Deal and World War II had assigned the federal government.
Acheson chaired the subcommittee on State Department reorganization.
The reorganization he devised and implemented revealed a great deal
about not only his conceptualizations of the office of secretary of state
and of the bureaucracy the secretary oversaw, but also his admiration
for the way the British conducted their foreign policy.[16] Briefly stated,
he streamlined channels of authority, centralized control in the hands of
the secretary, and reallocated policy responsibilities along geographical
lines much like those already in place in the British Foreign Office. It
is "fundamental that the Secretary of State should be in full command
of the Department and the Foreign Service," Acheson said in defense of
the reorganization, "so that the line of authority from the Secretary to the
Under and Assistant Secretaries to subordinate officials in the Department
and overseas is clear and unmistakable."[17]

Toward that end, Acheson eliminated centers of power that career
staffers had carved out for themselves over time, reduced the authority
of the undersecretary, and replaced the secretary's two political advisers
with nine assistant secretaries, much like the Foreign Office arrangement. Under the old system, the two political advisers had had, between
themselves, worldwide responsibilities, the one advising the secretary
on European and Near Eastern affairs, the other on Latin American and
Far Eastern affairs.[18] In place of this arrangement, Acheson created the
nine new assistant secretary positions already mentioned, giving six of

16. As Deputy Undersecy. John E. Peurifoy reported in October 1949: "We have just
completed a rather basic change in the structure of our organization. . . . This was the
result of the Hoover Commission survey and especially the task force study conducted
under the leadership of Secretary Acheson" ("The Department of State: A Reflection of
U.S. Leadership," *Department of State Bulletin*, Oct. 31, 1949).
17. Acheson, statement to House Committee on Foreign Affairs, Mar. 11, 1949 *(Foreign
Relations of the United States, 1949*, 1:2-3; hereafter cited as *FRUS)*.
18. For more information on State Department organization, see *U.S. Government Organization Manual* (Washington, D.C.: U.S. Government Printing Office, 1950). For the British
Foreign Office, see Donald G. Bishop, *The Administration of British Foreign Relations*.

the assistants geographically defined responsibilities and the other three oversight of public affairs, congressional relations, and economic affairs. For purposes of this study, the creation of one of the geographical bureaus, that of Near Eastern, South Asian, and African affairs, is particularly instructive. Within this bureau, headed under Acheson by George McGhee, there were two separate offices, one for Near Eastern, South Asian, and African affairs and the other for Greek, Turkish, and Iranian affairs. What this arrangement accomplished was to group together virtually all the areas of the colonial world where British power was or had been paramount. Under Acheson this bureau functioned as the American equivalent of the British Colonial Office. Acheson also eliminated any level of authority between himself and the subordinate assistant secretaries. The fact that they reported directly to Acheson rather than to the undersecretary gave the secretary a hands-on relationship with them and the policy matters they dealt with, thereby increasing the secretary's control over the formulation and implementation of policy.

These administrative arrangements, plus the appointment of his own men to key positions, ensured that the State Department functioned as Acheson wanted. To the key post of assistant secretary for Near East, South Asia, and Africa, Acheson appointed, as already noted, George McGhee, whose thinking on U.S. policy toward those parts of the world was more or less identical to his own. A self-described Texan of "Old South English stock," McGhee had studied at Oxford as a Rhodes scholar. There he learned to admire the empire and appreciate what he perceived as its civilizing mission. At Oxford, as he himself later said, he read the life of his "benefactor, Cecil Rhodes, and his success in expanding the British Empire in Africa," and of "Robert Clive and Warren Hastings, who spearheaded British interests in India." As a result of these readings, McGhee added, "Colonialism appeared to me not an instrument of oppression but the bearing of the 'white man's burden.' I regretted being too late to be part of the colonial era." McGhee carefully interjects that as he came to understand the racism behind imperialism he saw it in "quite a different perspective." Yet, he could not "fault the British attitude toward colonialism, since they had in my judgment adapted their colonial rule to changing circumstances and deserved credit for their accomplishments."[19] Acheson was rarely so straightforward in stating his views on the white man's burden or of British imperialism, but he and McGhee spoke with one voice on matters of policy toward the British colonial world.

19. McGhee, *Envoy to the Middle World: Adventures in Diplomacy*, 8-9.

The views of Acheson and McGhee no doubt encouraged the resolve in the Foreign Office to hold on to the empire. Some writers have suggested that after the electoral victory of the Labour Party in the elections of 1945 and the subsequent "loss" of India, the British gradually recognized their inability to maintain the empire and by the late 1940s and early 1950s were preparing, as gracefully as they could, to adjust to circumstances imposed by declining power. In the Foreign Office generally and the Colonial Office specifically, the reality was closer to the opposite of those hopeful assessments. There officials still regarded the colonies as economic and political assets and saw great opportunities for colonial development even after Indian independence. Those in the Colonial Office especially argued that the colonies were economic assets because they earned foreign exchange and provided raw materials and foodstuffs for Britain and were important markets for British products.[20] Although Acheson insisted that policy makers recognize and accept the world "as it is," neither he nor his British counterparts applied that thinking to matters related to the empire. None of them included indigenous nationalism as part of the reality to be embraced. Acheson, in particular, was never able to overcome the romanticism of the imperial mission in his worldview.

Had Acheson and his like-minded British allies listened, they could have heard responsible voices warning them that the economic as well as the political costs of empire had become prohibitive. Historian Peter Hennessy has pointed out that British economist John Maynard Keynes had uttered such warnings before the war ended in reports on financial policy prepared for no less a body than the British cabinet. "Our financial embarrassments have been and still are, and look like being even after the war, mainly the result of the cash expenditure of the Service [that is, military] Departments in Africa, the Middle East, India and the Southern Dominions," Keynes wrote in one such report. "There remains a vast cash expenditure overseas—local expenditure incurred on the spot . . . which is poured out, not only with no effective Treasury control, but without the Treasury knowing either beforehand or afterwards, what it has been spent on." If these costs are not brought "under drastic control at an early date (and perhaps it is not . . . [possible to do so])," Keynes continued, "our ability to pursue an independent financial policy in the early post-war years will be fatally impaired."[21]

20. Records of the Colonial Office, comments on Permanent Undersecretary's Committee (hereafter PUSC), doc. 79, on British Overseas Obligations, PREM 8/1202, PRO.
21. Peter Hennessy, *Never Again: Britain, 1945-1951*, 222-23.

Officials at the Colonial Office who might have been disturbed by the economic costs of the empire had no such doubts about the political advantages. "Politically, the Colonies provide centres in almost every part of the world which give us a direct claim to influence policies throughout the world," a Colonial Office staffer wrote in 1950. "If the United Kingdom were to withdraw from any Colony, our prestige would suffer in friendly and hostile eyes alike with serious effects on our position in the world. Moreover, we should be abandoning our responsibility for the welfare of a Colonial people."[22] Rather than dealing with the hard realities of the postwar world, the British were focusing on symbolic interests and fuzzy ideas of credibility.

It is important to recognize that these were views expressed in the *Labour* government of Clement Attlee and not the Tory government of Winston Churchill. Whereas the Labour prime minister, Clement Attlee, had some willingness to adjust Britain to changing circumstances, as evidenced by his acceptance of Indian independence, his foreign secretary, Ernest Bevin, was, as a contemporary noted, "at heart an old fashioned imperialist, keener to expand than contract the Empire." To officials with beliefs like Bevin's, the turning away from India was an opportunity to focus on what seemed to them the more malleable and durable African colonies. Symbolizing this continuing interest in colonial development was a new building to house the Colonial Office. Containing no less than 138,000 square feet of usable space, the building was to be "a Citadel to protect the Colonial Office communications and essential staff in war, a library, hall, garage, and storage space." Ironically, the government's financial situation killed the construction of the building, though the Colonial Office staff in London, which numbered 465 in 1939, had almost trebled by 1950 to 1,289.[23]

Evidence of continuing official support for maintaining the empire is abundant, especially concerning the African colonies. In March 1950, to cite one example, the American minister to Rhodesia and Nyasaland told a group of U.S. foreign service officers in Lourenço Marques, Mozambique, that British authorities in the two colonies were reluctant to accept U.S. aid because to do so might lead to American influence. "Where capital goes, influence goes," the minister said, summarizing not only British views but Acheson's views as well; "they want to stay British and do not welcome American participation in their affairs." The American minister

---

22. Records of the Colonial Office, comments on PUSC, doc. 79, PREM 8/1202, PRO.
23. Hennessy, *Never Again*, 233, 227.

in British East Africa voiced similar views. "It is very strange to note the way East African authorities seem to be still living in the age of Queen Victoria," he reported. "They appear to have a backward attitude and they do not realize how much the British and ourselves need one another or how closely cooperation has already developed."[24]

Acheson did little to discourage the British views reflected in these statements. From the outset of his tenure as secretary of state, he encouraged the British to rely on the special relationship he envisioned between the two countries and never tempered his encouragement with warnings to deal realistically with the colonial world. In his memoirs, Acheson described in dismissive terms Treasury secretary John Snyder's reaction to British overtures during talks in London for a substantial American loan. "He flew back like a modern Paul Revere crying 'The British are coming!'" Acheson said he and Snyder "had different attitudes toward Britain's troubles. [Snyder] was very wary about becoming involved in them, while to me it seemed both impossible and undesirable to avoid involvement. I saw them as part and parcel of larger problems that deeply concerned our interests and could be managed only under our leadership and with British association."[25]

The British for their part were encouraged by signs of increased American understanding of their concerns. In a study of the American relationship in 1950, an official in the Foreign Office was careful to recognize Acheson's commitment. "At a meeting at the State Department on the 14th September 1949," the official reported, "Mr. Acheson, when informing Mr. Bevin that the United States would appoint representatives to play an active role in . . . European strategic planning groups, added that this statement would not limit the 'ultra-secret global planning arrangements' which exist between the United States and United Kingdom." The official account went on to note that the British should not "refer to this assertion in any talks with the United States officials, not all of whom may be aware of it." Since "the United States and United Kingdom have to consider defence arrangements for areas outside the Atlantic Region, these special bipartite strategic planning arrangements are of high importance. This should be continued and developed."[26]

Bevin was pleased with the results of the first round of serious discussions he had with Acheson in September 1949, just after Acheson became secretary of state. The two men disagreed about China, but agreed to

24. Lourenço Marques Conference Papers, Feb. 27–Mar. 2, 1950, National Archives.
25. Acheson, *Present at the Creation*, 322-23.
26. Contained in a draft brief for bipartite talks with the American advance party during the week beginning Apr. 24, 1950, PREM 8/1204, PRO.

live with the disagreement.[27] "The talks with Mr. Acheson have been most helpful because they had served to make it clear that there is no fundamental difference in the objectives of the United States and the United Kingdom," Bevin told the Commonwealth ambassadors after the discussions. "It may be that the tactics pursued will be different and it may be also that elements in the Congress and the United States press will be critical of United Kingdom action but there now seems every reason to expect an understanding attitude on the part of the United States Administration."[28]

To enhance the Anglo-American relationship, Acheson proposed in March 1950 that new talks be held in London in May. Because Acheson intended these talks to cement a new and closer relationship, the talks and the preparations for them were central to his purposes. The London talks were to include parallel discussions with French representatives, and thus had three-party as well as two-party dimensions; nonetheless, Acheson's primary purpose was to use the talks to forge an Anglo-American agreement on specifics of the special relationship he envisioned. He noted his "immediate and intense displeasure" with a draft document spelling out American understandings of the special relationship—not because he disagreed with the understandings but because any such statement could be put to embarrassing use by critics. Even when he wrote his memoirs in 1969, Acheson was still answering critics of his policy. "Of course a unique relation existed between Britain and America—our common language and history insured that," he wrote then. "But unique did not mean affectionate. We had fought England as an enemy as often as we had fought by her side as an ally."[29] That later realization had not kept Acheson from having every copy of the offending document burned, however, and apparently no copy of it now exists.

Despite Acheson's endeavors to keep the terms of the special relationship secret and unwritten, the British were anxious to make those terms as specific and favorable for their purposes as possible. "The American suggestion that we should aim in the first place at establishing an understanding about the basic relationship between the two countries is an important development," a Foreign Office study prepared for the

27. Britain had recognized the Communist government of China, and the United States had not. Acheson was willing to overlook this difference of policy probably because without congressional pressure he would have favored recognition for China, too.

28. Note of a meeting between Bevin and the Commonwealth ambassadors in the British Embassy, Washington, D.C., Sept. 16, 1949, Records of the Foreign Office, 371/76024/ f14305/1024/61G, PRO.

29. Acheson, *Present at the Creation*, 387.

preliminary meetings said of Acheson's proposal. The study went on to note that recognition of the importance of Britain in the postwar world had been growing in the U.S. government. Viewing the United Kingdom as essential to U.S. security, the report argued that Americans recognized they "cannot get the main lines of their foreign policy right, whether in Europe, the Middle East, or Asia, without our help."[30] What the study does not say is that this *new* recognition of Britain's importance resulted from the rise of Dean Acheson to the position of secretary of state.

The author of this study urged his superiors in the Foreign Office to exploit this fortuitous circumstance. "We . . . have an unprecedented opportunity for discussing and perhaps reaching a wide measure of agreement with the Americans in the whole field of foreign policy. It is recommended that we should make the most that we can of this opportunity, and should not hesitate to discuss fundamental problems with complete frankness." Toward that end, the author suggested that it was best to speak bluntly to the Americans, but not to imply "that we know all the answers." A better approach was to pose a situation as a common problem, and suggest a sharing of ideas to resolve it. "The result of this joint approach to a problem is often that the Americans prepared themselves the solutions which we favor."[31]

In preparing for the upcoming talks, Sir Oliver Franks, the British ambassador in Washington, proposed to Ernest Bevin five bases for discussing the special relationship. The two parties, Franks suggested, should review and agree on their common objectives in the cold war world, determine what needed to be done and what each must do to get it done, agree on the special needs of the "United Kingdom–Commonwealth and sterling area" and the special role of Britain in Europe and other parts of the world, specify the nature of the long-term U.K.-U.S. relationship and the obligations of each government to the other, and agree on a mechanism to provide a "continuous survey of the world-wide commitments and capabilities of both partners to determine necessary adjustments" of the obligations and responsibilities of each.[32]

Despite the obvious care these proposals took of British interests, a document in the Foreign Office archives states that the proposals "were drafted by Mr. Acheson himself and it is thought that he attaches particular importance to these general items, the discussion of which he considers to be the main purpose of his visit to London." The document that includes this

30. Draft brief for bipartite talks, PREM 8/1204, 3, PRO.
31. Ibid.
32. Franks, telegram to Bevin, no. 1095, Apr. 4, 1950, PREM 8/1202, PRO.

revealing statement was generated by the Permanent Under-Secretary's Committee. This committee also reported that an Anglo-American sub-committee had produced a paper that would constitute the basis of further discussion of continuing consultation and policy coordination.[33] It was probably this committee that produced the offending document that Acheson had burned.

In preparing for the talks, this committee explored the means of getting an expansive U.S. commitment to support British interests. It hoped to get the two sides to pledge to "build up the strength and close unity of the non-Communist world," for in light of their combined "special responsibilities it is particularly desirable that . . . there should be continuous and close coordination of policy between" them. It was argued in committee that the principle of extremely close coordination had already been recognized by both sides concerning matters related to the Middle East because of arrangements agreed upon in World War II. Such a view, however, overlooks the crucial difference between establishing a peacetime coalition and one that was based on wartime necessity.[34]

This kind of "mission creep"—overlaying British interests with U.S. commitments, which the British sought and Acheson did little to discourage—illustrated the degree to which imperial concerns influenced both Britain's and Acheson's conceptualization of the special relationship. In fact, colonial concerns were primary with Foreign Office officials made anxious by the fear that their U.S. counterparts did not share their concerns. "Where divergent attitudes might result in weakening of each other's position in face of communist attacks," one of them said of disagreements over those concerns, neither side must lose sight of the necessity for cooperation and agreement. "It was felt that further discussion and consultation was [sic] desirable with the aim of avoiding misunderstandings and divergences both in general approach and in discussions in the United Nations," a Foreign Office official wrote summarizing an in-house discussion of the subject. "It was agreed that in this general category of questions the problem of Africa should receive special consideration." As if to balance this area of British concern with one of similar concern to the Americans, the official added, "Latin America was one of the areas mentioned on which closer cooperation might be developed."[35]

33. PUSC review papers concerning progress of conversations with U.S. and French officials in preparation for London Conference, May 4, 1950, PREM 8/1202, PRO.

34. Meeting of subcommittee on Anglo-American continued consultation on and coordination of policy, Apr. 26, 1950, PREM 8/1202, PRO.

35. Ibid.

To ensure the day-to-day cooperation the special relationship would entail, the committee proposed requiring British and American diplomats around the world to consult regularly and act cooperatively. "It was felt that in the coordination of policy constant day-by-day exchanges of view played an important part," a summary of the proposal reported. "This was particularly valuable before policies were finally formulated. Constant contact between officials at appropriate levels was an important factor. . . . To avoid situations arising in which one country found itself in the position of opposing or voting against the other" at the United Nations, British and American representatives should consult "prior to important meetings," and "delegations attending technical conferences" under UN auspices "might be briefed more fully in the light of the general common objectives."[36]

The effort by the subcommittee to make U.S. and British policies work hand-in-glove reflected the kinds of attitudes and atmosphere Acheson encouraged in the State Department. It would be an understatement of Acheson's control of policy formulation to suggest subordinates under his influence could or would freely attempt to work out this kind of relationship without the secretary's direction and support. It is also essential to understand that not everyone in the State Department saw the special relationship in the same positive light as Acheson.

The chief product of the subcommittee's deliberation was a document addressing the policies and processes that would constitute the special relationship. Arguing that the United States and the United Kingdom had common objectives not only in Europe "but throughout the world" as well, the document pointed to the necessity of defining those objectives both regionally and functionally. Not only should policy differences be avoided but governments should also recognize the essential principle in the "coordination of policy that it is contrary to the policy of either Government to injure the other or take advantage of the other. On the contrary, it should be their parallel and respective aim, within their agreed objectives, to strengthen and improve each other's position by lending each other all proper and possible support." The subcommittee recommended that Acheson and Bevin adopt their report as policy.[37]

Acheson's role in the May talks is better documented in British than American sources. Especially revealing are notes of a conversation Acheson and Bevin had on May 9 about the world situation. "The time had

36. Ibid.

37. "Continued Consultation on and Co-ordination of Policy," Records of the Foreign Office, 371/81645, PRO; revised subcommittee report, Bipartite U.S.-U.K. Relations, May 8, 1950, U.S.-U.K. Relations file, London, May 1950, RG 43, box 45, National Archives.

come for further major steps forward," Acheson told Bevin. "What was needed now was a determined effort by the Western Powers to show that they were not prepared to give way under the pressure of Russian communism. . . . In the old days, the British fleet by a show of force had been enough to maintain the peace of the world. It was just as essential now to be able to demonstrate to the peoples of Asia . . . that the West was strong, organized, and determined to maintain its way of life."[38] Significantly, Acheson conceived of the demonstration of power in imperial terms and against colonial peoples rather than in terms of cold war realism against the Soviet Union.

In the talks themselves, the British proposed the adoption of two position papers containing the ideas summarized above. In the kind of major steps he envisioned, Acheson endorsed the substance of these proposals in early discussions, but encountered vigorous objections afterward from several of his senior advisers, among them Philip Jessup, Averell Harriman, Charles Bohlen, and David Bruce, the last of whom was then ambassador to France. Jessup noted the "strong exception" the men took to the British proposals for institutionalizing consultation and coordination of Anglo-American policy. "The British evidently want you to approve this paper," Jessup wrote Acheson. "The issue involves the strong feelings which Bruce, Bohlen and Harriman have about the implications of this paper. It also involves what we think the British may be trying to read into the paper beyond its exact language. We recommend that you should not approve the paper as such before you have had a chance to study it in the light of indications of the British attitude." In writing this note, Jessup was trying to buy time to get Acheson to see the proposal in realist terms. "This particular paper is objectionable," Jessup and the others told Acheson in another note, "in that it smacks too much of a 19th century alliance on spheres of influence"—in other words, an outmoded imperial arrangement.[39]

The opposition of these weighty advisers caused Acheson to move cautiously. He assured the British on May 9 that he had no argument with the general proposition that the two governments "should work in the closest possible cooperation in every field and should have constant consultation to ensure common action." Bevin riposted that "it was vital to avoid conflict" over colonial questions. "What was needed was a constant exchange of view and opportunities for the Colonial Office to explain

38. Records of the Foreign Office, 371/81633/AU1027/4, PRO.
39. Memorandum for the Secretary, May 10, 1950, U.S.-U.K. Relations file, London, May 1950, RG 43, box 45, National Archives; Respective Roles United States-United Kingdom, U.S.-U.K. Relations file, London, May 1950, RG 43, box 45, National Archives.

its policies for the sympathetic consideration of the Americans." To this, Acheson "entirely agreed and he understood that the principle had now been accepted that we should have the closest consultation before United Nations meetings so as to be able to present a united front." Acheson and Bevin then agreed that the British proposals spelled out their own understanding of the need for consultation and cooperation but preferred not to adopt it as a policy statement. Jessup and the other critics, however, then began to prevail on this vital issue.[40]

A day after he accepted this personal understanding, Acheson confessed his entire support for the disputed paper and the principles of close consultation and policy coordination. "It was [nevertheless] quite impossible to allow it to be known that any such paper had been drawn up or that it had been agreed to," he told the British. "He was in complete agreement that it was vital that our policies should be aligned as closely as possible. He also thought that our interests were either the same or very close in all parts of the world." Still, Acheson "could not for obvious reasons admit any knowledge of a paper of the kind before him, but he would always be prepared to say quite openly that America must have the closest possible relations with Britain."[41]

These talks with the British were thus revealing. In the preliminary consultations, Acheson had evidently led the British to believe that he was open to an arrangement in the old spheres-of-influence tradition, an arrangement he had no authority to conclude on his own and for which he was called to task by his own senior advisers. Too committed to the principle to backtrack on the substance of the arrangement itself, he retreated to a verbal commitment to Bevin that left no written agreement of what he intended. This enabled him to deny that a special agreement had been reached while enabling Bevin to hope and expect that U.S. policy would move along lines as though it had.

Before the special relationship developed further, the crisis in Korea exploded on the administration. Both the British and the U.S. governments were immediately preoccupied with the crisis, which had the effect of enhancing their coordination of military policy, since the two supplied the largest contingents of men and material on behalf of the United Nations. Despite or because of this crisis, Acheson remained committed to his conception of the special relationship. In January 1951, he again broached the idea of formalizing the relationship, this time to Robert A. Lovett, despite a recent warning from Jessup and Paul Nitze of the Policy

40. Record of May 9, 1950, meeting, PREM 8/1203, PRO.
41. Fourth Bipartite Ministerial Meeting, May 10, 1950, PREM 8/1204, PRO.

Planning Staff of the pitfalls of such an agreement. "We could not commit ourselves to reach agreement with the British," Jessup advised Acheson. "That would be just one more obstacle in the way of getting decisions and actions." Acheson might tell the British, Jessup continued, that "we are perfectly willing to form the habit of calling them in to tell them that we are working on some particular problem and to inform them of how we are thinking."[42]

To try to win over Jessup and the other critics, Acheson attempted to portray the proposed agreement as one in which the United States would get the better of the deal. He stressed the reciprocal basis of the agreement he envisioned, pointing out its potential advantages for the United States. The British, he admitted, had recently been less forthcoming than the State Department about sharing information, but this agreement would solve that problem. Staff members, however, saw this British reticence as an obstacle rather than an opportunity, and remained unconvinced by Acheson's reasoning. Lovett reiterated the concern that there would be "very serious disadvantages if we were to make any commitments to the British." Acheson assured him that he was not proposing formal commitments, to which Lovett responded by asking the secretary to put a formal proposal in writing. In a follow-up memorandum, Acheson suggested a system of regularly scheduled talks between British and American diplomatic and military staffs. "My own view is that there is some merit in the idea," he wrote. To head off criticism, Acheson noted that the goal of such talks would not be joint decisions; rather, closer consultations with the British "might very well help in bringing U.K. thinking around somewhat more close to our own."[43] Since Acheson believed that U.S. and British interests were the same, putting the matter that way might have been disingenuous. Establishing a mechanism for regular consultation seemed to be his objective.

Lovett remained unconvinced. Backed by Jessup and Nitze, he repeated his objections to institutionalized consultations. "This might create the impression that we had formally re-established the Combined Chiefs of Staff organization," he told Acheson, referring to the unified military command of World War II. In further discussions, Lovett and Nitze convinced Sir Oliver Franks that the idea of institutionalized consultations should be shelved. Nonetheless, the two sides agreed to nonbinding informal talks

42. Memorandum of a telephone conversation, Acheson and Lovett, Jan. 18, 1951, Records of the Policy Planning Staff, box 17, Great Britain 1947-1953 file, National Archives.

43. Ibid.; Acheson, memo to Lovett, Jan. 18, 1951, Records of the Policy Planning Staff, box 17, Great Britain 1947-1953 file, lot 64D563, National Archives.

irregularly scheduled, with Jessup and Gen. Omar N. Bradley representing the American side, and Franks representing the British. By this time, Franks had already proposed that they begin the talks by discussing "Far Eastern problems."[44]

In his memoirs, Acheson described himself as "pro-British," and wrote of the "genuineness of the special relationship" and of "the real identity of British and American interests in Europe and elsewhere, however diverse they might appear." He traced the mutuality back to British acquiescence in the Monroe Doctrine in the early nineteenth century and to the British refusal to intervene in the American Civil War. In fact, British policy in both of those instances had been self-serving, but that was Acheson's point: the interests of the two nations had been identical in the nineteenth century and remained so in the cold war and the era of nationalist insurgencies against imperialism. Events soon proved Acheson wrong on the latter point. The fact that many of his contemporaries foresaw that problem and he did not is one measure of the unrealism that characterized his stewardship of U.S. foreign policy.[45] At the heart of Acheson's diplomacy was a determination to see much of the world not as it was but as he believed it should be.

44. Lovett to Acheson, Jan. 24, 1951, Records of the Policy Planning Staff, box 17, Great Britain 1947-1953 file, National Archives; Jessup to Acheson, Feb. 2, 1951, Records of the Policy Planning Staff, Great Britain 1947-1953 file, National Archives.

45. Acheson, *Present at the Creation*, 387-88. Acheson's admiration of the British for backing the Union seems a little strained. Britain did so only after a string of Union victories made it clear who would likely win the war. Because of the ties of British industry to Southern planters and the general dislike of slavery, the British were deeply divided over which side to support in the American Civil War.

3

Bonds of Loyalty

Historians have studied the relationship between President Eisenhower and his secretary of state, John Foster Dulles, in some depth.[1] In comparison, historians have given much less attention to the parallel relationship between President Truman and Dean Acheson. This neglect has limited the value of studies of Truman-era foreign policy, especially between 1949 and 1952, when Acheson was secretary of state. Acheson's influence over foreign policy in those years was extraordinary because of his success in "managing" Truman's decision making. Unlike Dulles, Acheson was more responsible for the foreign policy of the United States during his tenure in office than was the president he served, and it is to Acheson more than to Truman that the historian must look to understand the substance of that policy.

Acheson's influence explains the overriding concern in American policy to protect British imperial interests in the colonial world during his years in office. Historians have ignored, indeed failed to recognize, this elemental aspect of Acheson's stewardship of U.S. foreign policy, for practical as well as ideological reasons. Acheson's determination to obscure his purposes on key policy matters left little in the way of a "paper trail" documenting some of his most pressing intentions. In fact, the "trail" that remains hides some of the most basic of those intentions under a deceptive rhetoric of cold war realism. Among the reasons for Acheson's success in this deception, none has been more important than the shield provided him by McCarthyite charges that he was "soft" on communism and that the "softness" was part and parcel of a larger Anglophilia that

1. See Richard Immerman, "Confessions of an Eisenhower Revisionist: 'An Agonizing Reappraisal'"; Vincent De Santis, "Eisenhower Revisionism"; Mary McAuliffe, "Commentary: Eisenhower, the President"; Robert J. McMahon, "Eisenhower and Third World Nationalism: A Critique of the Revisionists"; and Richard A. Melanson and David Mayers, eds., *Reevaluating Eisenhower: American Foreign Policy in the Fifties*.

the McCarthyites found offensive. So offensive and insubstantial were the charges concerning communism—and the people who made them, including Sen. Joseph McCarthy himself—that people in and out of the foreign policy establishment not only rejected them outright but also refused to look into the nature or consequences of Acheson's Anglophilia. For the same reason, historians have done likewise. Everyone has thus viewed Acheson's foreign policy through ideological prisms that barred disinterested critique of his Anglophilia. Acheson would never have intentionally sacrificed essential U.S. interests for those of Britain. That basic fact is not a part of the equation in question here. The essential problem, which has never been sufficiently recognized, is that Acheson saw American and British interests as the same. Yet, that identity of interests did not always exist, especially in dealings with nationalist movements and aspirations in the decolonizing world. The implications of that circumstance for U.S. interests in the decolonizing world during Acheson's tenure in the State Department have therefore remained largely unexamined.

The same is true of Acheson's mentoring of Truman in matters relating to foreign policy, mentoring that was skillful, even adroit. As the mentoring metaphor suggests, the relationship between the two men had elements of the student-teacher model, with the worldly wise international statesman guiding the shrewd, domestically oriented politician. It was not that a calculating subordinate manipulated a naive superior; Truman was far too knowing and independent for that and Acheson too wise to attempt it. It was, rather, that Acheson knew his own mind and the intricacies of policy and bureaucratic machinations, and Truman welcomed the evident authoritativeness and apparent insight with which his secretary of state presented policy options to him.

The two men developed genuine respect for each other, a respect abundantly documented in correspondence between them, correspondence that continued long after their official relationship ended. Yet, it is possible that the United States never had a president and a secretary of state more different from Truman and Acheson. The continuing respect each man had for the other was, therefore, remarkable. "History, I am sure, will list Dean Acheson among the truly great secretaries of state our country has had," Truman wrote in his *Memoirs* in 1956. "The captain with the mighty heart," Acheson wrote eight years later of Truman, dedicating his own memoir, *Present at the Creation*, to the president.[2]

To Acheson, this kind of reciprocal loyalty was intrinsic in the patrician

2. Truman, *Memoirs: Years of Trial and Hope, 1946-1952*, 429; Acheson, *Present at the Creation*, v.

lifestyle he cultivated and in the aristocratic social class with which he identified. In a landmark work, *The Protestant Establishment: Aristocracy and Caste in America*, E. Digby Baltzell has described this class, and noted Acheson's place in it. His education at Groton, Yale, and Harvard Law, as well as his clerkship for Justice Brandeis, fit the pattern of this elite, and reinforced the sense of personal and social superiority Acheson displayed in his dress and demeanor and brought to his service in government.

Truman, by contrast, was small-town Missouri, Baptist, and a struggling bourgeois. He prided himself on his unpretentiousness and blunt honesty. With none of Acheson's advantages of birth, he rose in the world through hard work and self-discipline. A "common man" with little formal education, his formative life experiences included leadership of an artillery unit in World War I, collapse of his haberdashery business in the 1920s, and political alliance with the Kansas City "boss" Tom Pendergast.

Yet, Truman and Acheson had important similarities that need emphasizing. Despite their differing backgrounds, both men patterned their lives around American values of self-reliance and individual responsibility. Both grew up in small towns around the turn of the century, and the common experience gave them shared values that class and regional differences failed to obliterate. In memoirs published after leaving office, each man emphasized occasions on which he took unpopular but principled stands when more expedient actions would have been less difficult. Both men placed absolute value on loyalty. Thus, when "Boss" Pendergast died, alone and friendless, Truman attended his funeral despite widespread criticism and potential damage to his political career. Pendergast had befriended him in his time of need, Truman explained, and he owed the man's memory a token of respect. Similarly, when his colleague Alger Hiss was charged with passing secrets to the Soviet Union, Acheson rejected the charges, in part because of his confidence in Hiss and in part because of the disrepute in which he held his accusers. It was, in other words, a matter of personal honor involving a friend of his own class, not a matter for political calculation. "One must be true to the things by which one lives," Acheson wrote later of his stand.[3] Acheson submitted his resignation to Truman in the wake of this stance, but the president rejected it, noting that he, too, in the Pendergast case, had faced public criticism for loyalty to a friend.

Bonds of loyalty, then, bound the two men together. Historians of the Truman-Acheson years have acknowledged those bonds, and the influence they gave Acheson over foreign policy. However, they have never

3. Acheson, *Present at the Creation*, 360-61. See also Truman, *Memoirs, 1946-1952*.

spelled out the implications of that acknowledgment. In one of the earliest studies of the Truman presidency, journalist Cabell Phillips concluded paradoxically that Truman had "little creative genius" in foreign policy but "wrought the boldest and most profound changes" in that area of "any President in history." To explain that paradox—indeed, contradiction—Phillips credited Truman with "genius" in "his ability to seek good advice and act on it when he got it."[4] However valid that judgment might be, it hardly explains the Truman-Acheson foreign policy or Acheson's purpose in formulating it.

The most comprehensive studies of Truman's presidency are Robert J. Donovan's *Conflict and Crisis* and *Tumultuous Years*, the second of which covers Acheson's tenure as secretary of state. Donovan devotes an entire chapter to Acheson's foreign policy, stressing his importance in policy formulation. "The selection of Dean Acheson as secretary of state," Donovan wrote, "was the most important appointment Truman ever made, not only with respect to the direction of the foreign policy of the United States but also to the tenor of domestic political controversy." Famous for his domineering, overbearing attitude toward others, Acheson, in Donovan's reckoning, never had trouble with Truman. "Truman was the boss, and Dean played it that way," Donovan quoted Charles Bohlen as saying. "He never did anything without touching base with Truman." Truman repaid this solicitousness by giving Acheson wide latitude in policy formulation and implementation, but always with the understanding that Acheson was to do nothing that was contrary to Truman's expressed views or that would embarrass the administration politically. Tellingly, the example Donovan used to illustrate Truman's willingness to intrude himself into foreign policy and override his secretary of state came from James F. Byrnes's tenure in that office, not Acheson's. There is no evidence that Byrnes made the kind of effort Acheson did to "manage" Truman in order to bend foreign policy to his own purposes. Acheson's undersecretary, James Webb, recalled that Acheson studied the president "carefully in terms of how he could meet Truman's political needs . . . and still preserve his own standard as to what should be done in the international field."[5]

What oiled the Truman-Acheson relationship and made it run smoothly was, in Donovan's words, the "simple truth . . . that the two men liked each other." Acheson was too cerebral for Truman to seek out as a social

---

4. Phillips, *The Truman Presidency: The History of a Triumphant Succession*, 287.

5. Donovan, *Tumultuous Years: The Presidency of Harry S. Truman, 1949-1953*, 34-35. Donovan interviewed Bohlen on Jan. 25, 1973. See, for example, Robert Messer, *The End of an Alliance: James F. Byrnes, Roosevelt, Truman, and the Origins of the Cold War*. Donovan, *Tumultuous Years*, 36. Donovan interviewed Webb on Mar. 6, 1978.

companion, but he found Acheson's hardheadedness and mastery of issues indispensable in an adviser. Acheson, in turn, who had resented what he saw as Franklin Roosevelt's deviousness, admired Truman's straightforward frankness. Thus, Donovan concluded that Truman "needed a strong secretary of state and usually accepted Acheson's views on foreign affairs without being putty in Acheson's hands. Acheson, having no political following of his own, needed a president who would give him leeway and unquestioned support against his enemies. Each had found the right man."[6] The result was a happy alliance in which the strengths and needs of each man complemented those of the other.

Three recent well-received biographies, David McCullough's *Truman*, Robert H. Ferrell's *Harry S. Truman*, and Alonzo Hamby's *Man of the People*, assess the Truman-Acheson relationship in differing ways, thereby shedding light on the difficulties historians have had in understanding that relationship. McCullough's narrative study comes closer to recognizing the significance of Acheson's role in policy matters than does Hamby's analytical work. "Of the nine members of his Cabinet," McCullough observed, "none was so conspicuous or had more influence on Truman than the elegant, polished Dean Acheson," whose place at Truman's side "was unrivaled" in its influence on policy. Acheson was Truman's contact with the wider world, "his reporter and interpreter of world events."[7] As helpful as these and other observations are and as rich as the anecdotal evidence is that supports them, McCullough never probes into the substantive policies that Acheson used his unrivaled position to fashion. That is, he never explores the matter of Acheson's personal contribution to American policy as distinct from policy generated by the bureaucratic structures of the State Department and White House, or dictated by the political consensus that contoured cold war policy generally.

Ferrell and Hamby, on the other hand, downplay the significance of Acheson's role in policy formulation. Rather than presenting Acheson as the driving force behind Truman's foreign policy, Hamby relegates Acheson to a secondary and largely reactive role. Lacking George C. Marshall's stature, what Acheson had to offer was "absolute loyalty and a sensitiveness to the president's requirements." As Hamby put it, "Truman did not want to make foreign policy at the White House; rather he wanted close consultation and the right to veto final decisions." Acheson's influence was thus the product of Truman's temperament and sufferance, rather than Acheson's calculation or manipulation. "Vastly different from

6. Donovan, *Tumultuous Years*, 36.
7. McCullough, *Truman*, 751-56.

Truman in background and capabilities," Hamby wrote of Acheson, he "nevertheless possessed a temperament so similar to that of his chief that he easily functioned as an alter ego in charge of foreign policy." Similarly, Robert Ferrell places Acheson in the shadow of Truman and of George Marshall, the latter of whom he credits with the positive developments in the State Department in the Truman era, including the reorganization effected by the Hoover Commission. In his wide-ranging study of Truman, Ferrell's Acheson is one of many players in a large cast of characters revolving around the president.[8]

Hamby substantiates his assessment by pointing to instances in which Truman and Acheson had important policy differences and Truman overrode Acheson, among them the Point Four program and Truman's decision to meet Gen. Douglas MacArthur on Wake Island to discuss their disagreements over military strategy in the Korean War. Despite the significance of these episodes, Hamby's characterization of Acheson as simply Truman's alter ego in foreign policy matters relegates the secretary to a more subordinate role than he actually played. Hamby fails to acknowledge that Acheson withdrew his support from Truman initiatives such as the Wake Island talks so adroitly that Truman remained mollified. And without Acheson's support, Truman's proposals often foundered. Acheson also distanced himself more effectively than did Truman from the mounting controversy over MacArthur, which was politically costly to Truman.

The dispute over establishing diplomatic relations with the Vatican was an instructive example of how Truman and Acheson operated in matters on which they differed and how their mentor-student relationship worked. Shortly after Acheson became secretary of state, Truman, at the urging of Myron C. Taylor, who had been Franklin Roosevelt's personal representative at the Vatican, told Acheson that he intended to upgrade American representation at the Vatican. State Department bureaucrats supported the change, but Acheson did not. Acheson argued that the change would "surely start a religious controversy all over the country" and distract attention from "the growing Russian menace." After discussing the issues, Acheson later recalled, Truman "promised that he would do nothing to execute the plan until we had conferred again, regarding an appropriate time for doing so." It "was not difficult, amid the crowding events and crises of the ensuing years, to convince him

---

8. Hamby, *Man of the People: A Life of Harry S. Truman*, 510-11; Ferrell, *Harry S. Truman: A Life.*

that the appropriate time had eluded us." Literally, years went by as Acheson delayed the matter. Finally, in October 1951, Truman accused Acheson of using stalling tactics a Roman emperor might have admired. He told Acheson he had promised the pope he would upgrade the position and believed he was breaching a promise. "I was tempted to point out," Acheson later wrote, "that the Pope could give him absolution from the promise, if anyone could, but the President was in no mood to argue." No longer able to delay the inevitable, Acheson stepped aside with all the gracefulness he could muster. Truman "asked whether I would think it fair for him, after nearly three years, to recover his freedom to act without further consultation with me," he recalled. "Of course, I agreed."[9] In the aftermath, Truman, without Acheson's advice, nominated Mark W. Clark, whose army had liberated Rome in World War II, only to have the nomination blocked for personal and political reasons by the Texas congressional delegation. Many Texans, it seemed, had never forgiven Clark for decisions he had made during an attack on the Rapido River in the Italian campaign in which soldiers from Texas sustained unusually high casualties. In the ensuing political tempest, Truman withdrew the nomination. As usual, in the end, Acheson got what he wanted: no ambassador to the Vatican.

Historians whose research has focused on Acheson rather than Truman have also done little better in understanding the substantive particulars of the relationship between the two men, including the personal policy objectives Acheson used the relationship to further. Gaddis Smith has recognized Acheson as the most powerful secretary of state in the twentieth century, but rests that judgment on analysis of cold war policy with scant attention to the personal policy concerns Acheson brought to his position or used that position to push. Without systematic attention to the latter concerns, Acheson's relationship with Truman appears to hinge on nothing more substantial than his attentiveness to Truman's concerns. David S. McLellan similarly emphasizes personal factors in explaining the Truman-Acheson relationship. Truman took "an unfeigned delight in hearing Dean lay out a problem or take up the advocacy of some course of action," McLellan has written. However true that was—and it was true— it leaves one puzzled about the dynamics of, the motive power in, the relationship between the two men.[10]

9. Acheson, *Present at the Creation*, 574-75.
10. Smith, *Dean Acheson*, 391-95; McLellan, *Dean Acheson*, 95-96. The only historian who has written extensively on Acheson's post–secretary of state years, Douglas Brinkley, does not deal meaningfully with the Truman-Acheson relationship (see *Dean Acheson*).

General studies of the cold war have dealt effectively with the broad themes and global strategies of American policy, but they too have ignored the personal imperatives that drove major aspects of Acheson's policy formulation. In perhaps the best of those studies, Melvyn P. Leffler argues that Truman had little desire to control foreign policy and willingly gave Acheson wide discretion in even the most basic policy matters as long he kept Truman informed about what he was doing. In an even larger body of impressive work, John Lewis Gaddis does not address the mentoring relationship that existed between Truman and Acheson.[11] Rather, Gaddis presents Truman with leading rather than being led by a State Department and defense establishment firmly committed to realist goals through containment and other cold war strategies.[12]

In a more critical analysis than other historians, William E. Pemberton presents a more suggestive account of the Truman-Acheson relationship and its impact on U.S. foreign policy. In a harsh critique of the Truman administration, Pemberton distances himself from other historians of the subject, all of whom praise Truman's foreign policy generally and Acheson's role in formulating it specifically. This is not to say that Pemberton is always correct in his criticism, but works such as his may well lead to more balanced appraisal. Pemberton does not address the Truman-Acheson relationship comprehensively, but scattered through his study are insightful observations about Acheson's role in policy making. Pemberton believes that despite his self-image as a mover of men, Truman was easily manipulated by strong-willed subordinates who knew their own minds and purposes. "Dean Acheson," Pemberton asserts in a representative passage, "understood Truman's self-concept and could choose language and images that moved the president in directions Acheson wanted." Psychologically, Pemberton suggests, Truman needed a secretary of state to whom he could delegate authority and responsibility without worrisome second thoughts, but he needed equally strong assurances that he was

---

11. Leffler, *A Preponderance of Power: National Security, the Truman Administration, and the Cold War,* 268-69; Gaddis, *We Now Know: Rethinking Cold War History; The United States and the Origins of the Cold War, 1941-1947; Strategies of Containment: A Critical Appraisal of Postwar American National Security Policy; The Long Peace: Inquiries into the History of the Cold War;* and "Was the Truman Doctrine a Real Turning Point?"

12. See, for example, *The Long Peace* and in slightly different form, "The Long Peace: Elements of Stability in the Postwar International System" and "The Cold War, the Long Peace, and the Future." Other important cold war historians who do not specifically analyze the Truman-Acheson relationship include Randall Bennet Woods and Howard Jones, *Dawning of the Cold War: The United States' Quest for Order;* Thomas J. McCormick, *America's Half-Century: United States Foreign Policy in the Cold War;* Lloyd Gardner, *Architects of Illusion: Men and Ideas in American Foreign Policy, 1941-1949;* and Daniel Yergin, *Shattered Peace.*

himself the ultimate decision maker, "even if usually he was the ratifier" of decisions Acheson in fact made.[13]

Pemberton fails to follow up on these suggestive observations. His Acheson led Truman to better understandings of foreign affairs without threatening Truman's role as the ultimate arbiter of policy decisions. After going through notably unsuccessful relationships with James F. Byrnes and Edward R. Stettinius at State, Truman was eager to follow the lead of someone in whom he had the kind of confidence he earlier had in George C. Marshall. In Acheson, he had such a man and possibly more, someone with Marshall's reliability but with a surer, more sweeping vision of how the world should be and could be arranged. It was this vision that impressed Truman, as many of Acheson's colleagues have acknowledged. Secy. of the Treasury John Snyder, who was proud of his own relationship with Truman, later said of Acheson and the president, "He and Mr. Truman had great accord in views and worked together. He relied on Acheson; he believed in him." John D. Hickerson, an Acheson ally who served as assistant secretary for UN affairs among other posts, similarly acknowledged Acheson's profound influence on Truman. Asked whether Truman had had less than the usual degree of control a president has over foreign policy while Acheson was at the State Department, Hickerson responded, "I think that overstates it a little bit. I think that the [Truman-Acheson] relationship was an excellent one. Of course, that is based on the fact that there was very deep, close friendship between Acheson and President Truman. And it's also based on the fact that Acheson, I think, had excellent judgment."[14]

Acheson's strength of purpose bolstered his equally impressive bureaucratic skills. His memorandums to the president illuminate the careful way Acheson laid out problems, leading Truman logically and empirically to one reasonable conclusion, the one Acheson recommended. This method fit perfectly Truman's idea of the presidency as well as his sense of his own capabilities, at once giving him the advice and knowledge of a trusted aide while leaving final decisions to him. Truman was an intelligent as well as a shrewd man, able to read and absorb a great deal, follow an argument, and digest its meaning. He was not, however, a critical or original thinker, though he understood the value of critical and original thought. Skilled in the arts of the law, Acheson, for his part, had long ago mastered the techniques of persuasion. According to the unanimous testimony of those who observed the two men at close range, Acheson had the measure of

13. Pemberton, *Harry S. Truman: Fair Dealer and Cold Warrior*, 39.
14. Snyder, Oral History, 78; Hickerson, Oral History, 17.

Truman without the appearance of trying to push, or even to lead, him where he might not want to go. Richard Neustadt, a special assistant to Truman and later a noted scholar of the presidency, was one such witness. "When the people got around the table with the President going over the issues," Neustadt recalled, "toward the end, the Secretary of State had no hesitancy about coming in, taking off his jacket and sitting there and writing. Indeed, he felt quite confident that he could tell the difference between himself and everybody else and the President could tell the difference, too."[15]

The president and the secretary had a genuine sense of deference for each other. When Truman in late 1949 was leaving Washington for a brief vacation, Acheson surprised him by showing up at the airport to see him off. "It was good of you to see us off," Truman later wrote. "You always do the right thing. I'm still a farm boy and when the Secretary of State of the greatest Republic comes to the airport to see me off on a vacation, I can't help but swell up a bit." However one cares to read this incident, including Truman's reaction to it, the respect the two men had for each other is evident in it. "Your note touched me more than I can say," Acheson replied. "As I looked around that morning you spoke of, I saw no officials present—only a man to see off on vacation another, for whom he has the deepest respect and affection."[16] This handwritten reply made two points, which both men surely grasped, that no one else had come to see Truman off and that Acheson had come to see off not Truman the president but Truman the man.

The genuineness of this mutual respect spilled over into substantial matters of policy. One of the worst crises of the Truman presidency came in the initial days of the Korean War when the need for decisive action was imperative and the consequence of such action unknown. "Regarding June 24 and 25," Truman wrote in a longhand note to Acheson on July 19, 1950,

> your initiative in immediately calling the Security Council of the UN on Saturday night and notifying me was the key to what developed afterwards. Had you not acted promptly in that direction, we would have had to go into Korea alone. The meeting Sunday night at the Blair

15. Richard Neustadt, "Joint Oral History Interview: The Truman White House with Charles Murphy, Richard Neustadt, David Stowe, and James Webb," conducted on Feb. 20, 1980, in Washington, D.C., Harry S. Truman Library (hereafter HSTL), 91-92.

16. Truman to Acheson, Nov. 28, 1949; Acheson to Truman, undated, Acheson Papers–HSTL, box 180, folder 1947-1952.

House was the result of your action Saturday night and the results obtained show that you are a great Secretary of State and a diplomat. Your handling of the situation since has been superb.[17]

Acheson responded, also in a handwritten note, "I have just received your long-hand memorandum to me dated today. This is another of a long series of marks of your kindness to me and of your unwavering support and trust. I am deeply grateful for your note, and need not tell you that I shall treasure it. More than either, I shall do my best to deserve your confidence and serve you, and through you our country, with all that I have."[18]

This exchange underscores the nature of the relationship of close cooperation under stressful circumstances. Truman's letter, perhaps inadvertently, acknowledges Acheson's responsibility for the response to the North Korean assault. Acheson's letter shows his commitment and loyalty to Truman. The language about "serving" Truman seems a little archaic but was appropriate for a Victorian statesman addressing a superior with whom he had a close relationship. The mutuality of their sentiments grew in part on Truman's side from his recognition that he had much to learn from Acheson, a recognition that continued after he left office. "Been reading your book on Congress," Truman wrote Acheson in 1957. "Between you and Woodrow Wilson, I've been learning a lot—and hope to learn a lot more!" Six months later he wrote Acheson again: "Just received an invitation to attend some lectures you are giving at Tufts U in Medford, Mass. Wish I could be present. Will you send me the lectures? I'll read them and someday those back brain cells of mine may come up with a plagiarism."[19]

Acheson not only cultivated Truman but also carefully molded his colleagues and subordinates in the State Department into a policy-making apparatus responsive to his wishes. He spent much time discussing issues with his staff, making sure they knew his feelings and understood his purposes and what he expected them to do. Acheson thought originally and creatively, passed on his thoughts to his staff early in the policy-making process, and used the process to mold policy to his own ends. As Norman Graebner has observed in comparing Acheson to one of his predecessors in Truman's cabinet, "Unlike Marshall, he did not wait for his staff to settle on policies and then present them to him for rejection

17. Truman to Acheson, July 19, 1950, in ibid.
18. Acheson to Truman, July 19, 1950, in ibid.
19. Truman to Acheson, Apr. 8, 1957; Truman to Acheson, Oct. 7, 1957, Acheson Papers–HSTL, box 180, folder 1957.

or approval. Rather, he preferred to tackle the important questions earlier and influence the entire policy-making procedure."[20]

Acheson institutionalized this "hands-on" approach. Particularly important in that regard were his famous "9:30s." At that time each morning, Acheson assembled key members of his staff, and he and they discussed current issues and his thinking on them. In these "give-and-take" sessions, Acheson much preferred the "give" to the "take," which was one reason that other genuinely independent policy thinkers, among them George F. Kennan, left Acheson's State Department. In time, Acheson's influence reached beyond his own department into other agencies concerned with national security policy. Perhaps the best illustration of this was Acheson's clash with Defense secretary Louis A. Johnson. The details of that clash, which involved personality as well as policy differences, are not germane to this study. What is germane is that as a result of the clash, Truman sided with Acheson and dismissed Johnson from office. Acheson's influence over administration policy expanded impressively in the early years of his tenure at State.

A conflict in 1950 over the process of allocating scarce material resources among the allied nations illustrates Acheson's technique in bringing Truman to the decision Acheson desired. The example also illuminates Acheson's careful treatment of his chief allies, Britain and France. The flap surfaced at a meeting of NATO's Atlantic Council in Brussels at which British foreign sinister Ernest Bevin argued that only the Big Three—the United Kingdom, the United States, and France—should have a say in allocating resources, an argument certain to create problems with smaller allies. According to Acheson, this argument created a mistaken impression that "it would be the function of the three-power central group to buy up the world's raw materials and allocate them among other countries as they saw fit." That, Acheson said in reporting the flap to Truman, was "never the intention," though it is likely that Acheson disagreed mainly with Bevin's candor. In any case, Bevin's formulation of the matter created a dispute that Acheson took care to resolve. A successful resolution, he believed, would necessitate a careful balancing act. The British and the French were concerned with maintaining their interests in their respective empires, where many of the resources in question originated. American interests demanded not only that the British and the French be placated but also that the legitimate concerns of other allies be accommodated and the well-being of the Atlantic alliance itself safeguarded. This combination of concerns led Acheson to ask Truman for authority to settle the dispute

20. Graebner, "Dean Acheson," 276.

himself through negotiations with his British and French counterparts. Acheson recommended that Truman just put everything in his hands. "In view of the complexities of the subject and the difficulty of discussing it in full through correspondence," he wrote the president, "I believe it would be helpful if you would authorize me to sit down with Sir Oliver Franks and Ambassador [Henri] Bonnet and attempt to reach a solution of the problem." In the resulting negotiations, Acheson walked a tightrope between overtly protecting American interests and the interests of the cold war alliance while covertly accommodating the interests of the British and French Empires. He, Franks, and Bonnet, Acheson was sure, could settle the matter through understandings that obscured troublesome realities. "The British, the French, and ourselves are in full agreement that the central group would be merely an initiating and servicing mechanism," he told Truman of the proposed control group, "and that substantive recommendations would be made by the standing commodity groups representing all friendly countries having interest in the commodity concerned." The effect of Bevin's remarks had "been to arouse suspicions of domination by the three powers," Acheson continued; the more "representative central group would help to allay these fears."[21]

To the memorandum outlining this positive course of action, Acheson had already attached a note to British prime minister Clement Attlee for Truman's signature, asking Attlee to direct Bevin to agree to the course of action Acheson proposed. "This question presents many complexities which can only be fully explored across the table," the note read, adding that Truman was asking Acheson to sit down with British and French representatives to "arrive at some mutually acceptable understanding as promptly as possible." Truman approved Acheson's proposal and signed the note to Attlee.[22]

Acheson's determination to control policy formulation and implementation made him especially sensitive to organizational arrangements, not only in the State Department but in related executive agencies as well. He was therefore concerned that the chains of bureaucratic command be clear and respected, and that one individual be clearly responsible for making and implementing policy. His approach to the burgeoning problem of the imbalance of payments between the United States and its trading allies illustrated this facet of his conduct of policy. "The problem I would like to submit for your consideration," he wrote, raising the prob-

21. Acheson to Truman, Dec. 27, 1950, Memoranda to the President, Secretary's Memos, National Archives.
    22. Ibid.

lems with Truman in early 1950, "is how to develop an Administration policy and program for adjusting the balance of payments of the United States."[23] Here, as always, Acheson's language and tone were important. With no evident urgency or motive, he offered his thoughts on a matter about which Truman would have to make some decisions. In an equally straightforward manner, he sketched the problem of the dollar gap in world trade. Unless the United States boosted imports, especially from its European allies, the allies would have insufficient exchange to buy American goods, the manufacture and export of which were essential to domestic prosperity. If the problem was not eased, Acheson advised, the consequences might include a shift of power from "the democratic to the Soviet sphere."

What was needed was an immediate "affirmation" that "the importance of a successful economic system among the free nations is so great that the U.S. is determined to be a part of it." What was essential in the longer run was better coordination between domestic and foreign policy. "The whole machinery of government must be brought into play if we are to achieve success," Acheson told the president, and success would require Truman's direct involvement. After thus dramatizing the issue, Acheson placed Truman in the leading role: "Your personal direction is needed not only at the initiation" of a program to rectify the problem, "but throughout [the] development and implementation" of the program as well. "In order that such a direction should not claim too much of your time," Acheson assured Truman, "I recommend you consider using one of your staff assistants to assist you in directing and coordinating the Administration program to adjust the balance of payments of the United States."[24]

Acheson went on to point out the kind of person needed for the position, the bureaucratic role he should play, and the duties he might have. Those duties included responsibility for coordinating the activities of relevant executive agencies "in order to insure the fulfillment of assignment and the continuance of your leadership in the formulation of policy recommendations to you." This arrangement, Acheson assured Truman, would combine "flexibility, Presidential direction, and respect for line relationships with the capabilities of an experienced staff assistant who has your confidence and who has the skill required to stimulate and maintain teamwork among the responsible agencies."[25] Truman approved Acheson's initiative.

23. Acheson to Truman, Feb. 16, 1950, Memorandum to the President, Secretary's Memos, National Archives.
24. Ibid.
25. Ibid.

Acheson was not beyond intervening in meetings with important heads of state to steer Truman down the right path. In December 1950, British prime minister Clement Attlee rushed to Washington to discuss the situation in Korea, particularly American references to using atomic weapons in the war there. Truman had himself caused Attlee's unease by fumbling a press conference question to imply that use of atomic weapons was under "active consideration" in the administration. During the meeting with Attlee, the prime minister was being largely successful by presenting Truman with a series of leading questions. As Acheson noted, "[Attlee] early noticed a tendency of the President to show concurrence or the reverse in each statement of his interlocutor as he went along. Framing his statements to draw presidential agreement with his exposition, he soon led the President well onto the flypaper." Acheson resolved to prevent that from happening again. "At the second meeting, as the procedure started again," he later wrote, "I stepped on the President's foot and suggested that it might be helpful to the Prime Minister to let him complete his whole statement without interruption. It was far from helpful to the Prime Minister, as his glance at me indicated, but we fared better." Later, intervening "at the President's request," Acheson steered the discussion onto safer ground.[26] It is clear from the episode that Truman was often willing to step back and learn from Acheson, another reflection of the great deference he accorded the secretary.

This is not to say that Truman never acted on his own initiative or was unaware of what Acheson was doing. However, Acheson almost always was able to keep Truman on track on important policy matters. Acheson was sensitive to claims that his Ivy League education and sophistication enabled him to manipulate Truman. He often argued to the contrary, pointing out that Truman was a well-read and intelligent man. In any case, he continued, what was important about education was not the schools one attended but "what enters into your innards. Suppose somebody sits under John Galbraith for three years to get an education; a hell of a waste of time. Mr. Truman read every book in the Independence library, which had about 3,500 to 5,000 volumes including three encyclopedias, and he read them all the way through." Compared to an academic setting, Acheson believed that Truman "took in a hell of a lot more out of that effort, which he took out of farming when he did it, than he would listening to all of this crap that goes on at Yale and Harvard, and perhaps in other places—[such as a] Harvard Law School education." Acheson went on to argue that Truman's experience in Missouri politics had educated him in the most

26. Acheson, *Present at the Creation*, 481-82.

important subject, human nature.[27] When he said these things in 1971, the old Victorian was waxing nostalgic about the virtues of the school of hard knocks, which he believed proponents of modern education too readily dismissed. Nonetheless, his sensitivity to remarks about the difference in his and Truman's educations is evident. His touchiness suggests that there was some truth to the accusation that he had been able to "manage" Truman, more truth than he cared to admit.

Acheson himself testified to his ability to push Truman into decisions Acheson wanted him to make. In an appreciation of Truman published shortly after the president's death in 1972, Acheson was quoted as saying:

> On one occasion [Truman] cut me short in discussing an important presidential appointment, saying that he had already made up his mind and committed himself. When I continued to expostulate that he had not heard all the considerations he insisted that he had committed himself which, he said, ended the matter. Deciding to risk all, I suggested that it did not end the matter, since on the east front of the Capitol I had heard him commit himself to "faithfully perform the duties of the office of the President of the United States," which surely required full hearing of the facts before making a decision. For a moment the famous Truman temper rose with his flush. Then he said calmly, "Go ahead. You are quite right." His final decision was the opposite of his "commitment."[28]

The most convincing evidence of Acheson's ability to "educate" and "manage" Truman is in their extensive correspondence after the two men left office. They remained friends, though not social companions, and wrote frequently to each other. Because Acheson lived in Maryland and Truman was in Missouri, they rarely met. Acheson was unable to exert the same kind of influence over Truman he had while they were in office, which sometimes frustrated Acheson who, no longer Truman's subordinate, was less constrained in the advice he gave. "Dear Mr. President," Acheson wrote on January 15, 1957, "I wish it were possible for us to coordinate our efforts a little better on foreign policy matters. Your article in last Sunday's *New York Times*, the first of your North American Newspaper Alliance articles, has, I am afraid, cut a good deal of the ground out from under an effort to put some sense into the [Eisenhower] administration's foreign policy and to put some fighting spirit into the

27. Acheson, Oral History, 21-22.
28. *Economist*, special review section, Sept. 12, 1998, 5-6.

Democrats." Acheson continued that if it were true, as Truman argued, that Congress had no alternative but to go along with the president, then Acheson had spent "four useless hours before the foreign affairs committee and a good many useless days of work in devising what I thought an excellent alternative, and one which was thoroughly in accord with steps which had been taken during your administration." Acheson then went through Truman's article criticizing specific statements. "However, the main purpose of this note is not to stick on what has been done," he admonished, "but to urge that in the future we try to get together and not be at cross-purposes." Acheson's view of his role as guide and teacher comes through clearly in this letter. In a subsequent note, he not uncharacteristically softened the scolding in the earlier letter.[29]

Truman responded also typically, "I want your views frankly on any subject at any time," he wrote on January 28. "But I was somewhat flabbergasted when your formal letter, all beautifully typed, came on Jan. 17th. I felt the same way I do when Miss Lizzie [Truman's wife, Bess] gives me hell for something I know nothing about." Truman insisted that he and Acheson were encouraging the same result. "The final result of your statement to the committee and mine has been a proper reaction that both of us are hoping may create a foreign policy," he told Acheson. "I am going to send you a copy of all the statements I've made in the last week or so and then if you want to give me further hell—do it—and I'll continue to like it." Acheson's letter had evidently clarified Truman's thinking on the issue at hand, and he duly came to agree with Acheson.

Even marginal disagreements with Acheson continued to trouble Truman. Sending Acheson copies of his recent statements on foreign policy on October 14, 1958, he told his one-time aide, "While they are not exactly in conformity with the conversation which you and I had over the telephone, I did a lot of thinking after I talked with you, which no doubt I should have done before, and came to the conclusion that my fight for bi-partisan foreign policy ought to be rather consistent and I think if you will read these statements you will find that you and I are not more than an inch or two apart on the subject." The problem was what Truman regarded as the bumbling of the Eisenhower administration. "I am sure the foreign policy of the United States is in the doldrums," he told Acheson, "and has been ever since *you and I left the White House*." The emphasis is added because

<hr/>

29. Acheson to Truman, Jan. 15, 1957, Acheson Papers–HSTL, box 180, folder 1957. The second letter mentioned is not in the collection at the Truman Library and appears to be unavailable.

it is a revealing phrase about Acheson's important position in the Truman White House, a kind of co-occupancy of the executive mansion and an equal sharing of policy responsibilities.[30]

Acheson was happy Truman responded positively to his criticism; any other response "would be so unlike" the former president. "I think that perhaps we are a little further apart on the Quemoy issue than your letter suggests," he told Truman, concerning two offshore islands in the Taiwan straits then the subject of dispute between the rival Chinese Communist and Nationalist governments, "but it is of no moment. What seems to me of importance is this issue has a dual aspect" that Truman had failed to recognize. Truman responded appreciatively. "There is no way in the world for you to offend me—even if you'd hit me in the nose," Truman wrote. "I was very much afraid the offender had been this old man." Again he directed Acheson's attention to what they agreed upon. "I get so steamed up when I view what these executive numbskulls have done to a foreign policy that you and I left to them and a domestic policy that took twenty long years of sweat, blood and tears to establish."[31] The exchange shows the great deference that Truman still had for Acheson and his sense that they had been equal partners in the foreign policy they had created.

To continue his effort to mold Truman's thinking, Acheson wrote the former president a "Dear Boss" letter on June 28, 1960. The details in the letter concerning the presidential race in 1960, the African American sit-ins then sweeping the country, and certain foreign policy matters are especially revealing illustrations of Acheson's tutelage of Truman. In 1960, Acheson supported John F. Kennedy for the Democratic presidential nomination. Truman, on the other hand, considered Kennedy unqualified for the presidency, and said so in public. For this Acheson admonished Truman, providing him a list of "It's-not-dones" to guide Truman's conduct during the presidential campaign. "Never say that any of them is not qualified to be President," he told Truman of the Democratic candidates. "Never say that any of them can't win." "Never suggest that any of them is the tool of any group or interest, or not a true blue liberal, or has (or has used) more money than another."[32]

Concerning the African American sit-ins, Acheson was equally critical. "Do not say that they are communist inspired," he told Truman. "The evidence is all the other way; despite alleged views of J. Edgar Hoover, who you should treat as much as you would a rattlesnake." Also, "Do

30. Truman to Acheson, Oct. 14, 1958, Acheson Papers–HSTL, box 180.
31. Acheson to Truman, Oct. 24, 1958; Truman to Acheson, Oct. 31, 1958, in ibid.
32. Acheson to Truman, June 28, 1960, in ibid.

not say that you disapprove of [sit-ins]. Whatever you think, you are under no compulsion to broadcast it. Free speech is a restraint on the government; not an incitement to the citizen." Truman should keep his thoughts on such sensitive matters to himself. "Your views, as reported are wholly out of keeping with your public record. The discussion does not convince anyone of anything. And does the party great harm. If you want to discuss the sociological, moral, and legal interests involved in this issue you should give much more time and thought to them."[33]

Finally, Truman should be careful of what he said in public about foreign policy during the presidential campaign. "For the next four months do not say that in foreign policy we must support the president," Acheson urged Truman.

> The reasons: This cliché has become a menace. It misrepresents by creating the false belief that in the recent series of disasters [Eisenhower] has had a position or a policy to support. This just is not true. One might as well say "support the president" if he falls off the end of the dock. That isn't policy. But to urge support for him makes his predicament appear to be a policy to people who don't know what a dock is. So please, just for four months, let his apologists come to his aid.[34]

Acheson hoped Truman would agree to this "treaty of 'don'ts,'" but the feisty Truman was not easily leashed. Against Acheson's better judgment, Truman not only planned to go to the Democratic National Convention in Los Angeles in 1960 but also planned to speak out there against Kennedy. A family illness prevented him from attending. Acheson wrote Truman in the aftermath that had he known in advance what Truman planned to do, "I should have wasted the family subsistence on the telephone urging you not to do what fate was to prevent you from doing. . . . I am sorry that your sister-in-law [who had fallen ill] had to be sacrificed to keep you from so unwise a step. But it was in a good cause and I hope that she is now much improved." Acheson regretted that Truman had said anything against Kennedy, since his nomination was inevitable, "and that all you . . . said you . . . would have to eat—as you indeed have." Perhaps because events had not gone as he hoped they would, Truman seemed somewhat contrite. "Well," Truman wrote Acheson, "you told me what I ought to listen to and don't. Your letter of July 17th was a classic. . . . What I want to know is how much of a damphool [*sic*] can a man be—and still

33. Ibid.
34. Ibid.

think he might be right. That's this old man. You were right that I would have been in a better position if I'd said nothing."[35]

One more instance will complete this circle of illustrations of Acheson's "management" of Truman. In 1958, Acheson invited Truman to Yale University. Working with Yale officials, he carefully choreographed the visit, coaching Truman on how to conduct classroom discussions, and even how he should dress. "The ideal thing," he wrote Truman, "would be for you to take an important presidential decision—we talked this morning of Korea—and trace through how a president meets this responsibility and comes to his conclusion—how the facts, uncertain at first, gradually develop, how and from whom the president gets counsel, and how finally he does what only he can do, come to a decision." In the seminars, Acheson or the professor would break the ice, and "[o]nce they begin, the meeting rapidly becomes very informal and a great deal of fun." Truman wrote back on March 28: "The suggested program suits me perfectly and thanks to you I will remember to bring my dinner jacket."[36]

Such examples illustrate the care Acheson took to give Truman the central role in their relations, as he had always done in foreign policy decisions. However, they also document the mentoring role Acheson always had with the president. Acheson's success in both endeavors was impressive. He was thus able to impose his imperial vision on basic aspects of American policy toward the colonial world.

---

35. Acheson to Truman, July 17, 1960; Truman to Acheson, Aug. 6, 1960, in ibid.

36. Acheson to Truman, Mar. 25, 1958; Truman to Acheson, Mar. 28, 1958, in ibid. On Apr. 16, 1958, Truman wrote to Acheson saying how much he had enjoyed his visit to Yale. "The visit to Yale and a recent one to the University of Oklahoma were, I believe, my most successful." This reference equating Yale and Oklahoma must have given Acheson, the old Yalie, some discomfort.

4

The Ulster Connection

While the venerable Irish president Eamon De Valera was in the United States on an official visit in 1959, Dean Acheson wrote UN ambassador William Tyler, complaining about the conduct of foreign policy by the Eisenhower administration. As the Berlin crisis worsened, he told Tyler, "we clown around with the genial old man from Dublin, putting out green carpets, coloring the soup green at the White House, and chuckling while he kisses Mamie's hand." Clearly, the warm reception given De Valera irritated Acheson, but the coupling of his irritation with references to De Valera's Irish identity and his alleged irrelevance to U.S. foreign policy was a characteristic expression of Acheson's mind-set. So generalized was Acheson's scorn for the Catholic Irish that he applied it to Irish Catholics in the United States, at least to those in public life. In a typical reference to Irish American politicians, Acheson, in the words of Douglas Brinkley, described two of them, Joseph P. Kennedy, the father of John F. Kennedy and for a time FDR's ambassador to Britain, and Sen. Joseph McCarthy, as "two corrupt and criminal Irishmen cut from the same primitive political cloth." In fact, according to Brinkley, Acheson lumped the whole set of political Kennedys together and dismissed all of them as "uncouth Irishmen unfit for high public office."[1]

This animus carried over into Acheson's conduct of foreign policy. As secretary of state, he consistently supported British control of Ulster, his ancestral homeland, despite the growing tenuousness of that control, and the rising opposition to it. In dealing with Ireland and British policy toward Northern Ireland, Acheson was anything but a foreign policy realist. He was, in fact, a latter-day Victorian imperialist, a romantic traditionalist whose policy stances reflected a kind of provincialism,

1. Acheson to Tyler, Mar. 18, 1959, Acheson Papers, box 31, folder 404; Brinkley, *Dean Acheson*, 70.

even tribalism, incompatible with the wise conduct of modern foreign policy.[2]

The Republic of Ireland became an independent nation in 1949 when the Dail, the Irish parliament, severed the ties to the British Commonwealth. This act, and the Dail's subsequent refusal to join the North Atlantic Treaty Organization (NATO), opened a new chapter in the history of America's "special relationship" with the United Kingdom, and set the context in which Secretary of State Acheson had to deal with Ireland, Ulster, and the British presence in Northern Ireland.

The story of Ireland's centuries-long struggle for independence is well documented.[3] The circumstances Acheson confronted as secretary of state began with the Easter Rising of 1916 and the harsh British response to it, which had the effect of turning Irish public opinion strongly in favor of the rebels and the calls for independence. Within two weeks of the uprising, the British executed fifteen of the "leaders," including James Connolly, who was already so badly wounded he had to be propped up in a chair to be shot. The executions made heroes of the rebels, and violence against the British occupation increased exponentially. By 1920, Britain had more than forty thousand troops in Ireland. To quell the violence and the hemorrhaging costs of the occupation, the government of David Lloyd George in 1921 negotiated an agreement with Michael Collins and other leaders of the era's diverse independence movements. In this agreement, Britain recognized the independence of the Irish Free State, and the Free State in turn agreed to the partition of most of Ulster—the six counties of Down, Tyrone, Derry, Antrim, Armagh, and Fermanagh—and its annexation by the United Kingdom as Northern Ireland.[4] In these counties, a majority of the population was Protestant, descendants mainly of Scottish Presbyterians who migrated to Ireland during the British occupation, some of them as early as the reign of Elizabeth I.

2. This is a timely consideration. Writers are already turning their attention to this change in U.S. policy. See, for example, Conor O'Clery, *Daring Diplomacy: Clinton's Secret Search for Peace in Ireland.*

3. See, for example, Desmond Williams, *The Irish Struggle, 1916-1926;* Roger Hull, *The Irish Triangle: Conflict in Northern Ireland;* Godard Lieberson, *The Irish Uprising, 1916-1922;* Robert B. McDowell, *Ireland in the Age of Imperialism and Revolution, 1760-1801;* Francis James, *Ireland in the Empire, 1688-1770;* Goddard Orpen, *Ireland under the Normans;* Richard Bagwell, *Ireland under the Tudors;* Padraig O'Malley, *The Uncivil Wars;* and Thomas M. Gallagher, *Paddy's Lament: Ireland, 1846-1847, Prelude to Hatred.*

4. J. J. Lee, *Ireland, 1912-1985: Politics and Society,* 44. Ironically, Sinn Fein at the time of the Easter Rising held a moderate position and did not take part in the rebellion. When the British arrested its leader, Arthur Griffith, as part of their response to the rising, the party was transformed in public perception to a radical nationalist stance. The execution of the leaders of the rebellion then enhanced the status of Sinn Fein in the public eye.

The centuries-long political and economic dominance of British Protestants in Ireland, and the cultural prerogatives that accompanied it, rested on the systematic expropriation of Irish Catholics. Preservation of this Protestant "ascendancy," as it was known, had been the chief object of British policy since the days of Elizabeth I, and the Protestant settler population the chief instrument of that policy. Its ultimate prop, however, had always been the willingness of the British government to suppress ruthlessly any challenge to the ascendancy, a willingness exercised over the centuries on a number of spectacularly violent occasions. The results on both sides of the religious and ethnic divide in Ireland had been, among other things, the development of visceral animosities, and among the Protestant minority a siege mentality that encouraged exaggerated dependence on guarantees of continued union with Britain.

The 1921 agreement did not resolve those animosities: Irish nationalists continued to demand the absorption of Ulster into the Free State; Ulster Protestants and their British allies resisted that demand. In the wake of the agreement, a disgruntled nationalist assassinated Michael Collins, and some of the nationalists formed the Irish Republican Army to achieve their goal by terror if necessary. The British created a parliament to govern Northern Ireland and a constabulary to guard it, and assured the Protestants of Ulster that the Union was irrevocable. Irish nationalists, on the other hand, always considered the partition a temporary expedient to ward off British threats of "total war."[5]

Gradually, the Free State edged away from Britain, adopting its own constitution in 1938 and declaring its neutrality during World War II, and, in 1949, severing its ties with the British Crown, withdrawing from the Commonwealth, and proclaiming itself the Republic of Ireland. The British government accepted these changes, because it had no other choice, but in the Ireland Act of 1949, Parliament pledged that Northern Ireland would remain in the United Kingdom as long as its autonomous parliament wished.[6] Though this act granted citizens of the Irish republic special privileges in Britain, it made meaningful negotiations over Northern Ireland impossible by giving Ulster Unionists veto power over such negotiations.

This was the situation, still sporadically punctuated by acts of violence and retaliation on both sides, when British foreign secretary Ernest Bevin

5. Ibid., 54.

6. Lawrence James, *The Rise and Fall of the British Empire*, 533; Walter L. Arstein, *Britain Yesterday and Today*, 356; David Thomson, *England in the Twentieth Century*, 72-73. See also Henry W. Brands, *The Spector of Neutralism: The United States and the Emergence of the Third World, 1947-1960*; and Gary Hess, *America Encounters India, 1941-1947*.

and others proposed a set of new defense and security arrangements among the Western allies at the outset of the cold war.[7] The eventual outcome of the proposal was the North Atlantic Treaty Organization, which, among other things, committed the United States to an entangling alliance with its European and North American allies and, incidentally, to a series of arrangements that had the effect of strengthening the position of the British and the French in their respective empires. NATO had the enthusiastic support of President Harry S. Truman and Secy. of State George C. Marshall, and negotiations creating it were well along when Acheson became secretary of state.[8]

Geographically, of course, Ireland is in the middle of the NATO world, and the question of its membership and participation in the Western defense alliance arose immediately.[9] The United States and the other signatories of the Brussels Treaty who led the creation of NATO agreed on January 3, 1949, to invite Ireland and other small countries in the NATO area, including Iceland, Norway, and Portugal, to join the alliance.[10] To officials in Dublin the menace to Irish interests was not the distant Soviet Union but the next-door United Kingdom, and they responded to the invitation accordingly. "Eire has made it known," as the *New York Times* put it, "that she would consider membership in the projected North Atlantic pact only if partition of Ireland were abolished," and "only if an all-Ireland government were in a position to decide questions." Since that was not the case, Dublin declined the invitation "with regret."[11]

"Partition is our Palestine. Until that issue is settled we can go no further in our relations with Britain," Irish foreign minister Sean MacBride told a reporter following this decision. "The unjust partition of Ireland is as much an international problem as the Palestine or Indonesian questions," he also said, "and I am hopeful that Britain and the other countries participating in Atlantic co-operation realize that the ending of this undemocratic anomaly is vital to Atlantic co-operation."[12]

7. Leffler, *Preponderance of Power*, 208; Elizabeth D. Sherwood, *Allies in Crisis*, 7; Bradford Perkins, "The Truman Administration and Great Britain," in *The "Special Relationship": Anglo-American Relations since 1945*, ed. Wm. Roger Louis and Hedley Bull, 57-58.

8. Louis and Bull, *The "Special Relationship,"* 8-9. See also Alan Bullock, *Ernest Bevin: Foreign Secretary, 1945-51*, 57.

9. Gaddis Smith, for example, in his biography of Dean Acheson in the American Secretaries of State and Their Diplomacy series stated that Ireland hinted at an interest in joining the alliance. Smith recounts only the discussion held in mid-April 1949 between Acheson and MacBride. In Smith's treatment, the Irish issue is an inconsequential aside.

10. Hickerson, Memorandum of Conversation by the Director of the Office of European Affairs, Jan. 3, 1949, *FRUS*, 4:1.

11. *New York Times*, Feb. 2, 1949.

12. *New York Times*, Feb. 7, 1949. For an excellent biography of MacBride, see Anthony J. Jordan, *Sean MacBride: A Biography*.

"A very real difficulty presents itself by reason of the fact that the Pact, as at present drafted, is intended to 'protect the integrity' and the 'political independence' of the participating nations," MacBride said on another occasion of NATO. "Unless it be clearly recognized by the participating nations, including Britain, that the territorial integrity and political independence of Ireland is a matter which is the sole concern of the Irish people, our adherence to the Pact would be tantamount to sanctioning Britain's wrongful intrusion in our island." MacBride also argued with what seems in hindsight impeccable logic that the reunification of Ireland, the dissolution of the union of Ulster and the United Kingdom, was essential to political harmony and social stability in the geographical bosom of the NATO world; it was thus in the interest of the United States as well as of Britain itself. As Drew Middleton of the *New York Times* reported at the time, though the United States had no security interest in the separation of Ulster from the rest of Ireland, it had a vital interest in the cooperation of Ireland, "the bowsprit of Europe," with NATO. Ireland, Middleton argued, was a strategically obvious site for positioning NATO security forces. In fact, Irish ports were so strategically vital that secret British and U.S. military planners proposed that they be seized if a threat arose to them in an international crisis with the Soviet Union. These were the strategic considerations that prompted the State Department and the Joint Chiefs of Staff to recommend that Ireland be invited to join NATO.[13]

The Central Intelligence Agency (CIA) was similarly impressed by Ireland's strategic importance. "Ireland is potentially a valuable ally because of its strategic location athwart the chief seaways and airways to and from Western Europe," the CIA reported in an assessment for the president. Ireland's topography would permit the easy construction of airfields from which strategic bombers might attack "as far east as the Ural mountains. . . . Moreover, defense of such bases against air attack by European-based planes would be greatly facilitated by the need for such planes to cross the anti-aircraft defenses to Great Britain." In addition, the CIA study pointed out that bases in Ireland would extend the range and effectiveness of antisubmarine and convoy protection operations across the North Atlantic, as the lack of such bases in World War II had demonstrated. Finally, the manpower potential in Ireland was "not inconsiderable," and the denial of Ireland to an enemy "is an unavoidable principle of United States security."[14]

Despite these assessments, negotiations for Irish membership in NATO

13. *Irish Times,* Apr. 25, 1949; Feb. 15, 1949; *New York Times,* Feb. 2, 1949; policy statement for the Joint Chiefs of Staff by Adm. Louis Denfeld, Jan. 5, 1949, *FRUS,* 4:12.
14. Harry S. Truman Papers, President's Secretary's Files, box 261, Ireland folder.

were never promising. Acting Secy. of State Robert Lovett told George A. Garrett, the American minister in Dublin, to inform MacBride at the outset that should Ireland raise the Ulster issue in discussing the pact, Garrett should make clear the United States considered the two questions "totally unrelated and that we take their action in raising [the] partition question to mean they are not seriously interested in the Atlantic Pact and will accordingly not consult them further." Lovett sent the same message to the British representative in Dublin, and directed Garrett to inform the British representative of the "Irish government's reaction" to the American stance.[15]

This directive was Lovett's response to a request from British foreign minister Bevin asking for help in defending the British position in Ulster. "The Foreign Office would wish to concert policy with the US government," Bevin told Lovett, "in the event of any moves by the Irish government to make the ending of partition a bargain or quid pro quo in connection with Ireland's participation in the North Atlantic pact." He also asked Lovett to instruct Garrett to keep the British "informed of the reaction of the Irish government to his approach."[16] The wording of Garrett's instructions from Lovett paralleled that in Bevin's note to the State Department.

Throughout the negotiations, the Americans acted on the twin assumptions that the wishes and interests of Ireland were subordinate to those of Britain because the latter were tied to the national interest of the United States. Despite the fact that the Irish government had severed its ties to the British Commonwealth, U.S. negotiators dealt with their Irish counterparts within the framework of a Commonwealth perspective. As the negotiations proceeded, the Irish ambassador in Washington, Sean Nunan, told John D. Hickerson, Acheson's director of the Office of European Affairs at State, that Ireland wanted to join NATO, but wanted the United States to agree to mediate the Ulster problem as a preliminary to its doing so. Hickerson responded that NATO was a security system and admission to it "was not an appropriate means of settling problems of such long-standing duration as the question of partition." Nunan responded that that stance was inappropriate now that Ireland was a republic rather than a member of the British Commonwealth. Nevertheless, Hickerson held his ground, reiterating that Ulster was a matter for the United Kingdom and Ireland to settle as though it were an internal matter.[17]

15. Lovett to Garrett, Jan. 10, 1949, *FRUS*, 4:15.
16. Sean Cronin, *Washington's Irish Policy, 1916-1986*, 225.
17. Hickerson memorandum, Feb. 9, 1949, *FRUS*, 4:90-91.

Support for Britain's Commonwealth system was as much a matter of U.S. policy as this stiff-arming of Ireland. "As far as I can judge," wrote Mary Joy Tibbetts, an enthusiastic Anglophile in the London embassy at the time, "the British welcome our backing of the Commonwealth and consider our policy in this respect to be not only sound but essential in a troubled world" as well. In fact, so tied together were Britain and the Commonwealth in Tibbetts's mind that she argued that support for Britain was support of the Commonwealth. Any differentiation between Britain and the Commonwealth on policy matters, Tibbetts believed, would be "disastrous. In Commonwealth matters, as in everything else, the British are intelligent realists. They know that we will not be so childish as to attempt to wean members of the Commonwealth away from the British, and in all matters of serious concern, such as the Kashmir dispute, we have followed the policy of close consultation and have worked for the same ends."[18]

Tibbetts's letter reflects the enhanced Anglo-American relationship in the colonial world after Acheson took over the State Department. However, beginning in 1949 a series of events created new circumstances in which a reassessment of that relationship might have been fruitful. Among those events were the organization of NATO, the withdrawal of Ireland from the Commonwealth, and the emergence of nationalist and independence movements in various parts of the Commonwealth in the aftermath of Indian independence in 1947. These events, however, coincided with Acheson's appointment as secretary of state.

Following the example of Acheson himself, historians have generally applauded Acheson's appointment, and have emphasized the new spirit of creativity and realism they discern in his foreign policy. However much those qualities may have characterized other facets of Acheson's policies, they do not describe his policies concerning Ireland, Britain, and the British Commonwealth, and those concerning Britain's role in the colonial world.[19] The political changes that occasioned Ireland's withdrawal from the Commonwealth and the proclamation of the Irish republic also altered Irish foreign policy. The longtime leader of Irish neutralism, Eamon De Valera, lost political office in 1948, and the new government of Prime Minister John A. Costello developed a more assertive, anti-British foreign policy, as evidenced by the effort of Foreign Minister Sean MacBride to get the United States to mediate the Ulster issue as a condition of joining

18. Tibbetts to Satterthwaite, Dec. 20, 1949, Post Records, RG 84, 1949.350, box 184, London Embassy Confidential File B-C, National Archives.
19. See, for example, Acheson, "Apologia pro libre hoc," preface to *Present at the Creation;* and Isaacson and Thomas, *Wise Men.*

NATO. These changes brought no meaningful review of Irish-American relations in Washington, however, and no changes in American policy toward Ireland either before or after Acheson became secretary of state.

The refusal to become involved in the Anglo-Irish dispute was not an act of neutrality, but a calculated act to preserve the status quo by siding with Britain. Ireland was in no position to pressure Britain into negotiations. Feelers in that direction had been put out by Ambassador George Garrett, who had, in the words of one historian, a "common-sense view of politics." Specifically, Garrett recommended that Washington explore Dublin's request to mediate the Ulster dispute.[20] In a long dispatch in the spring of 1948, Garrett told Washington that Eire was open to compromise in return for help in getting the British to negotiate on the basis of "a realistic agenda." The Irish, Garrett wrote, seek "in their modest way to play a role" in opposing world communism, and "a situation is at hand which will bring unity to all Irishmen if the more local issue of partition is eliminated." Garrett argued, "The United States has more than a passing interest in the present phase of partition" because of the strategic advantages to be gained from Irish cooperation on matters related to cold war security. "The time would seem to be propitious to suggest to Westminster to carry forward an enlightened policy such as has been manifested in India, Burma, Ceylon, and other parts of the Empire." Garrett concluded, "It would also appear in England's best interests to take a look at its own front door with a view to collecting such good will as remains before the ultimate and presumably one-day inevitable solution of partition is resolved despite England's resistance to it."[21]

Robert Lovett, then the acting secretary of state, replied to Garrett by noting the "usefulness and desirability" of addressing the Ulster problem, but restating Washington's unwillingness to raise the issue with London. "The Dept. is interested in receiving the Legation's views and recommendations on this long-standing problem of partition," Lovett wrote to Garrett, "and is desirous of being informed promptly of any developments concerning it." In response to this expression of interest, the counselor at the Dublin embassy, Vinton Chapin, sent Washington a carefully argued memorandum that Garrett endorsed. Relations between Eire and Britain were now less troubled than they had been for years, Chapin noted, a circumstance that might encourage London to respond positively to a U.S. offer to mediate the Ulster dispute. Another circumstance that might also help was the common danger to both Ireland and Britain from the

20. Cronin, *Washington's Irish Policy*, 190-92.
21. Garrett to Secretary of State, box 16, 710–partition file, RG 84, 350/61/20/03, National Archives.

Soviet Union. That danger had thrust the Ulster dispute into a context "which transcends purely local interest," and "it would seem appropriate that the matter could be pursued" by the United States without "criticism on the score of interference or intrusion by Great Britain." The British government might therefore "be impressed with the wisdom of suggesting to Dublin and Belfast that considerations far more significant than those which enter into the border question make a settlement of special importance." Despite its global responsibilities, Chapin continued, Britain on its own seemed unable to take "a realistic view" of the Ulster question for reasons having to do with domestic politics. This was unfortunate, for "the longer [partition] remains a breach, the more difficult it will become of resolving and in this sense appears to be going against the stream where other places in Europe . . . are attempting to establish understanding."[22]

This was the situation when Acheson became secretary of state. The State Department was resisting suggestions that it raise the Ulster dispute with Britain, but had left the matter open by asking the Dublin embassy for updates on developments. Acheson at once ended that opening. Importantly, his chief deputy on European affairs, John Hickerson, had previously told Garrett that any interference in the Ulster issue would be an affront to the British. Britain had been America's ally in World War II, Hickerson reminded Garrett, whereas "Ireland's neutrality operated to the advantage of Germany."[23] The tone of Hickerson's note contrasted sharply with the measured language of Lovett's message, and reflected that Hickerson was one of Acheson's like-minded allies. A close friend of the new secretary of state, Hickerson was soon elevated from director of European affairs to assistant secretary of state.

However, Acheson's response to the situation went still further. In early 1949, he summoned Garrett to Washington for consultation. There is no record of the specifics of the consultation in State Department archives, but the letter Garrett wrote afterward to Livingston Satterthwaite, who handled British Commonwealth affairs at State, suggests that Garrett was dressed down for his handling of the Ulster issue. In defending his actions, Garrett wrote Satterthwaite from Dublin that he had always given "full weight to the Department's traditional position which was outlined to me in Washington before I proceeded to undertake my mission here." He had

22. Lovett to Garrett, Apr. 12, 1948, Records of the Dublin Embassy, box 16, partition file, 350/61/20/03, National Archives; Chapin to Garrett, Sept. 10, 1948, in ibid.

23. Hickerson to Garrett, May 4, 1948, RG 84, box 15, partition file, 350/61/30/03, National Archives. Hickerson is here reflecting a common cold war assumption that a country not aligned with the United States is arrayed against it. This approach caused problems for Sweden and India. In a bipolar world, the opposing camps saw little room for neutrals.

never been instructed to reject Irish overtures on the Ulster issue, and had never been told that Washington considered Ireland irrelevant on matters relating to the North Atlantic alliance. To the contrary, he responded to Lovett's letter in late 1948 expressing Washington's desire to ensure "the collaboration of Ireland as an ally with the Western Powers in any future conflict."[24]

It was that expression, Garrett told Satterthwaite, that prompted him to forward the Irish proposals to Washington and to recommend that they be studied carefully. However, in Washington, he had been "finally and definitively told that whether Ireland came in or stayed out [of NATO] was a matter of indifference and that her geographical position had little significance in respect to matters of strategy or in terms of the overall concept of Western defense and security." Garrett accepted that as the basis of U.S. policy but argued that had that been the case in 1948, he would have acted accordingly in his dealings with the Irish government.[25]

Though Garrett acquiesced in Acheson's policy, he clearly considered it shortsighted. He noted that Irish foreign minister Sean MacBride had raised the possibility of taking the Ulster issue to the United Nations, whereas other political figures in Dublin were predicting that British intransigence would sooner or later provoke violence from Irish nationalists. "Either action," Garrett warned Satterthwaite, "would start a train of consequences which could only be contrary to our best interests or those of England and less directly to those nations which are coming into association either under the Atlantic Pact or the Council of Europe." Acheson's new policy thus failed to convince Garrett. In a carefully worded note to Truman in July 1950, Garrett noted that he exerted no pressure on Ireland to enter NATO because the State Department had "instructed" him not to do so. Still, he let Truman know that he considered the partition of Ireland "unnatural" and the Irish refusal to enter NATO alongside Britain understandable. He also believed Washington should continue the effort to bring Ireland into the Western defense alliance.[26]

The new view in Acheson's State Department that Ireland was irrelevant to the strategic concerns of the alliance ran counter to assessments by the CIA and the Joint Chiefs of Staff, as well as Ernest Bevin. Since the strategic relevance of Ireland to NATO was geographically obvious, Acheson's stance is explicable only by the fact that he placed greater

24. Garrett to Satterthwaite, Mar. 14, 1949, RG 84, box 16, 350/61/20/03, National Archives.
25. Ibid.
26. Ibid.; Garrett to Truman, July 10, 1950, George A. Garrett Papers, folder 1.

weight on the British presence in Ulster than on any interests of NATO that that presence might jeopardize. Certainly, a man of Acheson's acumen in cold war matters could see the benefits of solving a thorny problem in the bosom of the NATO world. The Irish proposal was not that Britain abandon the Ulster Protestants to Catholic tyranny but that the people of Ulster be incorporated into the democratic Irish republic. Weighed against the costs of preserving the British presence in Ulster over Irish opposition, the gains to Western democracy the Irish proposal would likely bring, plus the benefits of strategically placed air and naval bases for NATO, a positive response to the Irish request for serious negotiations even against British opposition would surely have been better than rejecting it summarily.

To gain Irish cooperation with NATO, it may not have been necessary to solve the Ulster problem immediately but only to commence American mediation and British negotiation. U.S. pressure for either of those things would have angered the British and no doubt have stiffened their adamancy in the short run, but it may be worthwhile to speculate on what else such pressure might have produced. To be effective, the pressure would have to be sufficiently determined to convince the British of its seriousness at the same time American policy makers were preoccupied with their British counterparts in making NATO effective. That would have required the active support of Acheson and Truman, which was, of course, the rock on which the idea foundered. Acheson's commitment to British imperial interests never wavered, and Truman's reliance on Acheson's guidance in foreign policy was too complete to challenge Acheson on an issue Truman was indifferent to. Yet, without Acheson's support, the British were vulnerable to American pressure on this and other matters, as the huge U.S. loan had recently demonstrated and the future Suez crisis would illustrate much more dramatically. That crisis, which demonstrated Britain's inability to conduct a military operation in its own sphere of influence when faced with American opposition, humiliated the British. However, the British quickly cast aside the humiliation and did what they found necessary to preserve the Anglo-American relationship. Despite such acts of independence as recognizing the Communist government of China, the aftermath of the Suez crisis suggests that the British understood that the relationship with the United States was absolutely necessary for them. After initial outbursts of anger and resentment, the British would therefore likely have accommodated themselves to U.S. pressure on Ireland.[27]

27. The special relationship had, certainly, survived other earlier differences of opinion over policy, such as the Anglo-American naval rivalry after World War I, the trade war in the 1920s over rubber resources, and Britain's defaulting on its war debts in 1933.

Acheson's support for the British in Ulster thus ensured the loss of Ireland as a strategic asset for NATO without any counterbalancing gain for anyone except British imperialists and Ulster Unionists narrowly defined. A "realist" cost-benefit analysis of the outcome would surely have found this policy wanting. Critics of this reasoning might counter that Britain was perceived as a major power in its own right and that its support of NATO and other security endeavors was more vital to U.S. interests than the political status of Ulster Protestants or indeed of nationalist movements anywhere else in the empire or Commonwealth. That, indeed, was Acheson's calculation; nonetheless, to it may be answered that Washington need not have made an absolute commitment to the Irish side of the Ulster issue, but only to the search for meaningful negotiations. It was negotiations of any sort, not the absorption of Ulster into the Irish republic, that Acheson rejected.

The rejection evidences Acheson's contempt for nationalist movements everywhere in the colonial world, including Ireland. In the memoir of his tenure in the State Department, *Present at the Creation,* Acheson made a single reference to Ireland, and that one illustrated his bemused dismissal of the Ulster issue. "In August Secretary of the Navy Francis P. Matthews in a speech in Boston called for preventive war. He was made Ambassador to Ireland." The reference was to a political appointee whose views on foreign policy Acheson and Truman found too assertive, but the second part of the statement reflected Acheson's judgment that the embassy in Dublin was a place of political exile and policy irrelevance. The inattention to Irish affairs in Acheson's memoirs is consistent with his effort to steer attention away from his own Ulster background and from his personal history of dealing with matters related to decolonization. One result of this was more attention in his memoirs to Portugal, whose dictator, Antonio Salazar, Acheson admired, and whose empire was not yet under siege from indigenous nationalists while Acheson was in the State Department, than to Ulster, a trouble spot he had to deal with as secretary of state.[28]

Among the problems Acheson faced in dealing with Ulster was the political support in and out of Congress for the Irish position on the issue. Irish American politicians and others representing traditionally anti-British constituencies were especially critical of Acheson's handling of the Ulster matter, and tried to use their leverage in Congress to embarrass the administration. They introduced several bills dealing with the issue, the most important of them the Fogarty Resolution, named

28. Acheson, *Present at the Creation,* 478; Brinkley, *Dean Acheson,* 305-10; see also his epilogue.

for its author, Rep. John Fogarty of Rhode Island, an influential member of the Democratic caucus. The resolution called on Britain to allow a united Ireland, and threatened to end U.S. aid if it failed to do so. In debating the measure, the leader of the Democratic majority in the House, John J. McCormack, himself an Irish American representing a large Irish American constituency in Massachusetts, compared the Fogarty measure to a recently approved resolution "expressing the sense [of the House] that we believe in 'a free and democratic Palestine.' " McCormack had "fought for that resolution on the principle of self-determination," and the House, he argued, should approve the Fogarty Resolution for the same reason.[29]

Whether tied to traditional U.S. support for self-determination, as McCormack suggested, or to the demands of cold war policy, as others insisted, the Fogarty Resolution had considerable support. Those who emphasized its relevance to cold war policy, as did Fogarty himself, pointed to Soviet uses of Irish issues to embarrass the West politically, including the recent veto of Ireland's entry into the United Nations. "As far as weakening our strength in the world today," Fogarty told the House, "there is no question in my mind that resistance against communism would be strengthened all over the world if that outpost in the Atlantic Ocean . . . were a free and independent nation aligned with the cause of freedom." Another Irish American Democrat from Massachusetts, John F. Kennedy, added his support to the resolution. "A free, united, integrated Ireland," Kennedy said, "would provide an important bastion for the defense of the west, and would contribute to the strategic security of the United States." Rep. James Delaney of New York similarly believed that a unified Ireland would strengthen the free nations of Europe. "In the name of the freedoms which we cherish so dearly in our country," he told his colleagues, "this resolution ought to be adopted."[30]

The resolution had wide support from other influential or rising members of Congress from both parties, among them Republicans Jacob Javitts of New York, Albert Morano of Connecticut, and James E. Van Zandt of Pennsylvania. Prominent Democrats supporting the bill included Mike Mansfield of Montana, in whose subcommittee the resolution originated, Clement J. Zablocki of Wisconsin, Abraham Ribicoff of New York, and Alfred Sieminski and Peter Rodino, both of New Jersey. Chicago Democrat Adolph Sabath, then dean of the House, spoke compellingly on behalf of the resolution. Born in the Austro-Hungarian Empire in what later became Czechoslovakia, Sabath was himself an immigrant and a champion of

29. *Congressional Record*, 82d Cong., 1st sess., 1951, 97, pt. 12:283.
30. Ibid., 286, 276, 271.

the rights of subject peoples. By his own account, he had "abhorred and opposed oppression and discrimination" ever since he had himself been subjected to the "Austro-Hungarian imperialism that maintained a stranglehold on the Czech and Slovak peoples." The parallel between Austro-Hungarian and British imperialism was to Sabath exact. "Great Britain," he told the House, "has been telling us what to do for many years and has, in effect, forced us to do her will, not for our own good but to further her selfish imperialism and to insure the control of her possessions, control over which she secured through military and diplomatic conniving and trickery."[31]

Debate over the Fogarty Resolution provoked new expressions of the anti-British sentiment that always simmered beneath the surface of American politics, now reinforced by cold war concerns. "This tenderness for the feelings of England which I have observed during the debate today," Rep. John Shelley of California said of his House colleagues who opposed the measure, "arouses no sympathy from me. Neither does the argument that the United States should not inject itself into a controversy over partition of Ireland at a critical time in world affairs." He continued, "For us to sit back and refuse to take a stand in opposition to one of her gravest sins, the enforced partition of a sovereign nation, will only prostitute us in the eyes of those peoples who are teetering on the brink between democracy and communism. . . . A people enslaved care little whether their masters carry the hammer and sickle or the British lion as their standard."[32]

Despite the cogency of these arguments in hindsight, they failed to carry the day. The House rejected the Fogarty Resolution, which would have amounted to a major slap at a Democratic administration by a Democratic body, but did so by an unexpectedly close vote of 206 to 139, with one hundred members not voting. The chief argument against the resolution was that its adoption would embarrass and agitate the nation's most reliable ally. "The resolution is an interference in the internal affairs of Great Britain and none can deny it," insisted Democrat James Richards of South Carolina. Britain, a partner in NATO, was "exerting her utmost" in the common defense, whereas "Ireland has not seen fit to join this effort." Republican Leo Allen of Illinois argued, "Meddling in the affairs of our mutual friends can bring us nothing but disaster." Republican John Vorys of Ohio dismissed the resolution as "gratuitous, meddlesome advice" to a "friendly ally." Passage of the resolution, the two latter congressmen argued, would leave the United States open to similar

31. Ibid., 282.
32. Ibid., 277.

meddling regarding Hawaii, Alaska, and Puerto Rico. Nevertheless, an Irish newspaper reported, "The way in which these Congressmen voted and clapped Representative Fogarty of Rhode Island on the back after he spoke for Ireland and the way in which the galleries cheered indicated that there is support for Ireland that has never heretofore been permitted expression."[33]

In early 1949, the newly appointed secretary of state Dean Acheson was at the pinnacle of his career, respected by a president he admired and not yet burdened by the Korean War or the attacks of the McCarthyites. In Ireland, however, he faced a choice of the sort he often spoke of as "hard." He must endorse the status quo and with it the hostility to Irish nationalism that entailed, or he must initiate a new policy aimed at defusing a potentially dangerous issue that might eventually harm U.S. interests. Acheson did more than accept the concept of Hickerson noted earlier; he institutionalized a policy that uncritically supported Britain on the partition issue. He then cemented that policy through personal contacts in diplomatic channels, and through his influence with the president and his position on the National Security Council.

In the process, Hickerson, who supported the Unionist position on partition, rose to a position of power and influence in Acheson's State Department, whereas Secy. of Defense Louis Johnson, who recommended that the policy toward partition be reexamined, was eventually driven from office. Of course, many other factors contributed to both these eventualities, but given the importance of Ulster to Acheson, it would be a mistake to discount the role of the partition issue in either of them.[34]

In April 1949, Sean MacBride, the Irish foreign minister, met Acheson in Washington to discuss Irish-American relations, including Ulster and NATO. MacBride was a charismatic figure, much admired in Ireland for his family heritage and in diplomatic circles for his sophistication.[35] A child of the revolution that produced the Free State, MacBride was the son of Maud Gonne MacBride, a heroine of the struggle for independence, and of Maj. John MacBride, one of the fifteen men executed by the British following the Easter Rising in 1916. From his parents he derived a fierce commitment to Irish independence and unification, and he may not have known of Acheson's Ulster connection at the time of the 1949 discussions. In those discussions, MacBride and Acheson exchanged views on the Marshall

---

33. Ibid., 273, 272, 273; *Irish Independent*, Apr. 21, 1949.
34. As an Irish historian has noted, Johnson's "dismissal may not have been entirely unrelated to his recommendations on the Irish issue" (Ronan Fanning, "The United States and Irish Participation in NATO: The Debate of 1950," 40).
35. Cronin, *Washington's Irish Policy*, 193.

Plan, European unity and security, and the threat from communism before moving to the main subject of the exchange: Ulster and partition.

MacBride told Acheson his government endorsed the NATO alliance and would like to join it, but "no Irish government which had done this could have lasted two months as long as the partition question remained unsettled."[36] MacBride said his government was committed to resolving its problems with Britain, but British intransigence on the partition of Northern Ireland meant that the next step in the direction must come from London. If the Ulster problem were resolved, Ireland would become a friend of Britain, a ready supporter of North Atlantic unity, and an eager participant in NATO. The longer it was unresolved, MacBride predicted, the more explosive and difficult it would become. The organization and consolidation of the Atlantic alliance, MacBride suggested, furnished a window of opportunity for the United States to help resolve the issue with minimal offense to Britain. The sentiment in Britain for ending partition, he added, might be one basis for appealing to London.

Acheson was unmoved. "I said to the Minister," he recalled, "that we believed first that for us to become involved in the Irish partition question would be to bring us into a matter which was not an American concern, which would be resented in England and which in my judgment would cause far more harm than it could possibly do good."[37] The Ulster issue, he told MacBride, was unrelated to Irish membership in the Atlantic alliance, and the United States was unwilling to use that subject to meddle in the internal affairs of Ireland and Britain.

This posture of professed reluctance to meddle in the affairs of other nations was disingenuous. The United States had no similar reluctance whenever Washington convinced itself, however dubiously, that intervention was in its interest. While Acheson was himself secretary of state, the United States aided the French against nationalist rebels in Indochina and the British against a similar insurgency in Malaysia. It likewise helped Chiang Kai-shek establish his government on Taiwan over Chinese objections, and became embroiled in war in Korea. MacBride asked Acheson for no similar aid, but only for help in getting the British to negotiate meaningfully.

In late 1949, the British Embassy informed the State Department that the Ulster Society of New York wanted to honor Acheson as "the man of Ulster descent who has done the most for the United States during the year." Sir Basil Brooke, the prime minister of Northern Ireland, was

36. *FRUS, 1949*, 4:292-93.
37. Ibid.

to bestow the honor if Acheson agreed to accept it in person. Acheson's aides at State, however, urged him to refuse the honor. "Since Sir Basil Brooke is considered by the Southern Irish in the United States as the arch proponent of partition," one of them wrote, "your acceptance of the honor would undoubtedly cause a political storm in this country." Furthermore, it "might prejudice your effectiveness on the Hill where, as you know, Irish influence is great. The Ulster Society and the British Embassy will understand the reasons for your declining the honor and have had the delicacy not to ask you in writing."[38] Acheson evidently accepted the advice.

He did, however, meet in April 1950 with Brooke, while Brooke was on a tour of the United States. The Ulster government was erecting a statue commemorating the service of U.S. forces stationed in Northern Ireland during World War II, and Brooke wanted to present a replica of the statue to President Truman. For reasons that are not evident in the documents, Truman designated Acheson to receive the statue on his behalf, and Acheson agreed to do so. Luke Battle, Acheson's appointments secretary, noted that the Office of European Affairs recommended that Acheson see Brooke, accept the gift, but discuss nothing substantive.[39] Acheson agreed to this recommendation despite Brooke's stature as "a leading proponent of partition." To mute potential criticism, State Department spokesmen told the press the meeting was a routine courtesy call.

However, in the context of the partition controversy and Acheson's Ulster heritage, even a courtesy meeting with Brooke had more than symbolic significance. "There were no substantive matters of any kind discussed," read the official note on the meeting. "It was purely a courtesy call." Despite the absence of substance, Brooke described the meeting to the press as "delightful" because Acheson had "Ulster blood in his veins." To this impolitic reference, British ambassador Sir Oliver Franks, who had accompanied Brooke to the meeting with Acheson and to his subsequent encounter with the press, "quickly interposed: 'And some other relatives from South Ireland—the secretary said that.' "[40] Clearly, Franks understood the significance of Acheson's Ulster connection and the potential political damage a discussion of it by Brooke might cause. Franks's addendum to Brooke's remark made it appear that Acheson had connections to the Irish on both sides of the partition issue, which was

38. George Perkins to Acheson, Dec. 20, 1949, doc. 829, Memoranda of the Secretary of State, 1949-1951, and Meetings and Visits of Foreign Dignitaries, 1949-1952 (microfiche).
39. Battle to Acheson, Jan. 17, 1950, in ibid.
40. Memorandum of Conversation, Apr. 6, 1950, Memorandum of Conversation of the Secretary of State, 1947-1952 (microfiche); *Philadelphia Bulletin*, Apr. 7, 1950.

untrue but went unchallenged. This incident might explain at least in part why Sean MacBride never asked for another meeting with Acheson. It might also illustrate the sensitivity with which Acheson and his aides regarded his ties to Ulster while the partition issue remained controversial.

In the face of Acheson's intransigence, Louis Johnson, the secretary of defense, asked the National Security Council in the summer of 1950 to reexamine Irish-American policy, and assess the "desirability of undertaking diplomatic negotiations to encourage Ireland's participation" in NATO. The resulting policy paper, dated August 15, 1950, superseded one from 1948, that is, before Acheson became secretary.[41] By January 1950, Acheson had appointed Paul H. Nitze to take over the directorship of the Policy Planning Board, succeeding George Kennan, who had resigned the position. Nitze says he worked easily with Acheson, with whom he generally agreed on policy matters, and it is likely that he consulted Acheson in preparing the policy statement. As director of policy planning, he met with Acheson, and he knew that Acheson wanted all policy statements to reflect his own views regardless of who wrote them. Melvyn Leffler, the most authoritative student of national security policy in the Truman administration, emphasizes Acheson's hands-on control of policy formulation at State, and noted that Nitze and Acheson probably talked several times a day. "It is unlikely," Leffler has written of Nitze, "that he wrote any paper without first discussing the probable conclusions with Acheson."[42]

The statement Nitze prepared in response to Johnson's request concluded that the United States should refuse to involve itself in the Ulster matter. The Dublin government, Nitze complained, had repeatedly tried to "induce us to intervene with the United Kingdom to end partition by bringing about the forcible union of" Ireland. This, of course, misrepresents MacBride's request to Acheson, which was a "tactful" proposal for "assist[ance] in the solution of the problem." Nitze likewise prejudged the issue he was supposed to assess objectively by referring to the six counties of Northern Ireland as "an integral part of the United Kingdom." Ireland cannot be permitted "to play off the United States against Great Britain," Nitze wrote. "We should make it clear at all times that [a close

41. A footnote in *FRUS* notes that in a somewhat unusual circumstance all copies of the 1948 policy statement were apparently destroyed. Cronin in *Washington's Irish Policy* also notes an inability to find a copy of the document in the mid-1980s, including a search of the National Archives and the Truman Library. I conducted a similar search in 1997 with no success.

42. Leffler, *Preponderance of Power,* 313-14; Nitze to the author, Sept. 22, 1992; Nitze, *From Hiroshima to Glasnost,* esp. 94-96, 118-20; Leffler to the author, Oct. 15, 1992.

relationship with the United States] can form no substitute for healthy relations between Ireland and the United Kingdom." Disregarding actualities, Nitze insisted of Britain and Ireland that "history, economic conditions, and, above all, geography, have made those two countries irrevocable partners."[43] In fact, those things plus British imperialism had made the two countries enemies for centuries. The fact that the United States was the home of so many people whose forebears were victims of the resulting enmity was one basis of MacBride's appeal for U.S. mediation.

In siding with Britain and the Ulster Unionists, Nitze ratified the change in U.S. policy Acheson had introduced. The willingness of Acheson's predecessor, Robert Lovett, to consider Irish views on the Ulster issue has already been noted. It is worthwhile to point out here that the Acheson-Nitze policy did violence to the traditional U.S. stance on the issue. Back in 1938, to illustrate, Franklin D. Roosevelt had told his minister in Dublin that although the United States had to refrain from intervening in Ireland, "I quite agree with you that a final solution of Anglo-Irish relations, and of the Irish internal problem, would be an immeasurable gain from every point of view."[44]

The intransigence of the Acheson-Nitze policy, which contrasted with the implicit openness of Lovett and Roosevelt, encouraged Irish Americans to criticize Acheson's handling of the Ulster issue and to raise for the first time the matter of the growing criticism in Ireland of the United States. To blunt this criticism, State Department policy makers launched a modest informational and educational program "designed to present US policy [in the Irish republic] through the press, radio and films; to increase knowledge of American life through a US Information Library, and by educational exchanges; and to give in music, lectures and literature a true picture of American culture." The United States "should avoid being drawn into discussions of the rights and wrongs of such issues," the policy makers wrote of the Ulster problem, "and demonstrate by words and actions our neutrality on the partition."[45] It would certainly have been obvious to the Irish, no less than the British, that an American "neutral" position supported continued partition.

Just how much influence Acheson's Ulster heritage had upon his Ulster policy cannot, of course, be calculated precisely, in part because the heritage cannot be separated from the larger worldview of which it was an

43. *FRUS, 1950*, 3:1469, 1476.

44. Roosevelt to John Cudahy, Feb. 9, 1938. Cited in "United States Policy on the Irish Partition Question," research project no. 73 of the Division of Historical Policy Research, July 1948, box 15, RG84/350/61/30/03, National Archives.

45. *FRUS, 1950*, 3:1469, 1476, 1470-71.

integral part.[46] Nevertheless, that its influence was considerable seems obvious, in the extent to which the policy deviated from the realism Acheson so often praised and in the testimony of associates concerning his style and manner of policy making. According to the most astute of those associates, George Kennan, Acheson "was a man who dealt, in his inner world, not with institutions but with personalities; and he was not always, I thought, a good judge of the latter." As already noted, Acheson endeavored to ensure that policy recommendations counter to his own thinking never reached him. Kennan wrote:

> The thought of consulting the staff as an institution and conceding to it as did General Marshall, a margin of confidence within which he was willing to respect its opinion even when that opinion did not fully coincide with his own—the thought in particular of conceding to the staff a certain function as the ideological inspirer and coordinator of policy, bringing into coherent interrelationship the judgments and efforts of the various geographic and functional divisions of the department—all this would have been strange to him.[47]

In place of the institutional resourcefulness Kennan proposed, Acheson substituted close personal associations such as those he had with British ambassador Oliver Franks and with the closest members of his staff such as Paul Nitze, whom he had chosen in the first place because they agreed with him and who in turn affirmed his thinking during frequent contacts with him. This formula worked perfectly in providing Acheson the Ulster policy he wanted, affirming the correctness of that policy, and helping him resist critics of it.[48] This is not the arrangement a statesman committed to realism would have constructed or presided over. It is instead one that enabled Acheson to generate and sustain policies in Ulster and elsewhere that bolstered outmoded ethnic and political—and economic—hierarchies to the detriment of U.S. interests in the long run.[49]

46. William P. Bundy, Acheson's son-in-law, said it was his judgment that "Dean Acheson was first and foremost a statesman, whose personal likes among nations and their nationals were distinctly secondary, though not wholly without influence, when he weighed what policy should be toward such nations. In the case of the Republic of Ireland, I–and more important those closest to him–would judge the influence to have been nil" (letter to the author, Mar. 26, 1992).

47. Kennan, *Memoirs, 1925-1950*, 426-27.

48. See also Fred I. Greenstein and Richard H. Immerman, "Can Personality and Politics Be Studied Systematically?" 105-28; Immerman, "Eisenhower Revisionist," 319-42; and Robert Jervis, *Perceptions and Misperceptions in International Relations*.

49. Immerman, "Eisenhower Revisionist," 325. Also helpful for this passage was Peter Novick, *That Noble Dream: The "Objectivity Question" and the American Historical Profession*.

5

The Kashmir Connection

Dean Acheson's responsibilities as undersecretary of state after World War II involved basic matters of policy formulation. When Secy. of State James Byrnes was away from Washington, as he often was in 1945 and 1946, Acheson's role in policy decisions was often primary, even definitive. Unlike Byrnes and Byrnes's successor, George C. Marshall, under whom he also served, Acheson intervened in the policy-making process at the outset rather than the conclusion. As a result, the policies with which he concerned himself reflected his own way of thinking.[1] This pattern does much to explain the handling in Acheson's State Department of matters relating to the independence of India, once the jewel in the crown of the British Empire.

In early November 1946, as Anglo-Indian discussions of Indian independence grew increasingly volatile, Acheson discussed the subject with Sir Girja Bajpai, the Washington representative of the Indian National Congress Party and later Indian foreign minister. India was not yet independent, and Bajpai thus had no official standing in Washington, but he wanted Acheson, and through him the State Department and the administration, to know firsthand that the Indians were committed to independence and would like to have American goodwill and assistance in achieving it. Bajpai told Acheson that the impending independence of India provided the United States with a unique and historic opportunity for establishing an era of friendship and mutually beneficial cooperation between the two peoples and their governments. "Conditions in India made it possible for an American ambassador, if he so desired, and if he were well qualified, to exercise a peculiarly important influence at this time," Bajpai told Acheson. Whatever ties continued between in-

1. Graebner, "Dean Acheson," 276. Although Graebner noted Acheson's technique of early intervention in the policy process, he did not elaborate on the potential implications.

101

dependent India and the United Kingdom would be loose ones, more like those of Ireland than of Australia, he said. An independent Indian government would never rely on Britain for guidance in domestic or foreign affairs. "In the light of these conditions," Bajpai continued, "an American Ambassador might exercise very considerable influence in the direction of friendly and helpful advice," and that influence would likely grow if wisely exercised after Indian independence.[2] Evidently, Acheson received these views without responding substantively to them; there is no archival evidence that Bajpai's remarks generated any discussion in the State Department. That, however, was significant in itself.[3]

Despite the informality of the exchange with Acheson, Bajpai was proposing a radical realignment of U.S. foreign policy, which had never been deeply concerned with the Asian subcontinent, and of the external relations of India, which had been dominated by Britain and the empire for two centuries. Had Bajpai's proposal been treated seriously, and acted on, it is possible a new policy wedded to enlightened views of U.S. and Indian interests rather than to British imperialism might have emerged and avoided some of the problems that have plagued Indo-American relations ever since. A policy sensitive to Indian circumstances and imperatives, and less accommodating to those of Britain, might have made India less resistant to alignment with the West during the cold war, and less insecure (and bellicose) in its dealings with Pakistan.

Acheson's worldview precluded these possibilities, and Washington never explored the opportunity offered by Bajpai's proposal. Instead, American policy toward the subcontinent remained tied to Britain, with consequences detrimental to America's strategic interests and to the well-being of the people of South Asia. One result of the lost opportunity was Washington's inability to influence India during the Kashmir crisis that Acheson faced as secretary of state. A look at his handling of that crisis will show the dimension of the loss, and the extent to which here as in Ulster Acheson adhered to his imperial vision.

In proposing a new relationship between India and the United States, Bajpai used the example of Ireland to suggest how independent India would deal with an interfering Britain. The usage was ironic in view of

2. Memo of Conversation by Acheson, Nov. 8, 1946, *FRUS*, 5:96-97.
3. Robert J. McMahon, *The Cold War on the Periphery: The United States, India, and Pakistan*, is an important contribution to the field of U.S. relations with South Asia. Other valuable studies of the Indo-American relationship include Dennis Kux's *Estranged Democracies: India and the United States, 1941–1991*, Dennis Merrill's *Bread and the Ballot: The United States and Indian Economic Development*, and Henry W. Brands's survey *India and the United States: The Cold Peace*.

Acheson's Ulster connection and of which Bajpai was no doubt ignorant, and may have been impolitic on Bajpai's part. However, the Irish struggle for independence and its upcoming secession from the British Common-wealth contained parallels with the situation of India, which Bajpai if not Acheson considered instructive. Indians educated under British auspices were well acquainted with "the Irish problem," whether through Jonathan Swift's satire, Charles Stewart Parnell's Home Rule movement, or the history of the Irish struggle against the British presence there. Gandhi was intimately familiar with the Irish struggle for independence, and whatever he thought of the violent methods of some Irish nationalists, he cited that struggle as an example for subject peoples elsewhere, including those in India. Gandhi was impressed by the Irish success in using legal and political approaches to loosen the bonds of empire. More significant for this study, Jawaharlal Nehru, with whom Acheson had to deal as secretary of state, also saw significant similarities between the Irish and the Indian struggles for independence. Nehru's willingness to take what the British considered extreme positions on matters relating to Indian independence was influenced by what he had seen during two visits to Ireland while studying in England. "He at once felt an affinity with the Sinn Fein movement, the aggressive, self-reliant new kind of Irish nation-alism," one of his biographers has written of the experience. "Ireland and India presented identical pictures to Jawaharlal. In both countries people were listless, numbed by rhetoric into inaction. Irish parliamentarians and Indian liberals seemed alike to him." In Dublin in October 1907, shortly after an outburst of violence, Nehru had expressed disappointment at missing the rioting, but, in the words of his best biographer, he "had felt first-hand, the force of nationalist agitation and was impressed by the Sinn Fein movement. . . . The parallel in India was, of course, obvious, and Jawaharlal's visit to Ireland and his understanding of her politics seem to have strengthened his Extremist sympathies."[4]

Acheson, too, saw similarities between the Irish and Indian nation-alisms but drew from the similarities entirely different lessons. Acheson's worldview, rooted in the Ulster Protestant ascendancy, included a large degree of appreciation for the social orderliness he credited to the imperi-alist presence. Acheson therefore scorned nationalism except among the Great Powers. He never understood why indigenous peoples resisted the benefits he saw in Western influences, even when those benefits came with the trappings of imperial power. He expected gratitude, not the

---

4. B. N. Pandey, *Nehru,* 42–43; Sarvepalli Gopal, *Jawaharlal Nehru: A Biography,* 1:22. Gopal's three-volume study is the best work on the Indian statesman.

resentment cropping up everywhere in the colonial world after World War II, and his attitudes toward Indians were not unlike those he had toward Catholic Irish. "I know I ought to like them, and, indeed, have liked some," he wrote a British friend. "But by and large they and their country give me the creeps." Acheson thus saw in the Indian struggle for independence what he had already seen in the Irish struggle, and believed the one struggle deserved the same response as the other.[5]

In the struggle for Indian independence, no problem was more intractable than the chasm between Hindus and Muslims. The failure to solve that problem led, among other things, to the Kashmir crisis that Acheson confronted as secretary of state. The problem involved the status of minority Muslims in a majority-Hindu India or, alternatively, the partition of India into separate Hindu and Muslim states. Gandhi and other Hindu leaders, including Nehru and the Congress Party, wanted a unified, democratic, secular India that guaranteed the rights of all groups. Muslim leaders, on the other hand, including Mohammed Ali Jinnah, rejected the idea of a single Indian nation in which Hindus would be an overwhelming majority, and favored partition. Despite intense negotiations with active British involvement, the two sides were unable to agree on the issue. Jinnah insisted on partition, which Nehru just as adamantly rejected, and by the summer of 1946, the two sides were at an impasse. "We have exhausted all reason," Jinnah said. "There is no tribunal to which we can go. The only tribunal is the Muslim nation." At this point, Jinnah's Muslim League proclaimed August 16 "Direct Action Day," which launched the "Great Killing." In Calcutta alone more than five thousand people were killed, more than twenty thousand injured, and one hundred thousand left homeless.[6]

In a last-ditch effort to find a compromise agreement, Nehru and Jinnah flew to London in December to meet Prime Minister Clement Attlee and other officials. Attlee urged Nehru to compromise, that is, to accept partition, and when he refused the talks collapsed. Back in India, Nehru was conciliatory to the Muslims but defiant toward the British, who were still pressuring him to accept partition. "Whatever form of Constitution we may decide in the Constituent Assembly will become the Constitution of free India—whether Britain accepts it or not," he declared. "We have

---

5. Acheson to Desmond Donnelly, Mar. 18, 1959, Acheson Papers, box 7, folder 96; Bottigheimer, *Ireland and the Irish*, 220-21.

6. One of the best studies of the Indian progress to independence is S. M. Burke and Salim al-Din Quraishi, *The British Raj in India: An Historical Review*. For an account of events at the end of 1946 and early 1947, see esp. 451-84. See also the classic work by Stanley Wolpert, *A New History of India*, 340-49.

now altogether stopped looking towards London. . . . We cannot and will not tolerate any outside interference."[7]

The substance of this outburst takes on added significance for this study because it came only a month after Girja Bajpai's proposal to Acheson that the United States reassess its policy of deferring to Britain on Indian and South Asian affairs. Nehru needed an ally untainted by an imperial past. The American Revolution as a triumph over imperialism was clearly on Nehru's mind when he addressed the Constituent Assembly on December 13, 1946, and discussed among other things the history of successful revolutions.

Already, though, Nehru and other Congress Party leaders were becoming suspicious of U.S. machinations. In December, one of those leaders, the blunt-spoken and influential Sardar Patel, discussed U.S. policy toward independence with George Merrell, the American chargé d'affaires in India. Showing, in Merrell's words, "considerable animation when stating his case," Patel complained of the pro-British nature of statements Acheson had recently made on the subject, and "did not seem to be inclined to accept the view that U.S. Government's attitude was not determined by policy of supporting the British whenever possible." Another Congress leader told Merrell that Nehru considered U.S. policy to be "a strong endeavor to support [the] British."[8]

Acheson rejected Patel's characterizations of his own views and of U.S. policy as British inspired, assuring Merrell that his recent statements on the Indian situation "were made solely on US initiative." It was important, Acheson continued, that Merrell "dispel any Indian belief US actions [are] inspired at instance of British." Merrell thereupon raised the issue with Nehru, who denied believing U.S. policy was British inspired.[9] Nevertheless, Indian leaders remained convinced that London had undue influence on U.S. policy concerning Indian independence, and Acheson did nothing to allay that suspicion.

The suspicion was valid. In early 1947, the State Department issued a Policy and Information Statement on India that included views objectionable to Acheson. The statement expressed fear that the British would be unable to maintain their influence in independent India, that in indepen-

7. Quoted in Michael Brecher, *Nehru: A Political Biography*, 330. See also Hector Bolitho, *Jinnah: Creator of Pakistan*, 171.

8. The characterization of Patel is from Wolpert, *New History*, 351. D. V. Tahmankar, *Sardar Patel*, provides a valuable review of the statesman's career. Merrell to Acheson, Dec. 10, 1946, *FRUS*, 5:101-2.

9. Acheson to Merrell, Dec. 11, 1946, *FRUS*, 5:103; Merrell to Secretary of State, Dec. 14, 1946, in ibid., 105. With Byrnes in Europe, Acheson was in charge.

dent India the British would be targets of nationalists and communists, and that the tilt in U.S. policy toward the British left the nationalists with no one to appeal to in the West.[10] The implication of this formulation was that Britain's position in India was a liability for the West generally and for the United States particularly.

To counter this argument, and its disturbing implications, Acheson asked Merrell for help in the form of a positive assessment of the future British role in India. Addressed to "My dear Mr. Acheson," Merrell's assessment argued that the distrust of the British among Indian leaders was a temporary product of passions and expectations generated by the politics of independence and would soon subside to manageable levels. British behavior, Merrell told Acheson, "has taken most of the wind out of the sails of the politicians who in the past have specialized in charges of British perfidy." Acheson should therefore give little weight to Jinnah's recent "pronouncements regarding the necessity of ridding India of the British. I believe he would really prefer to have them remain." Merrell knew of no basis for the contention that "bitterly anti-British sentiment" was widespread in India. On the contrary, he sensed "no obvious signs of bitterness against the British among the Indian politicians now in the Interim Government."[11]

Merrell's assessment confirmed Acheson's understanding of subject peoples and how they were likely to behave toward imperial overlords. This enabled him to discount contrary views. Similarly, when ambassadors such as George Garrett in Ireland, Chester Bowles in India, and Henry Grady in India then in Iran expressed such contrary views, Acheson did not consider the arguments on their merits but either removed them or marginalized them to the fringes of the policy-making process. Only the skillful and respected Jefferson Caffery in Egypt of the ambassadors who appear in this study managed to hold on to his influence while criticizing British behavior to Acheson.

Acheson's influence over U.S. policy in India diminished somewhat in June 1947 when Henry F. Grady replaced Merrell in Delhi as ambassador to the newly independent India. Chosen for the post because of his knowledge of trade and economics, Grady already had wide experience in government and diplomacy. With doctoral degrees in both economics and law, Grady had worked for the Bureau of Planning and Statistics of the United States Shipping Board and as a U.S. trade commissioner to London

10. Merrell to Acheson, May 23, 1947, Records of the Director, Office of South Asian Affairs, Regional Conference and Country Files 1951-1954, India File, 59/250/50/11/04-5, National Archives.
11. Ibid.

and continental Europe after World War I, and then became professor of international trade and dean of the College of Commerce at the University of California from 1928 until 1937.

Unlike Merrell and Acheson, Grady was suspicious of British purposes in India, and favored an independent U.S. role in the subcontinent. His communications to the State Department reveal sympathy for India's efforts to become independent in fact as well as in name. At a conference in Washington of top U.S. diplomats then serving in South Asia, Grady reported "a strong anti-British feeling among top Indians" who "want the British out and the sooner the better." So strong was this sentiment that, according to Grady, the Indians were willing to risk the spread of communist influence rather than side with the British. Grady was thus concerned that U.S. support for the British presence would result in nationalist animosities directed against the United States. As to suggestions that the United States pressure Indian leaders to remain in the Commonwealth, Grady said, "We are already accused of pulling British chestnuts out of the fire." The United States should accept the independence of India and Pakistan and urge the two countries to cooperate with each other, but it should also acknowledge that the future of those countries did not depend on ties with the Commonwealth. "There is no anti-American feeling in India," he added, "but there would be if we identified ourselves with the Commonwealth cause."

Grady noted that in matters relating to India, the British were less accommodating to U.S. concerns than Americans were to those of the British. They "have made no attempt to consult with us on common problems or to ask our advice," Grady reported. None of the British officials in India, including Gov.-Gen. Lord Louis Mountbatten, "thinks of us in any way as partners. They have over three hundred people working on trade relations. I have expressed more sympathy for British trade than the British have for American trade. On more than one occasion, Mountbatten has warned Nehru against dollar imperialism."[12] Clearly, Grady considered the effort to accommodate U.S. policy to British concerns counterproductive to U.S. interests, including the British effort to get Washington to pressure India and Pakistan to remain in the Commonwealth. American interests in South Asia were not those of the British, Grady insisted; in fact, the two were often in conflict.

Grady's thinking thus clashed with that of Acheson, who wanted to meld U.S. policy in South Asia with that of the British. To Acheson, the

12. Memorandum by Joseph S. Sparks, Division of South Asian Affairs, Dec. 26, 1947, *FRUS*, 3:175-78.

United States should defer to Britain in South Asia, and membership in the Commonwealth was the proper response of India and Pakistan to the gnawing sensitivities of their indigenous nationalists because it ended formal political control but not the stabilizing influence of Britain. Acheson's desire to shore up the Commonwealth was at the heart of his unwillingness to challenge the British in South Asia, even at the risk of alienating the nationalistic governments there and jeopardizing U.S. strategic interests. As Grady and others warned, pressure from Washington to keep India and Pakistan in the Commonwealth created problems, and not necessarily the problems Washington anticipated. In the event India and Pakistan did, that fact did not sustain the kind of relationship to Britain that the British hoped it would.

In the summer of 1949, Joseph S. Sparks of the Office of South Asian Affairs spelled out the consequences of the changed circumstances. "It has become apparent that India's membership in the Commonwealth is not an unmitigated good source of strength so far as either the UK or the US is concerned," Sparks noted. The problem was that Britain perceived "unnatural constraint" in dealing with India on sensitive matters such as Kashmir "for fear of straining the Commonwealth ties." The United States had supported British efforts to maintain political influence in South Asia, and in return expected Britain to restrain India on matters such as Kashmir and keep it tied to the West in matters of strategic concern. "The UK is of little value in this connection so long as it greets each specific case in which its intervention would be of assistance with the attitude that playing such a role is out of the question because it might strain India's ties within the Commonwealth," Sparks pointed out. "It is difficult to see the value of these ties, at least from our point of view, if they can never be utilized for fear of straining them." In fact, Sparks suggested, India's membership in the Commonwealth might actually be an Indian ploy to influence other members to distance themselves from the Western alliance.[13]

One of Acheson's immediate concerns when he became secretary of state was to stanch the spread of such thinking in the State Department, and toward that end one of the first changes he made in the diplomatic corps was to move Grady from India to Greece, ostensibly to take advantage of his economic and financial expertise in overseeing the Truman Doctrine aid program designed to combat the spread of communism there. In Grady's place in Delhi, Acheson appointed Loy Henderson, a loyal

13. Sparks to Mathews, Memorandum on Significance of India's Retention of Its Commonwealth Membership, July 8, 1949, Records of the Office of South Asian Affairs, box 17, UK File, 59/250/49/33, National Archives.

confidant.[14] Henderson's loyalty to Acheson on matters relating to Britain and the empire was such that one historian has said of him, "Henderson must have thought he spent half his life picking up the pieces of Britain's Empire." Henderson was "favourably disposed towards the British," in the understated words of William Roger Louis, the historian of the British Empire. "The British Empire [to Henderson] was a stabilizing force in most parts of the world." British defense minister A. V. Alexander said after a meeting with Henderson, "I feel we have a very loyal friend, one with very sane views from our point of view."[15] Now ensconced in the State Department, Acheson had in Henderson and George McGhee, in charge of the Bureau of Near East, South Asian, and African Affairs, two lieutenants who seconded his approach to the colonial world.

When Acheson took office in January 1949, one of the pressing problems he faced was the struggle between Pakistan and India over Kashmir.[16] Located in northwest India at the juncture of China, Afghanistan, and what was then West Pakistan, the province of Kashmir was strategically, as well as economically, significant for both India and Pakistan. The watershed for various drainage systems, including the Indus River, the province had under the British Raj been a defensive outpost against the Russian Empire, and the locus of a series of short, bloody wars with the Russians.[17]

The problems Acheson confronted there stemmed from the partition of the subcontinent into India and the geographically divided nation of West Pakistan and East Pakistan. In the division of territory between Hindu India and Muslim Pakistan, the choice of each princely state to join one or the other lay with each reigning prince rather than with the people.[18] The

14. Acheson, *Present at the Creation,* 170. Acheson admired Henderson's loyalty and took the opportunity to praise his handling of the Palestine issue as well as his "shrewd" evaluation of the problem. Acheson was praising Henderson, then head of the Near East Office, for advocating a neoimperial policy. Henderson tried to persuade Secretary Byrnes that Britain, the United States, the Soviet Union, and France should first agree on a plan for Palestine, and then "consult" the Jews and Arabs before implementing the plan.

15. Henry W. Brands, *Inside the Cold War: Loy Henderson and the Rise of the American Empire, 1918-1961,* 233; Louis, *The British Empire in the Middle East, 1945-1951: Arab Nationalism, the United States, and Postwar Imperialism,* 37-39. See also Louis, *Imperialism at Bay: The United States and the Decolonization of the British Empire, 1941-1945.*

16. This discussion of the origins of the Kashmir crisis rests chiefly on McMahon, *Cold War on the Periphery,* 20-25; Michael Brecher, *The Struggle for Kashmir;* Sisir Gupta, *Kashmir: A Study in India-Pakistan Relations;* Charles H. Heimsath and Surjit Mansingh, *A Diplomatic History of Modern India;* B. R. Nanda, ed., *Indian Foreign Policy: The Nehru Years;* and Raju G. C. Thomas, ed., *Perspectives on Kashmir: The Roots of Conflict in South Asia.*

17. See, for example, Peter Hopkirk, *The Great Game* (New York: Kodansha International, 1994).

18. Jammu is a subordinate state in the province of Kashmir. The two are hereafter referred to as Kashmir.

princes generally chose according to the religion of their subjects, but the maharaja of Kashmir, Hari Singh, a Hindu prince, equivocated despite the fact that a considerable majority of his subjects were Muslims. The maharaja was still undecided on August 14, 1947, the deadline set by the independence negotiators, despite visits by Lord Mountbatten, Gandhi, and Mohammed Ali Jinnah, each urging him to make up his mind. When independence and partition became realities, the resettlement of millions of Hindus and Muslims took place, to the accompaniment of widespread violence and bloodshed. As this occurred, on October 22, 1947, armed Muslim tribesmen, mainly Mahsuds, moved from Pakistan into Kashmir, occupying territory and terrorizing the Hindu population. It was not clear at the time that the invaders were acting on behalf of Pakistan, though Pakistani officials expressed support for what they were doing. Its military forces soon in retreat, the government of Kashmir requested aid from India, and on October 27, Indian forces entered Kashmir in time to save the capital city, Srinagar, and most of the province from capture. Battle lines then stabilized, and the positions of India and Pakistan on the conflict hardened, each blamed the other for the continued fighting. The failure of the United Nations and the refusal of the United States to condemn Pakistan as the aggressor and to treat India as the victim of aggression angered the Indian government. In January 1948, while Acheson briefly held no office in the State Department, India appealed to the UN Security Council for help in ending the now stalemated war. Secy. of State George C. Marshall instructed UN ambassador Warren Austin to work out with the British a response to the Indian appeal. A few days later, Commonwealth secretary Philip Noel-Baker asked Washington to take the lead in making that response, since any proposal by the British might seem to India or Pakistan, or both, self-interested. Marshall resisted the British overture, and the Indian initiative came to nothing.[19] To break the military stalemate, Pakistan in May 1948 sent three army brigades into Kashmir to reinforce the irregular Muslim forces. Despite this, the stalemate continued until December, when the two nations agreed to a cease-fire to take effect on January 1, 1949. There the situation stood when Acheson returned to the State Department as secretary of state in late January.

Several aspects of the situation demanded immediate attention. One of these was a proposed plebiscite to determine the wishes of the people of Kashmir. India and Pakistan had earlier agreed that a plebiscite might

---

19. Marshall to Austin, Jan. 6, 1948, *FRUS*, 5:272-73. Memo of Conversation, Lovett and Noel-Baker, Jan. 10, 1948, in ibid., 1:276-78. See also McMahon, *Cold War on the Periphery*, 23.

solve the dispute, but they disagreed on ground rules for it, and the plebiscite never took place. Pakistan wanted all Indian and Pakistani troops withdrawn from Kashmir and replaced by UN peacekeepers as a precondition to the voting. India rejected this, claiming Kashmir was Indian territory, and pointing to the request of the Kashmiri government for Indian assistance against Pakistani aggression. India thus saw no reason to object to the presence of its troops during the plebiscite. The United Nations Commission on India and Pakistan was formed in mid-1948 with members appointed by the two involved parties and the UN.[20]

Acheson might at this point have ordered an assessment of U.S. policy as it affected either Kashmir specifically or South Asia generally for purposes of determining whether the policy of deference to British interests contributed to the stalemate in the war or otherwise compromised American interests in the region. In July 1949, Bajpai, then the Indian foreign minister, discussed Indo-American relations with Loy Henderson. He told Henderson that the Indian government was troubled by impressions that Washington blamed India for the failure to hold the Kashmir plebiscite. Were the impressions correct, Bajpai asked, and if so what did Washington suppose India should do to remove the blame? He requested a frank response, assuring Henderson that frank answers would give no offense. The Americans were beginning to behave like the British, Bajpai observed, and he hoped the United States "would not fall into British habit of taking [an] evasive attitude when unpleasant or disagreeable matters developed."[21]

Henderson responded that there was no "crystallized" judgment in the State Department concerning Indian policy in Kashmir. However, Washington did have problems with some of India's actions. India seemed insufficiently conciliatory, Henderson told Bajpai, especially since its forces controlled most of the contested province. He would convey the substance and spirit of their conversation to Washington, and ask for a frank statement of U.S. views. In doing so, however, he told Acheson that he knew the difficulty of putting together such a statement because an "utterly frank statement might morbidly offend Nehru." Acheson's response emphasized his conviction that India's insistence on its legal right to Kashmir was not useful in the present situation, and greater flexibility on India's part was needed. Acheson also told Henderson to inform his

20. Despite some resistance from Marshall, an American delegate, J. Klahr Huddle, had been named to the commission. Other delegates were Josef Korbel of Czechoslovakia, Ricardo J. Siri of Argentina, Egbert Graeffe of Belgium, and Alfredo Lozano of Colombia.
21. Henderson to Secretary of State, July 29, 1949, *FRUS*, 6:1726.

British counterpart of his exchange with Bajpai and with Washington if he believed it desirable to do so.[22]

Nehru responded angrily to Acheson's message. "He was tired of receiving moralistic advice from the US," he told Henderson after reading it. "India did not need advice from [the] US or any other country as to its foreign or internal policies." The issue between India and Pakistan concerned religion, he continued. India was a secular state in which all citizens participated without regard to their faith; Pakistan, on the other hand, was a religious state trying to use religion to incite Kashmiris against India. Henderson replied to Nehru's "tirade" by reminding him that Bajpai had asked him for a frank statement of Washington's views, and in making those views known he could hardly be accused of offering unwanted advice. Nehru agreed that some of his remarks had been "somewhat over-forceful," and begged Henderson's pardon for the outburst.[23] Nonetheless, the exchange demonstrated the depth of emotions underlying not only India's conduct in the Kashmir crisis but also its determination to pursue a foreign policy independent of Western pressure.

Despite these problems, U.S. and British policy makers continued the search for policies that melded their interests in Kashmir and South Asia. Driven by Acheson's sense that U.S. and British interests were similar, the State Department pushed that search. In doing so, however, policy makers in Washington came increasingly to believe that the United States must be more assertive and more independent of the British. Excessive concern during the Kashmir crisis with placating the British, they came to believe, was preventing Acheson from taking the steps necessary to bring South Asia into the strategic alliance against the Soviet Union. With India and Pakistan at each other's throats, it was impossible to reach a strategic accommodation with either without incurring the enmity of the other. In fact, an accommodation with either would probably cause the other to drop out of the Commonwealth, the ultimate disaster for British policy makers and an eventuality that would compromise Acheson's effort to preserve as much of the old imperial framework as possible.

Despite the policy deadlock this produced, Acheson refused to challenge, or even pressure, the British. U.S. and British representatives met at least twice in Washington in September 1949 to discuss South Asian policy without significant results. The most significant point in the discussions

---

22. Ibid., 1727-28; Memorandum by the Secretary of State to the Embassy in India, Aug. 5, 1949, in ibid., 1729-31.
23. Henderson to Acheson, Aug. 15, 1949, in ibid., 1732-33.

might have been a remark by M. E. Dening of the British Foreign Office that Acheson, Ernest Bevin, and British ambassador Sir Oliver Franks had recently discussed the Kashmir problem. Presumably, the discussion had been outside formal channels and any decisions reached amounted to private understandings. "No record of a separate discussion of the Kashmir problem has been found," the editor of the relevant volume of the *Foreign Relations of the United States* notes of Dening's remark. There is likewise no record of the discussion in the Foreign Office archives. However, an off-the-record meeting made sense given Acheson's relationship with Franks, his conviction that Anglo-American interests were the same in South Asia, and his desire to keep the specifics of the special relationship to himself. Dening implied that Acheson, Bevin, and Franks had discussed Nehru's proposal for a permanent seat for India on the UN Security Council, and Bevin had stated his intention to recommend that Prime Minister Attlee reject it. The on-the-record meetings reviewed the Kashmir situation, including the handling of the issue in the Security Council, and India's role in the crisis. Conferees agreed that "the UK and the US would continue to maintain close contact and to exchange views on the Kashmir issue."[24]

Not surprisingly, Acheson's relationship with Nehru, the embodiment of Indian nationalism and anti-imperialism, and, his Western critics said, of its self-righteousness as well, was an uneasy one. When Nehru came to Washington in October 1949, he came, in the words of Acheson's confidant George McGhee, with "a chip on his shoulder." According to McGhee, Nehru believed that officials in Washington could not understand someone with his background. "He appeared determined to appeal to the American people over the heads of their government," McGhee concluded, after studying briefing papers from Loy Henderson on "how to handle" Nehru.[25]

This estimate was hardly conducive to fruitful negotiation. Henderson, in fact, seems to have looked upon Nehru with something bordering on contempt. The friction between the two men had become such that it was unwise for Acheson to keep Henderson in Delhi—except for the fact that Henderson's thinking on Nehru, and on larger issues concerning South Asia, matched that of Acheson himself. The Indian ambassador in Washington, Vijayalakshmi Pandit, who was also Nehru's sister, was among those who recognized the problem. Madame Pandit "was disturbed by

24. Memorandum of Conversation of Mr. F. D. Collins of the Division of South Asian Affairs, Sept. 19, 1949, in ibid., 1743-44, 1745, 1747.
25. McGhee, *Envoy to the Middle World*, 46-47.

the fact that Loy Henderson and Nehru do not get along well together," she told Philip Jessup of the State Department some months after Nehru's trip to Washington. "She said she had frequently watched her brother freeze up in talking to Loy." The result of the incompatibility, she continued, was that in Delhi Henderson dealt with Bajpai rather than Nehru, and "while she feels Bajpai is an excellent person, he is not Nehru."[26]

This assessment was correct. "Nehru is a vain, sensitive, emotional, and complicated person," Henderson told Acheson at the time of Nehru's trip to Washington. "Mixed with his vanity appear to be certain furtive doubts regarding his own ability to carry on constructive work. He is at his best when playing the role of a critic and in making appeals to persons and groups who are his intellectual and social inferiors." Henderson believed Nehru's thinking had been molded by his education in England, where he learned the "anti-American" attitudes that influenced his foreign policy. His views had "been hardened by the influence of a group of Britishers who have gone out of their way to prejudice him against things American," Henderson told Acheson. "There is no doubt that people like the Mountbattens have had some success in strengthening his convictions that Americans in general are a vulgar, pushy lot, lacking in fine feeling, and that American materialistic culture dominated by the dollar is a serious threat to the development of a higher type of world civilization." In Henderson's estimate, those who had worked to confirm these attitudes in Nehru included Winston Churchill, Ernest Bevin, Harold Laski, and Bernard Shaw.

The curious result of Nehru's anti-Americanism, in Henderson's calculation, was a cautious Anglophilia. "I am glad that they have succeeded in making him pro-British," Henderson told Acheson, as close relations between Britain and India were in the American interest. Henderson hoped exposure to U.S. democracy and enterprise during his visit would capture Nehru's imagination "instead of getting on his English-strung nerves."[27]

Henderson's assessment of Nehru, like the hope he expressed for Nehru's visit, contained more than the ordinary amount of miscalculation and wishfulness. What Henderson labeled "pro-British" in Nehru's thinking had to do with ideals Nehru learned in Britain about political

26. Memorandum of Conversation, Aug. 17, 1950, Decimal File, 611.91/8-1750, National Archives.
27. President's Memoranda Book Regarding Nehru Visit, Office Files of George McGhee, box 13, India 1949 file, 59/250/49/31/01-03, lot 53D468, National Archives.

independence and democratic self-government, not about the glories of empire or the benefits of the Commonwealth. Nehru's goal was an independent India respected in international circles, and his attitude toward the United States reflected his assessment of Washington's disdain for that goal. Henderson's belief that Nehru was unable to think independently or creatively reflected his failure to understand the Indian statesman. To whatever extent Washington worked to pull British chestnuts out of postimperial fires or otherwise sought to shore up the British presence in South Asia was the extent to which Nehru would be "anti-American." Whether Henderson or Acheson, or both, understood this is unclear. What is clear is that both believed they could manipulate the prickly Nehru for U.S.—and British—purposes.

One of the puzzles of Acheson's stewardship of U.S. foreign policy is the absence of a clear policy toward India by the time of Nehru's visit to the United States. "The lack of clarity among American planners is stunning," historian Robert McMahon has written of this situation. "For all the talk in Washington of India's centrality in the muddled Asian picture, the administration had made no hard decisions before Nehru's arrival." McMahon's judgment is valid within the parameters of conventional assessment. But Acheson would have rejected it. In his mind, U.S. policy toward the subcontinent was clear. It was to follow the British lead in the interest of protecting British, and thus American and Western, interests by preserving as much as possible of the old imperial order in South Asia. During Nehru's visit, Acheson lectured Nehru on what he might learn about leading a newly independent, democratic nation from such figures as Washington, Jefferson, Lincoln, and Andrew Jackson. Acheson believed Nehru had much to learn from such men, and was pleased with his lecture, though Nehru, evidently, was not. "The result was very definitely a change from routine and caught our distinguished Visitor unprepared," Acheson wrote of his effort. "He was not pleased." Nehru found it equally difficult to communicate with Acheson. "He talked to me, as Queen Victoria said of Mr. Gladstone," Acheson wrote of Nehru after the Washington discussions, "as though I were a public meeting." After their extended discussion of the Kashmir issue and the world situation during the Washington talks, Acheson wrote afterward that the talks had left him "a bit confused," implying that Nehru's understanding of the issues made little sense. "I was convinced," Acheson said of the discussions generally, "that Nehru and I were not destined to have a pleasant relationship. He was so important to India and India's survival so important to all of us, that if he did not exist—as Voltaire said of God—he would have to be invented. Nevertheless, he was one of the most difficult men with whom I have ever had to deal."[28]

Not everyone agreed with Acheson that Britain was the central player in South Asia or should be the focus of American policy there. One of those who disagreed with him was H. R. Mathews of the South Asia Office, who made a realistic assessment of the strategic situation there in the aftermath of Nehru's trip to Washington. The independence of India had left the British unable to defend the subcontinent against Soviet penetration, Mathews began. The British Indian Army was gone, and Britain was unable to provide the military assistance India needed to fill the resulting power vacuum. In addition, the residues of imperialism and the flowerings of nationalism had diminished British influence in the region to the point that only the United States could influence the situation positively. Indian leaders recognized this, as their requests for U.S. assistance showed, and the United States thus had a historic opportunity to influence India not only in the Kashmir crisis but in other regional matters and in larger strategic matters as well. "We have at present," Mathews suggested, "an unusual opportunity to strengthen such anti-Soviet tendencies as exist in South Asia with a limited outlay of US resources." He recommended that the United States "provide at least the minimum assistance [the Indians] deem essential for internal security." Otherwise, "we will have lost these opportunities, and contributed to their dependence on the Soviet countries." Without mentioning Britain, Mathews wrote that India should be the focus of U.S. policy. "India is the natural, political, economic and military center of South Asia," he noted. "In all of Asia it is now the only nation that is large enough and has the power potential to resist a determined Communist military effort with any possibility of success. . . . If we are to have effective policy in Asia, therefore, India must be the Keystone of that policy."[29]

Mathews's recommendations had no immediate impact, and in January 1950 Ambassador Philip Jessup was still arguing for a policy centered on Britain, even to the extent that U.S. aid to India be funneled through Britain.[30] By this time, however, Acheson moved to seize the diplomatic initiative. He proposed that Kashmir be demilitarized, and India recon-

28. McMahon, *Cold War on the Periphery*, 54-55; Acheson, *Present at the Creation*, 334-35, 336.

29. Memorandum, Mathews to McGhee, Nov. 1, 1949, Records of the Office of South Asian Affairs, 1939-1953, Military Affairs file, box 23, lot 54D341, 59/250/49/33/04-6, National Archives.

30. Records of the Office of South Asian Affairs, box 15, lot 54D341, 59/250/49/33/04-6, National Archives.

sider earlier U.S. proposals for UN mediation and a UN supervised plebiscite to decide the future of Kashmir. Should India continue to reject UN mediation, the United States would support whatever "Security Council action [was] necessary to overcome [the] present deadlock" in Kashmir.[31] Acheson had Ambassador Warren Austin place this proposal before Bajpai and Madame Pandit, both of whom were at the UN at the time. Acheson had probably cleared this proposal with the British—at least Bajpai and Madame Pandit assumed as much, and were upset by the presumed collusion. Bajpai told Austin gruffly that he "assumed that the reference in the message to [the U.S.] intention to support [the Security Council] action was not intended as a threat." Austin responded that "it was simply a statement of fact."[32]

Acheson's attempt to bully the Indians backfired. A few days after the Austin-Bajpai exchange, Nehru responded to Acheson in a terse, angry note reiterating the Indian position on Kashmir and rejecting the premises of Acheson's proposal as false and self-serving. India had behaved reasonably in Kashmir, he insisted, despite the fact that Acheson and other critics ignored the reality of Pakistani aggression. "The Government of India would be false to their trust and to both moral and legal obligations resting on a civilized government," Nehru lectured Acheson on the well-being of the Kashmiris, "if they were to leave these people exposed to a repetition of the violence and danger from which [they] were rescued."[33]

The impasse thus continued. The "US continues to believe UK should bear major responsibility for promoting settlement," Acheson cabled the London embassy in February 1950, "and accordingly will urge UK to assume [the] leading role in consultations with [Security Council] members to New York to work out solution." Acheson would still defer to Britain on Kashmir, this time citing the overly legalistic nature of the Indian position in the dispute, which rested on the legality of the decision of the Hindu maharaja of Kashmir to attach his majority-Muslim province to India rather than to Pakistan at the time of partition. "The U.K. as the senior member of the Commonwealth is in the best position to take the necessary leadership in the consultations in New York to work out a practical program of action for the [Security] Council," Acheson told Ernest Bevin in a personal note, also in February 1950. "We will of course

31. Acheson to Austin, Jan. 13, 1950, *FRUS*, 5:1367. See also Austin to Acheson, Dec. 16, 1949, in ibid., 6:1761. General McNaughton, a Canadian, was an important international figure during this period because of his role within NATO. For more on his role at the UN, see John Swettenham, *McNaughton* (Toronto: Ryersen Press, 1968).

32. Austin to Acheson, Jan. 13, 1950, *FRUS*, 5:1368-69.

33. Austin to Acheson, Jan. 16, 1950, in ibid., 1369-70.

work closely with your delegation and cooperate fully in developing a joint plan."[34]

Nationalist forces undermined this policy in India as they were doing in other disputes in other parts of the British colonial world. Events, in other words, were undermining Acheson's policy, a fact that Acheson himself understood but was unable to accept. "The first half of 1951," he later wrote in language that illuminates his understanding of the problem, "was particularly notable for tasks that distracted us from the main constructive work of rebuilding, out of the ruins of the nineteenth-century European imperial system, a free world." "Rebuilding" was Acheson's metaphor, not replacing old empires with newly free nations and peoples treated equitably and respectfully as their conduct deserved. It was instead Acheson's way of obscuring his support for a reconstituted world order in which neoimperialists conceded what they had to concede to local elites, oriented toward the West and toward capitalism one hoped, while preserving what they could of the old imperial order.[35]

Acheson's stance disappointed Bajpai, who had once hoped for closer Indo-American relations. In early February 1950, Loy Henderson discussed the Kashmir crisis with Bajpai, who in Henderson's estimate had recently "been somewhat distant when we have encountered each other at various social and official functions." He continued, "It is evident that Sir Girja feels deeply what he considers to be the decision of the Government of the United States to support the Pakistan approach to the Kashmir dispute." Yet, it is likely that what bothered Bajpai was not so much Washington's "Pakistan approach" to Kashmir as the general deference to Britain, prompted in this case by Britain's desire to keep Pakistan in the Commonwealth.[36]

Bajpai also objected to Henderson's harsh language, and he must have sensed the disparagement Henderson had for Indians. "Indian leaders, particularly Nehru, have been cajoled and treated as spoiled children for so long," Henderson told Acheson, "that they have tendencies to become outraged when they encounter opposition on the part of Western countries to any of their cherished schemes. They must eventually become

34. Acheson to U.K. Embassy, Feb. 11, 1950, in ibid., 1382-83; Acheson to Bevin, Feb. 13, 1950, in ibid., 1385.
35. Acheson, *Present at the Creation*, 499.
36. Henderson to State Department, Feb. 4, 1950, decimal file, 611.91/2-650, National Archives. Mary Ann Heiss, in *Empire and Nationhood: The United States, Great Britain, and Iranian Oil, 1950-1954*, argues that the United States and Britain used racial stereotypes in dealing with Iranians. Similarly, Acheson and Henderson, in particular, saw Nehru and other Indians as emotional and childlike, certainly not capable of responsible self-government.

sufficiently adult to recognize that disagreements of this character are an inescapable part of international life."[37]

Sir Girja resumed his conversation with Henderson in April. Detecting what he called a growing "resentment" among Indians toward the United States, Henderson suggested to Bajpai that this attitude was the result of misperceptions that U.S. aid to India was ungenerous, that Washington was on Pakistan's side in the Kashmir dispute, and that the United States was pressuring India to drop the socialization of its economy. Bajpai agreed that there was a problem in Indian perceptions of the United States, but suggested that "disappointment" was a better description of the perceptions than "resentment." "Indian people on attaining independence had assumed [the] US would give them considerable assistance in effort to develop their economy," he told Henderson, "and now realizing the falseness [of] these assumptions they were disappointed and disillusioned."[38] Neither man mentioned the Anglo-American relationship as a factor in the problems.

H. R. Mathews of the South Asia Office summarized the nature and substance of that relationship in April. U.S. and British representatives had met frequently since Indian independence to exchange views on South Asian problems, Mathews noted, and "when possible, agree on tactics and procedures to be followed with respect to specific questions. . . . Consultations have been most frequent concerning the Kashmir dispute." On occasion, he continued, "we have concerted with the British in special diplomatic appeals to the Governments of India and Pakistan," and the cooperation has included personal frequent exchanges between Acheson and Bevin. "In all our exchanges," Mathews noted, "the United States has endeavored to accommodate British views, and it is believed that the reverse is true." Yet, the exchange of views had never been entirely complete. "We have never told the British," Mathews pointed out, "that we believe that the British Commonwealth should be utilized more fully as an instrument for the attainment of our common objectives. We have never told the British that we do not wish to compete with them in the Indian subcontinent, or that we prefer to supplement rather than to supplant them."[39]

Such views, which Acheson encouraged and undoubtedly expressed to his staff and personally to his British counterparts, underlay a new

37. Ibid.
38. Henderson to Secretary of State, Apr. 12, 1950, decimal file, 611.91/4-1250, National Archives.
39. Mathews to Hare, Apr. 17, 1950, Records of the Office of South Asian Affairs, box 22, 59/250/49/33, National Archives.

statement of State Department policy. "The Indo-British relationship is the strongest link between India and the West," read the India Policy Statement of October 1950, "and it is our policy to maintain and strengthen it. . . . British objectives closely parallel our own, and in its relations with India, Great Britain enjoys certain advantages over the United States, hence it is our purpose to supplement the British in India, not to supplant them." Britain would thus "take the lead" in matters related to India, as the two governments had agreed the previous May 1950 in London. The "British Government is aware of our basic views regarding the relative roles of the United Kingdom and the United States," and the United States should "scrupulously avoid . . . adopting a position of leadership in a United Nations effort to press partition on the parties [in Kashmir], continuing [instead] to rely on British or Commonwealth initiative." This close cooperation "should be increasingly exploited," the statement continued, though there "remains the task of more completely and carefully coordinating United States and British activities in India." That task should be attended to in joint discussions, in order to achieve "greater understanding and mutual agreement." However, this arrangement must be kept secret. "Great care should be taken to prevent the Government of India gaining knowledge of such United States–British collaboration."[40]

It was evidently a desire to preserve this arrangement that led Henderson to reject a proposal from Washington to create machinery for "systematic consultation between India and the United States" on regional and world issues. The problem with formalizing consultations, he told Acheson, was the attitude of Indian leaders. The "desire for better relations with US are [*sic*] not shared by various governmental and Party leaders, including apparently Nehru, who as Pri[me] Min[ister] and Fo[reig]n Min[ister], is in position [to] exert strong influence on India's fo[reig]n policies." Nehru was also "at present a powerful factor in fanning unfriendly feelings toward US."[41]

Anglo-American cooperation thus remained the centerpiece of Acheson's South Asian policy as the Kashmir crisis dragged on and South Asia specialists in the State Department became increasingly concerned about the threat of communism. War raged in Korea, and the position of the French degenerated in Indo-China. In discussions in London in early 1951, the two allies reiterated the terms of their cooperation in South Asia, including Kashmir, but there surfaced signs of impatience

40. India Policy Statement, Oct. 1950, decimal file, 611.91/10-2350, National Archives.
41. Henderson to State Department, Aug. 23, 1950, decimal file, 611.91/8-2350, National Archives.

among some U.S. policy makers. Donald Kennedy, deputy director of South Asian affairs, asked his British counterparts if they still agreed that London "should continue to have the major responsibility for seeking a solution to problems on the Indian subcontinent." When the British answered affirmatively, Kennedy noted that the "American assessment of the present situation in the area was that it called for positive action now." He asked if the British agreed with that assessment, and again the answer was yes. However, after a meandering discussion focusing mainly on the perceived reluctance of India to recognize the reality of the communist threat in the area, the British rejected Kennedy's suggestion that the time to act had arrived. "We must exercise patience and moderation," they said; "any attempt to force the process might land us in disaster." To Kennedy's request for workable suggestions for solving the problems, one of the Britons responded lamely that it was "imperative that the Kashmir dispute and other difficulties between India and Pakistan be settled." Kennedy continued to probe, asking whether the British "thought it would be helpful at this time to make a clear and perhaps more positive statement than any hitherto on the US and UK policy toward Asia." Could the two allies, he asked, "by such a statement, help to allay Asian suspicions over such issues as colonialism, the fear that a new type of imperialism was being fostered through economic aid, developments in Indo-China, and US efforts with respect to Formosa?"[42] The British believed this would be counterproductive. It would be better to delay a statement and allow the statement when made to "flow in time from the course of events." It seems clear the British were engaging in what Bajpai once called "the British habit of taking an evasive attitude when unpleasant or disagreeable matters developed."[43] Discussion then proceeded to problems of defending the region against the communist threat. Kennedy reviewed a list of policy objectives centered on making the region resistant to communist attack or subversion or both. The British agreed with Kennedy's objectives, but believed the more pressing need was improved relations between India and Pakistan, tenuous members of the Commonwealth.[44]

There the Anglo-American dialogue rested in late February 1951 when George McGhee, Acheson's assistant for Near Eastern, South Asian, and

---

42. Memo of Conversation, Feb. 6, 1951, *FRUS*, 6:1654, 1655, 1657. It warrants mention that Kennedy had been an American representative at the February 1950 Colombo (Ceylon) Conference of Commonwealth nations. He was certainly familiar with British policies toward its Commonwealth members.

43. Henderson to Acheson, July 29, 1949, *FRUS*, 6:1726. The use of this tactic has been well documented in Ireland, Iran, and Egypt.

44. Memo of Conversation, Feb. 14, 1951, in ibid., 1658.

African affairs, convened a meeting of the chief U.S. diplomats concerned with the region. The conference convened in Nuwara Eliya, Ceylon, the lush surroundings of which provided a setting reminiscent of parallel events in the days of the British Raj. On his way to the conference, McGhee drove through "many tea plantations which looked like vast, perfectly manicured parks," and the Grand Hotel that hosted the conference had, in McGhee's words, "wide verandas and large rooms with high ceilings reminiscent of the colonial era, when the prosperous tea planters would gather here with their families to escape the heat of the plains."[45] The purpose of the conference was to review South Asian policy against the backdrop of a growing realization that deference to Britain was creating problems. Parallel difficulties with the British in Iran and Egypt fueled the concerns of many of those present.

The conference was an opportunity, McGhee said in his opening re-marks, to ask fundamental questions. "Who are our friends? On whom can we rely in a crisis?" Britain, McGhee acknowledged, could no longer play the international role it once played, and its recent role in South Asian affairs reflected declining influence rather than confident strength. In the Kashmir crisis, McGhee noted, the chief British concern was to keep the Commonwealth together, which precluded an assertive response toward either Pakistani aggression or Indian intransigence. This was not conducive to the kinds of bold initiatives necessary to protect the strategic interests of the Western alliance, which demanded the orienting of South Asia toward the West and away from the communist bloc.[46]

Henderson challenged McGhee's assessment of the situation as it con-cerned India. It is a mistake, he argued, to say that India is not a friend of the United States in matters of vital concern. Beneath the veneer of criticism Indian leaders make of U.S. policy, Henderson said, lay a deep reservoir of friendship and common interest. The way to Nehru's heart, he suggested, was through patient persuasion alternating with confrontation on matters in which the Anglo-American allies were likely to prevail.[47]

Despite these assurances from Henderson, one of the major policy initiatives explored at the conference was the possibility of an alliance with Pakistan. U.S. interests in the area, according to those who proposed the initiative, required development of strong flanks in Pakistan, Burma, and Indochina to enhance the defense of South Asia from Soviet aggres-sion. Responding to the proposal, the conference recommended that U.S.

45. McGhee, *Envoy to the Middle World,* 278.
46. Brands, *India and the United States,* 61.
47. Ibid., 62-63.

"military authorities should consider on an urgent basis the desirability of the United States entering into an early understanding with Pakistan which would provide for equipping and building up Pakistan's military forces and insure the availability of Pakistani forces on the western flank [of South Asia] at the outset of war." The conference recommended that a similar understanding with India be explored, though discussions indicated that the conferees believed those prospects far less promising than the understanding with Pakistan.[48]

Despite the criticism of Britain and the recognition of its inability to play the role of suzerain in South Asia, the Ceylon conferees concluded that "the United Kingdom should continue to take the lead in pressing for a settlement of the Kashmir dispute." They also concluded that Washington should consult London before discussing Kashmir with India or Pakistan, and should assure Pakistan of U.S. assistance against Indian military attack. If India or Pakistan rejected the proposed Kashmir settlement then before the Security Council, "the United States should look to the United Kingdom for leadership as to the next step which should be taken in connection with the dispute."[49]

What was the impact of the Ceylon conference? It appears to have been twofold. First, a larger number of the diplomats responsible for making and administering U.S. policy in South Asia had met together and in the course of discussing matters of common interest had voiced their very real concerns about the ill effects of continuing to defer to the British. If there had been a code of silence on that subject, that code had been broken. Second, despite the concerns expressed, only Acheson could make such a fundamental change in U.S. policy, and he, like McGhee, his key adviser on the subject, was prepared to make no such change. So, after some serious grousing, U.S. diplomats stayed on Acheson's course, and the conference had no major effect on U.S. policy.[50]

At the end of March 1951, India rejected the proposals before the UN to resolve the Kashmir dispute, and Bajpai reiterated his complaint to Henderson that the United States still refused to treat India as an independent player in diplomatic matters. The occasion for this latest reiteration was the fact that India had recently received a copy of the drafted peace treaty with Japan formally ending World War II not from

48. Ceylon Conference, Feb. 26–Mar. 2, 1951, *FRUS*, 6:1669.
49. Ibid., 1667-70.
50. Anita Inder Singh, *The Limits of British Influence: South Asia and the Anglo-American Relationship, 1947-1956*, recognizes this element of dissatisfaction but mistakes it for a genuine change in policy, which does not happen until the Eisenhower administration (see, for example, 117-20).

the United States but from the United States through Britain, as though it were still a political appendage of London. India, Bajpai told Henderson, "would prefer discussing matters of this kind directly with U.S. rather than through the U.K. Although India is a member of the Commonwealth, it was not a UK dependency." Henderson professed not to know why the draft came through Britain, but he was certain it was not "with the idea that members of the Commonwealth are in the British sphere of influence."[51] Nonetheless, that was exactly the idea Acheson wanted to encourage, as Bajpai clearly understood. Bajpai was therefore unimpressed with Henderson's response to his complaint.

By the summer of 1951, Acheson's policy of following the British lead in traditional spheres of British influence produced a crisis in Iran. Apart from its Iranian specifics, the crisis there, combined with the problems the policy produced elsewhere, signaled the bankruptcy of Acheson's policy. Acheson recognized this fact, but in a triumph of ideology over realism, he clung to the policy. "My own colleagues in the State Department and in Treasury and Defense," he wrote later, "had come to the conclusion that the British were so obstructive and determined on a rule-or-ruin policy in Iran that we must strike out on an independent policy or run the gravest risk of having Iran disappear behind the Iron Curtain." Acheson resisted the move, fearing that a fundamental policy change in Iran would undermine Britain's—and his own—ability to deal with postcolonial crises there and elsewhere. "Recent events in Iran and Turkey indicate [a] deterioration of UK prestige [in the] Near East," Acheson cabled the U.S. Embassy in Islamabad in 1951, "with probably similar results in [Pakistan] and consequent lessened effectiveness US-UK collaboration re Kashmir." The Foreign Office was "well aware" of these problems "but not yet ready [to] propose solutions."[52]

This was a significant admission on Acheson's part, but he undertook no policy changes in its wake. To be sure, fundamental changes of the sort needed would have been difficult to make, and by 1951 may not have had the desired results. The Western allies were preoccupied by the war in Korea, and war is not always the best time to reexamine policy basics. Acheson's policies had so alienated Nehru that Nehru was unwilling to be

51. Henderson to Acheson, Apr. 5, 1951, *FRUS*, 6:1764-65. It is interesting to note that Acheson had a similar problem in his relations with Ireland. The Irish wished to be treated independently and even broke away from the Commonwealth to prove this point. The Irish also hoped that this would defeat the American argument that the Ulster question was a domestic issue and hence out of bounds for U.S. involvement. Acheson, nevertheless, continued to view Anglo-Irish relations as a domestic affair.

52. Acheson, *Present at the Creation*, 682; Acheson to Embassy in Pakistan, July 14, 1951, *FRUS*, 6:1774-75.

helpful in Korea, and the British were determined to take no substantive action over Kashmir. In fact, British diplomats were criticizing Americans for being unwilling to "let events take their course and influence them unobtrusively from the side-lines."[53] There was a strong sense among the British that Acheson would do nothing antagonistic to their own sense of British interests.

Wanting a man of like mind to handle the Iranian crisis, Acheson moved Loy Henderson from Delhi to Tehran in early 1952, and replaced him with Chester Bowles. Bowles, a foreign service veteran, was an independent thinker, and his prompt criticism of Washington's handling of South Asia took State Department staffers by surprise.[54] In February 1952, Bowles dispatched to Washington a five-page "personal report" he titled "The Crucial Problem of India." In it, he stressed India's centrality to the well-being of South Asia and its importance to the West in the cold war, and urged Washington to pursue policies with those priorities in mind. Bowles never mentioned Britain, and his report may have been a plea to Washington to drop the policy of deferring to Britain in India and elsewhere in South Asia.[55] Bowles's plea, if that is what it was, had no effect in Washington, though his presence in Delhi, where he worked effectively to make U.S. policy palatable to India, helped narrow Indo-American differences and placate the sensitive Nehru. After Henderson's hostility, this amounted to a breath of fresh air. In November 1952, Bowles asked Acheson to withdraw U.S. support for a resolution then before the Security Council to give UN sanction to the presence of Pakistani as well as Indian troops in Kashmir after a cease-fire. U.S. support for the resolution "is a serious mistake," Bowles told Acheson. Nehru believed the resolution struck "deliberately at the Indian position," considered the Churchill government "clearly responsible" for it, and saw it as an attempt to "restore former UK prestige in the Middle East following failure in Iran and elsewhere." Nehru thus found U.S. support for the resolution "puzzling," and Bowles warned that a vote for it would compromise the progress he had recently made in convincing Indians of U.S. sympathy and willingness to help solve their problems.[56]

53. S. J. L. Oliver of the Foreign Office to F. S. Tomlinson in British Embassy, Washington, D.C., Sept. 7, 1951, Records of the Foreign Office, FO92884/10345/8, PRO.

54. A note jotted on one of his early 1952 communications from a startled desk officer: "This is an amazing statement for an ambassador. Does he realize how far he is from Department policy?" Bowles, as ambassador to Spain during the Spanish civil war, had been sharply critical of America's policy of "malevolent neutrality" in that conflict.

55. Bowles to Charles Murphy, Feb. 4, 1952, President's Secretary's Files, National Archives.

56. Bowles to Acheson, Nov. 17, 1952, *FRUS*, 11:1302-3.

Achesonian policy toward South Asia thus ended where it began, still deferring to the British, still offending the Indians. Support for the British-authored resolution on Kashmir, which passed the Security Council 9–0, with the Soviet Union abstaining, on December 23, 1952, was Acheson's last initiative on South Asia. As already noted, Nehru rejected the resolution because it failed to acknowledge Pakistani aggression, to recognize Kashmir as a part of India, and to require the removal of Pakistani troops from Kashmir as a precondition to peace negotiations. Nehru was also incensed by the "obviously anti-Indian presentation" in which the British delegate, Sir Gladwyn Jebb, an ardent imperialist, had defended the resolution in the Security Council, and by the acquiescence of the U.S. delegate in that defense.[57]

David Bruce, Acheson's undersecretary, responded to Bowles's report without addressing its substance. Washington continued to support the British effort to solve the Kashmir crisis, Bruce told Bowles, but recognized that no solution was possible without Nehru's cooperation. The department "considers Nehru [the] key figure in settlement [of the] Kashmir issue," Bruce wrote. "Until he is willing [to] make some agreement there of course can be none." Bowles refused to accept such rationalizations. In a reply to "the Department of State," he telegrammed, "we disagree at vitally important points." The result of U.S. support for the British resolution, he said, would be growing embitterment in India, and increasing distrust of U.S. motives. Pending a more realistic approach, Bowles again recommended that the United States withdraw its support for the resolution.[58] The recommendation fell on deaf ears.

One of Acheson's favorite aphorisms was that statesmen must deal with the world as it is, not as they would like it to be. However, Acheson's South Asian policy foundered on the shoals of his own idea of how that region should be. Acheson's determination to deal with the South Asia that should be reflected an inability to understand—literally, a failure to comprehend realistically—the motives and imperatives of a postimperial world leader such as Nehru. Acheson was thus unable to assess or deal realistically with his Indian counterpart. The circumstances in which the two men encountered each other thus widened the misunderstandings their differing experiences and mind-sets made inevitable.

Acheson ignored the realistic evaluations of Nehru that his staff sometimes presented to him. "As an Asian nationalist, [Nehru] resents our

57. Ibid. For Lord Gladwyn, see Louis, *British Empire in the Middle East*, 30-31, 100-101.
58. Bruce to Bowles, Nov. 20, 1952, *FRUS*, 6:1304-6; Bowles to State Department, Nov. 24, 1952, in ibid., 1306-7.

support of European metropolitan powers which retain colonies in Asia," read one such evaluation in November 1950, a clear warning of the dangers of subordinating U.S. policy to British interests. Acheson's private disparagements of Nehru were no adequate response to such warnings.

It might be objected that the characterization of the South Asian problem presented in this study ignores perceived necessity at the time of preserving the Anglo-American alliance in the cold war world. Yet, a realist alternative to the way Acheson perceived that necessity was possible, even preferable, and available as examples from the administrations of both Franklin Roosevelt and Dwight Eisenhower illustrate. Roosevelt's dislike of French and British imperialism is well known. Long before India gained its independence, Roosevelt spoke bluntly on several occasions to Winston Churchill about the necessity of Britain accommodating itself to a postcolonial world. Although willing to accommodate the immediate needs of his wartime allies, Roosevelt nevertheless made his anti-imperialist views clear.[59] And after Acheson and Truman left office, John Foster Dulles and Dwight Eisenhower, their immediate successors, scuttled Acheson's deference to the British in South Asia and entered into military alliance with Pakistan.[60]

Whatever the wisdom of that move, it showed the availability of policy options that Acheson refused to consider. The strategic significance of India in South Asia was such that Acheson clearly had an obligation to make it a central feature of his policy calculations. Given Nehru's commitment to Indian national interests, it is reasonable to believe that a policy accommodating those legitimate interests without regard to British desires might have been more successful than Acheson's adherence to British interests, in Kashmir specifically and South Asia generally. "The fact of the matter is that India wields a terribly disproportionate share of power in the South Asian region," historian Robert G. Wirsing has recently written, "and, when it comes to a settlement in Kashmir, cannot be treated as the equal of Pakistan."[61] A policy embodying that principle

59. An excellent exposition of these attitudes is in Louis, *Imperialism at Bay*.
60. Robert J. McMahon, "United States Cold War Strategy in South Asia: Making a Military Commitment to Pakistan, 1947-1954," 812-40. Although McMahon does detail much of the decision-making process, he has little to say about the Anglo-American alignment. As in his book *Cold War on the Periphery*, McMahon addresses the confused strategic formulation in the region. This confusion, I believe, was spawned by the indecision generated by Acheson's effort to tie U.S. policy to Britain's outdated imperial approach.
61. Wirsing, *India, Pakistan, and the Kashmir Dispute: On Regional Conflict and Its Resolution*, 259. Wirsing, however, recommends a process and plan for a solution that, although of necessity favoring India's position, addresses concerns of both sides. McMahon, highly critical of the Eisenhower alliance with Pakistan, has argued that the best approach would

may have placed India in the role Acheson gave Britain in his South Asian policy. Further, it would likely have recognized the strategic actualities in the region, and insisted that India and Pakistan, no less than Britain, accommodate themselves to those actualities.

---

have been one of steady evenhandedness, with no favor for one side or the other. McMahon makes a strong case, but such a policy would be most valuable if it were adopted on the basis of U.S. interests and not simply created to follow British policy, as during the Acheson years (*Cold War on the Periphery,* 337-47).

6

The Iran Connection

∞

In October 1952, U.S. policy toward Iran was in shambles. The moderate, pro-Western prime minister, Ali Razmara, had recently been assassinated by an Iranian nationalist, and his radical, unpredictable successor, Mohammed Mossadeq, had severed diplomatic relations with Britain and nationalized the British-owned Anglo-Iranian Oil Company (AIOC). This series of catastrophes came on the heels of a long effort by Secy. of State Dean Acheson to shore up the long-tottering position of Britain in Iran, and keep Iran, which shared a border with the Soviet Union, under the umbrella of the Western alliance. "I think this tragedy can be laid at the feet of Mr. Acheson," exclaimed an exasperated Henry F. Grady, who had recently resigned as ambassador to Iran. Grady's resignation expressed his frustration over the shortsightedness of Acheson's policy of deferring to British concerns in Iran and the failure of President Harry S. Truman to heed Grady's warnings about that policy. "If Acheson tells Truman the moon is made of green cheese," Grady exclaimed, "Truman believes it." For fourteen months Grady had struggled with Washington and London alike over the terms of a new agreement on the division of AIOC revenues between Britain and Iran. He had likewise fought for Anglo-American support for Razmara, and warned Washington of the perils of allowing the British to set the terms of its dealings with Iran. "Had Britain and the United States backed Razmara, the former Iranian Prime Minister who was a friend of the West and who was fighting the nationalization movement, this present situation would not have developed. Nor would Razmara have been assassinated," Grady said. "During my tenure as ambassador to Iran I made at least half a dozen recommendations, all of which were ignored or flatly turned down by our government, under British influence and insistence." Throughout that time, the United States had leverage with the British because of greater financial and other resources, but "we just yielded" to British intransigence, Grady complained.

129

"Acheson didn't see it. He has always been very tender toward the British. Actually, my recommendations were made directly to Acheson. And they annoyed him greatly. They were accompanied by top secret information, and an insistence on my part that I wanted the record to show we were heading for disaster. One doesn't do that to Acheson, I have gathered. And while one doesn't like to be vindicated by disaster, there it is."[1]

Grady's lament as well as his finger-pointing were justified; the bases of both are amply documented. Yet, historians of American-Iranian relations have largely ignored them.[2] The reason for this appears to be twofold: the tendency of historians to take Acheson's "realism" at his word, thereby blinding them to the imperial paradigm that underlay his policies, and the tendency of scholars to skip over the Razmara period, June 1950 to March 1951, and go directly to the Mossadeq era, April 1951 to August 1953. The preoccupation of American scholars with the role of the Central Intelligence Agency in Mossadeq's overthrow in August 1953 also contributes to the neglect of the earlier period, when the opportunity to prevent much of the later turmoil was present.[3]

Grady was an important figure in American diplomacy during the early years of the cold war, but other, more prominent men overshadowed him at the time, and historians have never given him the attention he deserves, perhaps because of his criticism of Acheson and the lack of success of U.S. policy in Iran. Grady was, nonetheless, a figure to be reckoned with.[4] As

1. *Philadelphia Bulletin,* Oct. 18, 1952. Based on a copyrighted story from the *San Francisco Call-Bulletin.*

2. For example, Heiss, *Empire and Nationhood.* Neither Leffler, *Preponderance of Power,* nor Daniel Yergin, *The Prize: The Epic Quest for Oil, Money, and Power,* mention Henry Grady despite his eventful fourteen months as ambassador in Tehran.

3. Most of the literature on the postwar problems in Iran center around the Eisenhower administration's struggles with Mossadeq. Some books that center on the earlier and more important (in terms of a missed opportunity) Razmara period include James F. Goode, *The United States and Iran, 1946-1951: The Diplomacy of Neglect;* Mark H. Lytle, *The Origins of the Iranian-American Alliance, 1941-1953;* James A. Bill, *The Eagle and the Lion: The Tragedy of American-Iranian Relations;* Barry Rubin, *Paved with Good Intentions: The American Experience and Iran;* and Richard Cottam, *Iran and the United States: A Cold War Case Study.* Most of these studies generally accept that the early cold war in Iran was a time of missed opportunities, but none of the authors clearly recognize the existence and enormous impact of Acheson's imperial paradigm. An older work that remains useful is Benjamin Shwadran, *The Middle East, Oil, and the Great Powers.* See also Francis D. Gavin, "Politics, Power, and U.S. Policy in Iran, 1950-1953," *Journal of Cold War History* 1:1 (summer 1999). Acheson plays a minor role in Gavin's still valuable account that stresses continuity rather than change in U.S. policy toward Iran.

4. For example, he was a special expert in the Bureau of Planning and Statistics of the United States Shipping Board, 1918-1919; U.S. trade commissioner to London and continental Europe, 1919-1920; and acting chief of the Division of Research, Bureau of Foreign and Domestic Commerce. Grady's background has been gathered from various sources in the Henry F. Grady Papers at the Truman Library.

noted in an earlier chapter, President Truman had named him ambassador first to India and then to Greece, where he received much of the credit for directing the administration's successful effort to prevent Greece and Turkey from falling under communist influence. Because of that success and his knowledge of economics, he was a logical choice to serve in another economic trouble spot, Iran. Given his experience and expertise, his commitment to U.S. interests, and his independent judgment, Grady's stance on policy matters deserved far more attention than they received in Acheson's State Department. The policy failure Acheson and his British counterparts brought on themselves in Iran was not inevitable, but was the result of bad choices consciously, even calculatingly, made against the advice of men such as Grady. Without factoring in Acheson's romantic attachment to Britain's neoimperial vision and using that attachment to read the record of his commitment of U.S. policy to British objectives, the real meaning of the Anglo-American fiasco in Iran is not fully intelligible.

In February 1948, Secy. of State George Marshall asked the embassies in London and Tehran whether it was desirable to tell the Iranian government that "there is no rivalry" between Britain and the United States on matters relating to Iran, and that Tehran "would make a great mistake in basing any part of its policy on supposition of conflict between" the two. The London embassy responded that British officials would welcome such a statement. The embassy in Tehran, however, replied that a statement to that effect "would not be entirely warranted in fact," and in any case Iranians would be more impressed by actions than by statements.[5] The statement therefore was not issued, and it seems clear from the exchange that during Marshall's tenure as secretary of state British and American cooperation in Iran was less complete than it became under Acheson.

In fact, the close relationship that developed in military matters during Marshall's tenure as secretary of state had no parallel in diplomacy. As late as November 1948, only two months before Acheson replaced Marshall, Joseph Satterthwaite, who oversaw Near Eastern affairs at State, asked Ambassador John Wiley in Tehran for his views on the desirability of consulting the British on questions of policy in Iran.

That coordination with and deference to the British was not U.S. policy when Acheson assumed office in late January 1949 is confirmed by the State Department policy statement on Iran dated February 1, before Acheson had control of the policy-making apparatus. Iran had maintained its political independence by balancing competing pressures upon it "in a spheres-of-influence regime imposed by the Russians in the north and

5. Marshall to the Embassy in the United Kingdom, Feb. 4, 1948, *FRUS*, 5:105.

the British in the south," the statement noted. "Recently, however, as American encouragement and support began to replace British power and influence in the area, Iran has found it possible to achieve and maintain an effective degree of national independence."[6] The bases for this hopeful assessment were the growing threats to British oil concessions in the face of declining British power and the parallel willingness of Iranian nationalists to regard the growing U.S. presence as friendly. In these circumstances, American and British interests did not appear to be the same.

On the date of this statement, February 1, 1949, less than two weeks after he took office, Acheson took the first step to change that assessment of the relationship between U.S. and British interests in Iran. The British ambassador, Sir John H. Le Rougetel, was in the process of making "urgent, energetic representations" to the Iranian sovereign, Shah Muhammad Reza Pahlavi, to institute no constitutional reforms or other initiatives that might be contrary to British interests. Acheson directed the embassy in Tehran to "concert closely" with Le Rougetel in this effort, and to assure the Shah and his government of the identity of Anglo-American interests in the matters under discussion. In a follow-up telegram, Acheson reiterated the instructions and emphasized the concurrence in them of Ambassador John Wiley, who was then in Washington. Acheson further instructed the embassy that "parallel" representations, requested by the British Foreign Office, should be made to the Shah's government to demonstrate U.S. support for Le Rougetel's initiatives. To make certain there was a unity of approach, the State Department in another telegram on February 7 asked the embassy to make certain that Ambassador Le Rougetel "emphasize the full concurrence of Ambassador Wiley in his representations."[7]

Acheson thus set in motion a reorienting of policy in Iran, tying U.S. interests to those of Britain and informing the Iranians that the United States would do nothing contrary to British interests. Very quickly, Iranian nationalists of all stripes began directing the resentments they had long had for the British to Americans as well. The change was soon a major factor in Iranian-American relations, as many in the State Department recognized at once. "Iranians, traditionally suspicious of British imperialistic motives, would not welcome any tendency on our part to follow the British lead in Iran," read a briefing memorandum prepared for the Shah's visit to Washington in November 1949, "and are inclined to believe rumors of

---

6. Policy statement on Iran prepared in the State Department, Feb. 1, 1949, *FRUS*, 6:474-75.

7. Secretary of State to the Embassy in Tehran, in ibid., 476, 478. See also 477 n. 2.

Anglo-American rivalry in that country."[8] If the rumors referred to were erroneous, the premise of the memorandum was nevertheless valid.

The source of the problem, the root of the burgeoning anti-Western sentiment in Iran, was the heavyhandedness with which the British endeavored to maintain their suzerainty and the exploitiveness of the oil concessions they had wrested from the government. It was this structure to which Acheson was tying U.S. interests. The symbol of the problem to Iranians was the British-owned AIOC and its determination to continue to funnel the lion's share of the revenues from Iranian oil into British coffers. The AIOC was at the time the fourth-largest oil producer in the world, and its refinery at Abadan, the world's largest, provided a significant portion of Europe's petroleum, including much of the fuel used by the Royal Navy. The company controlled more than one-third of the industrial output of Iran.[9]

The company's—and Britain's—control of Iranian oil dated back to 1901, when an Australian entrepreneur, William Knox D'Arcy, obtained from the Iranian government an exclusive concession to exploit whatever oil resources he located in a 480,000-square-mile area of the country. In return, D'Arcy agreed to pay the government what turned out to be very modest royalties on the vast oil deposits he found.[10] Out of this new agreement came the Anglo-Iranian Oil Company, which owned the oil revenues throughout the area of D'Arcy's concession in return for payment of 16 percent of its revenues to the government. This division of revenues was still in effect when Acheson became involved in the issue.

In the aftermath of Acheson's directive to the Tehran embassy mentioned above, British ambassador Le Rougetel, on behalf of the United States and the United Kingdom, met with the Shah and warned him to act cautiously on matters he was then considering, including the reallocation of revenues generated by the AIOC. Despite the united front, the Shah told Le Rougetel that he intended to dissolve the Majlis, the Iranian parliament, and order the election of a constituent assembly to consider the question of oil revenue. Emboldened by U.S. support in the face of the Shah's intentions, the British evidently believed they could defuse the situation by making small concessions. Le Rougetel therefore acquiesced to the

8. Background Memoranda on visit to the United States of His Imperial Majesty Mohammad Reza Pahlavi Shahinshah of Iran, November 1949, Office Files of George McGhee, box 15, Iran folder, lot 53D468, National Archives.

9. Ibid. Heiss, *Empire and Nationhood*, provides an excellent brief history of the AIOC (1-14).

10. Heiss, *Empire and Nationhood*, 5-6.

Shah's decision, saying it was necessary to avoid a nationalist overthrow of the government and the ouster of the Shah.[11]

These developments took the State Department by surprise. The Shah's sudden decision to take the momentous step of convoking a constituent assembly to deal with oil revenues was puzzling to Washington in the face of recent British assurances. In addition, the department found Le Rougetel's sudden about-face on the issue and his comment that the Shah and his government were in danger "incomprehensible."[12] The department found itself tied to policies the British had decided on unilaterally. By the end of February, the department was attempting to strengthen Anglo-American cooperation while undoing the damage caused by the initial effort with Le Rougetel.

On February 22, Acheson attempted to clarify the situation. The Shah, he said in a message to the Tehran embassy, had mistaken Le Rougetel's joint representations to mean that the United States opposed constitutional reform in Iran. The department's concerns were only that the reforms be timely, responsible, and calculated to encourage political consensus. The department had been in regular communication with the Foreign Office on the issues, and Acheson directed Ambassador Wiley to "consult with Le Rougetel with view to making observations to [the] Shah or his emissaries when and as you consider it desirable."[13]

The merging of American and British policy in Iran was done subtly and appears to have gone almost unnoticed for a time. Questions about it may have prompted the memo justifying it in January 1950 by F. Garner Ranney of the Office of British Commonwealth and Northern European Affairs. The memo traced Anglo-American cooperation in the Near East back to wartime arrangements.[14] In April 1944, Washington had notified U.S. missions in the region that "the conduct of Anglo-American relations throughout the area [should be] in the spirit of cooperation based on mutual frankness and good will." A spirit of "mutual frankness and good will" during World War II was, of course, a far cry from the subordination of U.S. to British interests in time of peace. Equally problematic as background support for Acheson's initiative was an informal agreement of October 1947, which Ranney also cited, in which the State Department and the Foreign Office agreed that neither country would try to improve

11. London Embassy to State Department, RG 59, 891.00/2-1449, National Archives.
12. State Department to Tehran Embassy, Feb. 15, 1949, RG 59, 891.00/2-1449, National Archives.
13. Acheson to the Embassy in Iran, Feb. 22, 1949, *FRUS*, 6:484-85.
14. Memorandum by Ranney, Office of British Commonwealth and Northern European Affairs, to the director, Labouisse, Jan. 30, 1950, *FRUS*, 5:123-24.

its position in the Near East at the expense of the other. This agreement had been an attempt to limit conflict, not coordinate policy. Finally, Ranney cited recent talks in which George McGhee of State and Michael Wright of the Foreign Office had reiterated "the importance of cooperation." It was Acheson who had prompted these talks, and the agreement acknowledged in them may be taken as the point at which Acheson's reorienting of Anglo-American policy in Iran was in place.

The cold war provided the context in which this reorienting took place, and that context provided the basis on which Acheson defended it as a realist. The Soviet Union's interests in Iran at the time were, like those of Britain and the United States, strategic and economic, and like those of Britain, they had a long history.

Back in 1907, Russia and Britain had divided Iran into spheres of influence, Russia in the north and Britain in the south, and in 1921 Russia's successor, the Soviet Union, had pressured the Iranian government to agree to permit Soviet troops to enter the Soviet sphere under extraordinary circumstances. Recognizing the volatility of the area, British foreign secretary Ernest Bevin and Secy. of State James F. Byrnes had reached an agreement with Soviet premier Josef Stalin in 1945 that all foreign troops would leave Iran. Citing the 1921 agreement, Stalin, seeking access to Iranian oil, in March 1946 dispatched an armed force into northern Iran. U.S. protests and Iranian resistance led Stalin to remove the troops, but the danger of Soviet intrusion remained.

The lingering effects of this history, including the imperious attitude displayed by the British in dealing with Iranians, already concerned Ambassador Wiley when Acheson began reorienting U.S. policy. Unlike Grady, Wiley never challenged Acheson's policy, despite his conviction that American interests in Iran were not the same as those of Britain and were, in fact, likely to be damaged by too much deference to the British. He warned Acheson especially about British imperiousness, cautioning that unless it were tempered significantly it would "in the end be fatal to British interests in this country and possibly in the long-run to world peace."[15]

Acheson could not ignore Wiley's warning concerning British attitudes. "We . . . share your concern over indications in some quarters of [a] nostalgic British propensity to [want to] return to [the] 1907 regime," he wrote to Wiley. Acheson was similarly concerned about the "legalistic approach" of the British to the 1921 treaty mentioned earlier, according to which they might acquiesce in the presence of Soviet troops in northern Iran "as

15. Wiley to Acheson, Apr. 22, 1949, *FRUS*, 6:508.

[a] means of promoting [the] revival of [the old] 'spheres-of-influence regime' and thereby solidifying British control of southern Iran." Yet, Acheson refused to raise these issues with the British, or otherwise rein in their hopes of maintaining their traditional position in Iran.[16] Certainly, Acheson and the British knew that President Truman would never agree to the absorption of northern Iran into the Soviet sphere in order to shore up Britain in the southern part of the country. Such a proposition was fantastic on its face, and Acheson's failure to dismiss such talk with blunt action and even blunter language to the British was another measure of his tolerance of Britain's yearning for imperial renewal.

As the British dreamed of saving their expiring hegemony, Washington found itself in a dogfight with Iranian officials over financial assistance. Behind the growing Iranian demand for increased assistance was an implicit threat to defect from the West in the cold war, and behind U.S. calculations concerning increased assistance was an effort to know just what was necessary to maintain Anglo-American influence in Tehran. In July 1949, Iranian negotiators characterized U.S. aid offers as "measly," demanding parity with Turkey, to which American aid had recently ballooned in response to the Soviet threat there. The Iranians submitted a request for economic assistance totaling about $147 million. When that was not forthcoming, their requests for military aid ranged between $175 million and $200 million.[17] These rising sums reflected increasing boldness. The Iranians were in effect soon insisting that the amount of American aid was not something for the United States to decide but for them to negotiate, and they would judge its adequacy by, in the State Department's words, "invidious comparison with other recipients irrespective of specific needs." The State Department demurred. "Whether this attitude derives from [a] view [that] aid is obligatory largesse owed by [the] rich to [the] poor, or is due Iran in payment for alignment to our side," read a State Department memorandum of the situation, "it is based on complete misconception since no obligation rests with U.S. in the matter." The memorandum continued, "Being neither charitable distribution largesse nor payment of obligation," American aid "is not subject to bargaining. Being [a] voluntary contribution, [the] US alone can determine [the] amount and character of such aid."[18]

16. Acheson to Tehran Embassy, Apr. 29, 1949, in ibid., 514; Paper on Desirable Course of Action toward Soviet-Iranian Treaty of 1921, in ibid., 534-35.
17. Wiley to Acheson, July 12, 1949, in ibid., 540-41; Acheson to Tehran, Aug. 30, 1949, RG 59, 891.20/8-949, National Archives.
18. Memorandum by Henry L. Deimel Jr. to Division of Greek, Turkish, and Iranian Affairs, July 15, 1949, RG 59, 891.20/7-1549, National Archives.

Six months later, in January 1950, George McGhee reviewed the Iranian problem, venting his, and no doubt Acheson's, frustration about this situation. Recent Iranian demands had "caused a feeling of irritation in high levels of [the] United States Government," McGhee noted. "The frequency with which aid was requested had no bearing on the amount it received and, indeed could serve as an irritant in relations." Iranian requests now outnumbered all other requests from the Middle East combined. What was more, "many" of the requests were "ambiguous, overlapping and not well justified, could only make a very unfavorable impression on United States officials and were therefore not in Iran's best interests." McGhee concluded, "It would not be profitable for Iran to continue to press this point."[19]

The number and persistence of the requests may have reflected an Iranian understanding of Acheson's determination to prop up British influence in Iran. It may equally well have reflected an understanding of the importance of Iran for each side in the cold war and the precariousness of Iran's commitment to the West. In any case, in July 1949, the National Security Council stressed the importance of Iran and the rest of the Middle East in the conflict with the Soviet Union, and took note of the danger to the West of an overthrow of the Shah's government by elements open to Soviet overtures. This "would have a crippling effect upon the economy of the UK, and would place increased demands upon the dollar area."[20]

Ambassador Wiley argued for increased U.S. aid to Iran. Despite the propping up of the British, Wiley argued, it was American power and influence that was having an impact on Iran. There was no real unity among Iranian leaders concerning the Soviet threat, and without U.S. leadership there was little hope such unity could be achieved. American interests in the region were vital, and protecting Iran meant, among other things, winning support from Iranians.[21] This growing realization of the difference between U.S. and British interests was underscored in late 1950 when, to protect the pound sterling, the British announced drastic reductions in oil and gasoline imports into Britain and its overseas territories, and other countries in the sterling bloc followed suit.

As these events transpired, there was little movement in the effort to achieve a more equitable division of oil revenues between Britain and Iran. By January 1950, when Le Rougetel prepared to leave Tehran for another assignment, the British had agreed to minor concessions that failed to

19. Memorandum of Conversation, Jan. 26, 1950, RG 59, 788.5, National Archives.
20. Report of the National Security Council on the Position of the United States with Respect to Iran, NSC 54, *FRUS, 1949*, 6:549.
21. Wiley to Acheson, Aug. 9, 1949, RG 59, 891.20, National Archives.

satisfy the Iranians. Le Rougetel insisted, however, that the agreement containing the concessions "must be submitted to the Majlis as it is, or should not be submitted at all," because Britain would make no further concessions. Noting that even some in the British Embassy considered this inflexibility unwise, Wiley reported to Acheson that he had suggested to Le Rougetel that a " 'take it or leave it' policy might be too inelastic."[22]

This rigidity complicated the problems Wiley saw in a looming change in the Shah's government. The ailing sixty-eight-year-old prime minister, Mohammad Sa'ed was losing political support, and the scramble to find a successor was under way at the beginning of 1950. Wiley told Acheson the position would probably go to Gen. Hajeb Ali Razmara, chief of the Iranian General Staff, about whom Wiley had mixed feelings. A graduate of the French military academy at St. Cyr, the forty-nine-year-old Razmara was honest and had considerable political support, but Wiley believed he wanted to remain out of the political fray until the dispute over oil revenues was resolved. As prime minister, Razmara, Wiley estimated, "would probably want to play the role of Richelieu. He is ambitious, utterly cold-blooded, ruthless and cinquecento," and in office would see himself as an agent of change.[23]

Deteriorating economic conditions exacerbated these political uncertainties. To deal with both sets of problems, Wiley asked Acheson in February 1950 to consider increasing economic assistance to Iran. American assistance had had "the dimensions of a bag of peanuts," Wiley said, and substantial increases would help anticommunists such as General Razmara cope with problems of subversion. That reasoning grew out of Wiley's recent discussions with Razmara, who warned Wiley of the problem of subversion and the growing inability of the Shah's government to deal with it. "This, from him, is startling," Wiley told Acheson. Acknowledging that the Iranian economy was archaic and the government corrupt, Wiley nevertheless pressed for increased aid. "We should face the facts and on the highest level re-evaluate the position of Iran in the mosaic of our strategic thinking," he told Acheson, urging him to support "effective" levels of assistance. "Effective" meant "economic measures based on adequate financial support through grants and credits which under American control and direction could alleviate any crushing distress of the masses."[24]

Acheson raised Wiley's concerns at his daily staff meeting on March 1,

22. Wiley to Acheson, Jan. 30, 1950, *FRUS*, 5:460-64.
23. Ibid.
24. Wiley to Acheson, Feb. 15, 1950, in ibid., 470-71, 481.

only to hear from Raymond A. Hare, an assistant for Near Eastern affairs, that although the situation in Iran was not good, there was no cause for alarm. "We periodically receive cries of 'wolf' from that area and we are never quite sure when there is a genuine cry," Hare told Acheson. In this case, "the cries of 'wolf' have been received before the facts of the situation." Acheson asked "if this was not a case of corrupt and incompetent government which no matter how much equipment or money we put into it would be doomed to fail." Hare believed "this was somewhat the case."

While Acheson prevaricated, the situation continued to worsen in Iran. Sa'ed was seen by many in Iran as pro-British, and he had been named prime minister with instructions from the Shah to secure ratification of the supplemental oil agreement. As time went by without ratification, Sa'ed's position became increasingly insecure. Finally, on March 19, Sa'ed failed to win a vote of confidence in the Majlis, and the Shah replaced him three days later. The new prime minister was Ali Mansur, and unlike Sa'ed he was not popular in Iran and was widely believed to be weak and corrupt. Moreover, he was even more unlikely than Sa'ed to be capable of pushing through the Majlis an agreement with terms acceptable to Britain.[25]

Acheson's reply to Wiley, more than three weeks after the exchange with Hare, voiced his impatience with Wiley's repeated calls for aid and for a more assertive U.S. policy in Iran. Rejecting those calls once more, Acheson suggested instead that if Wiley considered it "useful" he could "speak frankly" to the Shah about concerns Acheson had about the situation in Iran. Tell the Shah, Acheson suggested, that "you have heard reports from several sources that secret negotiations with [the] Russians are in progress and that they were undertaken because Iran failed [to] receive what it considered adequate Amer[ican] assistance. You would be glad to know whether these reports [are] correct. If so, you wish [to] point out [that] history has shown neither Iran nor any other country can expect anything but disaster from enlisting aid of [the] Russian bear." Wiley might also, Acheson continued, express "regret" that the "Shah's recent attitude and actions, if correctly reported has [*sic*] given [the] impression he has faltered in his previous determination to show his people [the] road to progress."[26]

On the day Acheson dispatched these instructions to Wiley, March 25, the State Department reiterated the policy of cooperation with Britain. In advisories to embassies across the Middle East, the department extended

---

25. Shepherd dispatch, Records of the Foreign Office, FO 371, 82310/EP1016/10, PRO. See also Heiss, *Empire and Nationhood*, 20-22.
    26. Acheson to Tehran, Mar. 25, 1950, *FRUS*, 5:504.

the cooperation between the two governments to private businesses as well. "The Department believes that cooperation between British and American business communities in the Near East is also desirable," the advisories noted. However, since that policy if publicly known might "not have the desired effect and on the contrary might lend itself to misrepresentation and misunderstanding," ambassadors should use discretion in encouraging it.[27]

Four days later, on March 29, Acheson sent a follow-up note to Wiley. He had discussed the Iranian situation and Wiley's concerns with "the appropriate Department officers," and had learned "that the Department's position regarding our aid programs for Iran has been fully reviewed for you in several communications during the past few weeks and I do not believe I have anything further to add at present."[28] In a communication meant to be personal, this seems unnecessarily harsh language. More important, it effectively closed the door on Wiley's effort to change Acheson's Iranian policy.

Wiley's concerns, however, did not go away, and State Department staffers, no doubt at Acheson's direction, continued to monitor the situation. In April, they acknowledged that the controversy over U.S. assistance continued to simmer. According to one of their evaluations, the " 'lack of American aid' had to some extent already replaced 'British intrigue' as the whipping boy of Iranian politics." They acknowledged the danger of political unrest, accounting for it by economic conditions. Iran was the only "free country" bordering the Soviet Union not receiving economic assistance designed to keep it outside of the Soviet orbit. In light of these circumstances, the authors of this evaluation suggested that State reconsider the aid issue, place an enlarged aid program in the hands of an on-the-spot administrator, open additional consulates in Iran, expand information programs, and otherwise enlarge the U.S. presence in Iran. The United States should also pressure the Shah to reform his government, and even designate by "name the Iranian official who it believes most effectively could" accomplish what the situation demanded.[29]

What was striking about these recommendations was the movement they suggested in the direction John Wiley had urged, and the absence of expressed concern for the British role in Iran. Notably, Acheson "indicated he was in general agreement with the paper," but wondered whether the proposed changes in policy "brought in the British as far as we can and

27. Ibid., 505.
28. Acheson to Wiley, Mar. 29, 1950, in ibid., 506-7.
29. Paper prepared in the State Department, undated, in ibid., 510, 515-16.

whether the program will meet the evil which it is intended to meet." Acheson believed the chief problem in Iran was the situation in the Shah's government, not the lack of U.S. aid, but he conceded that because of economic weakness "it would not be feasible for the British rather than ourselves to take the lead" in addressing the problem. Still, he added, "we intend to consult fully with them." Thus, Acheson subtly thwarted the effort to institute a more realistic policy by burdening it with British concerns.

As he made these grudging concessions to reality, Acheson named a new ambassador to Iran, Henry F. Grady. The reason for Wiley's removal is unclear, but the removal itself came little more than a month after his call for new policies had provoked Acheson's displeasure. Grady went to Tehran fresh from his success in Greece, and no doubt expected equal success in Iran. However, circumstances in the two countries differed. In Greece, Grady had had a relatively free hand to deal with the problems he encountered. George Marshall gave his ambassadors more leeway than Acheson, and Britain was less committed to maintaining political and economic suzerainty in Greece than in Iran. Grady had not therefore had to reckon with Acheson's support for the British imperium. Grady owed his new appointment not only to his success in Greece but also to the recommendation by George McGhee and support from Philip Jessup, Paul Nitze, and John Peurifoy, all close advisers of Acheson. "I believe that the best qualified person to head the mission would be Henry F. Grady, now ambassador to Greece," McGhee wrote Acheson of the Iranian post. "His extensive experience, particularly in economic matters, and his background dealing with similar political problems . . . would make him ideally suited for this difficult task." In McGhee's estimation, "the major problems in Iran at this point appear fundamentally of an economic nature," and he believed "there would be great advantages in the designation of Mr. Grady as Ambassador." McGhee wrote as if the new ambassador would be free to address those Iranian problems on their merits, not on how his doing so would impinge upon Britain's efforts to hold on to its oil concessions and political influence.[30]

The controversy over oil revenues still smoldered when Acheson endorsed the recommendations for a larger U.S. role in Iran and named Grady ambassador. In late April, the retiring Iranian ambassador in Washington, Hossein Ala, a British-educated aristocrat whose loyalty to the Shah was unquestioned, tied together the issues of economic aid and oil

---

30. McGhee to Acheson, Apr. 12, 1950, Records of the Policy Planning Staff, box 18, Iran file, National Archives.

revenues in discussions with Acheson's key advisers. After outlining the needs of his government for assistance, Ala asked for help against the British on oil revenues. For the first time a senior Iranian official requested "American good offices in the AIOC negotiations to ensure a fair deal for Iran," specifying that a fair deal meant "to increase royalties to a 50–50 basis." McGhee responded that "it would be invidious for the United States to intervene" in the Anglo-Iranian negotiations, and in any case "the 50–50 royalty basis" Ala proposed "existed only in Venezuela" and not in the more analogous contract recently negotiated with Saudi Arabia. One of Ala's delegation countered that a 50–50 split was now customary on long-term concessions like those of the AIOC. Despite McGhee's demurral, Ala insisted that public opinion in Iran would accept nothing less than 50–50, noting that the British government received more in revenue from the AIOC concession than the Iranian government. Moreover, increased revenues were necessary to fund economic developments planned by the Shah's government.[31]

The logic as well as the equitableness of Ala's argument resonated with staff officials, who contrasted it with the inflexibility of the British. Accordingly, those in the Near Eastern affairs office proposed that the issue be raised at the upcoming meeting of Acheson and Bevin. "It is felt desirable to express to the British our concern over the failure of the Iranian Parliament to ratify the Anglo-Iranian Oil Company concession," the staffers explained, "a failure the Department believes attributable in large measure to a too rigid stand by the company and the British government." The "Company thus far has refused to concede" anything significant to the Iranian negotiations, especially on the 80–20 split in oil revenues called for in the draft agreement then before the Majlis. "We feel that there is considerable justification in the Iranian demands," the staffers concluded, noting the Shah's pressing need for funds to implement his Seven-Year Development Program. They recommended not that the United States involve itself in the AIOC negotiations, but that Washington press London to "do everything in its power to bring the matter to a speedy conclusion."[32]

At the May conference, Bevin's aides rejected the proposal, refusing even the suggestion to restudy the issue. The matter was already "over-surveyed," they insisted. "What Iranians need is not more information but general 'gingering up.' " They also needed, or so the British believed,

31. Memo of conversation with Iranian delegation, *FRUS, 1950*, 5:526-29.
32. May Foreign Ministers Meeting Position Paper on Iran, Apr. 27, 1950, in ibid., 5:529-32.

to ratify the new AIOC agreement as negotiated. Raymond A. Hare, one of Acheson's deputies, voiced American concerns about this "take it or leave it" attitude. To this, one of Hare's counterparts in the Foreign Office responded that his government had considered the question from all points of view and was "sure it is taking [the] right stand in pressing for ratification [of the AIOC agreement] in [its] present form."[33]

While diplomats debated, the situation in Iran deteriorated. Still in office when the May conference ended, Wiley reported that the government of Prime Minister Ali Mansur would likely fall soon, citing Gen. Ali Razmara as the source of reports to that effect. Razmara's repeating of rumors may or may not have been self-serving, since he was himself a possible successor to Mansur. "With [the] present muddled political and economic situation," Wiley told Washington, "there is growing sentiment for [a] Razmara premiership even among some of his former political enemies." In Acheson's absence, State left to Wiley what if anything he might do in the situation, suggesting that a hint from Wiley might result in Mansur's dismissal. Because of his earlier chastisement for assertiveness, Wiley refused to take any action without the British. "I think that to avoid crossing wires with the British," he replied to State's suggestion, "we should for [the] moment pursue policy of negative politeness toward Mansur."[34]

Wiley's hunch that Razmara would be the next prime minister seemed more certain than ever by the end of May. Wiley told Washington on May 26 that the Shah would likely ask Razmara to form a broadly based government unless the British vetoed the idea. Razmara was prepared to deal equitably with the British, Wiley believed, meaning he would likely acquiesce in the recently negotiated agreement with the AIOC increasing Iran's share of oil revenues from 16 percent to 20 percent provided the British could show that its share was equal to or no better than those of other Middle East oil concessions, and provided too that the AIOC agree to replace the large number of Indian nationals in its labor force with Iranians.[35] With these conditions satisfied and Razmara in office, passage of the new agreement would be likely. Still out of office, Razmara deflected criticism from both Britons and Iranians that

33. U.S. delegation at the London Tripartite Foreign Ministers Meeting to the Acting Secretary of State, May 16, 1950, in ibid., 5:546-47.

34. Wiley to Acheson, May 22, 1950, in ibid., 548; Acting Secretary of State to the Embassy in Tehran, May 22, 1950, in ibid., 549; Wiley to State Department, May 27, 1950, in ibid., 556.

35. As in other parts of the empire, the British often imported Indians as workers. This was because they had learned valuable skills in India and language was less of a problem. Further, having few local ties, they could be expected to be loyal to the British. Gandhi, for example, after leaving India to study law in England found work as a lawyer in Africa.

he planned a "dictatorship" by pointing to his proposal to decentralize power by placing local police forces under the control of popularly elected governments. He also proposed to dissolve the current parliament and replace it with a more democratically elected one.[36]

In June 1950, as the economic situation worsened, Grady replaced Wiley and Razmara became prime minister. Razmara was a hard-nosed military man who some in the State Department feared would move Iran toward neutralism in the cold war and resist necessary political reforms. In politics, Razmara was something of a polarizing figure. The British especially disliked him, which might have been the basis of his appeal among Iranians. "God forbid that he become Prime Minister; he is too sinister for our taste," said Lancelot F. L. Pyman of the Foreign Office.[37] Yet, when he became prime minister, Razmara rose to the challenges of the office, accepting some of the reforms the Americans considered necessary and resisting pressures to throw out the British.

There is evidence that the United States calculated that Razmara would act as he did, and was influential in having the Shah name him prime minister. Prior to the appointment, Razmara, the Shah, and Max Thornburg, an American businessman, had met regularly to discuss economic problems. Like other American businessmen in Iran, Thornburg was at odds with Acheson's strategy of propping up the British, at least in matters concerning oil. An executive at Standard Oil, Thornburg had advised the State Department on petroleum matters during World War II, and since 1947 had assisted the Shah's government in the same area. Viewing the situation from an Iranian rather than British perspective, he questioned the usefulness of the AIOC, and argued that the 20–80 split in oil revenue was inequitable because it denied Iran money from its own resources necessary to finance essential economic development. As historian Linda Wills Qaimmaqami has noted, Thornburg believed the best development model for Iran was one in which Americans with experience in the oil industry develop and operate oil-producing enterprises in underdeveloped countries so that "a systemic identification would occur between the host producing nation's economy and the American economic system." As a result of the model, the "United States would gain highly compatible trading partners, foreign investment would be encouraged, the continuing penetration of American business would be guaranteed, and American strategic interests would be served."[38]

36. Wiley to Secretary of State, May 26, 1950, in ibid., 558-59.
37. Pyman to William Strang, Records of the Foreign Office, FO 371/81668/1156/4, PRO.
38. Qaimmaqami, "The Catalyst of Nationalization: Max Thornburg and the Failure of Private Sector Developmentalism in Iran, 1947-1951," 4-8.

Thornburg had come to Iran from Venezuela, where he had helped restructure the oil industry and been instrumental in negotiating the agreement that split oil revenues 50–50 between the government and the international oil companies. This was the most favorable agreement in the industry at the time for the government of a developing nation, and the example inspired the Iranians to resist the 20–80 split on which the British insisted. In Iran, Thornburg worked exclusively with American consultants, which had the effect of alienating the British and freezing them out of the Shah's planning for the future of Iranian oil. This was, of course, a calculated move on the part of both Thornburg and the Shah's government, and reflected the primacy Thornburg gave Iranian economic development over British concerns about political spheres of influence and economic self-interest. Thornburg reckoned, however, without considering Acheson's support of the imperial structure defended by the British. By 1951, Britain complained to the State Department that Thornburg was the Shah's "chief adviser on nationalization," and protested his presence in Iran. The State Department soon ordered Thornburg to return to the United States.[39]

As the spat over Thornburg played itself out, Acheson worked to find an Iranian government that would accommodate British interests. In the early summer of 1950, he had cabled the embassy in Tehran that the United States was sympathetic to the reforms proposed by Razmara, hoping they would "start Iran on [the] road to progressive, efficient, democratic government." He added that the British were "in full agreement" with this position, and expressed his willingness to act as a go-between should the British and the Shah's government have difficulties working out differences over such issues as land reform, corruption, and trade unions. Acheson was even willing to work as an intermediary between Razmara and the British. Yet, in none of the mediative roles was the embassy to raise the issue that mattered most, the adjustment of oil revenues. The "Department," Acheson wrote, meaning Acheson himself, was "reluctant [to] press" the British on the matter of increasing the Iranian share of the revenues since London had "now gone considerably further in this direction than contemplated six months ago" and the department had already "made its views thoroughly known to high UK officials including Bevin." This willingness to push the Iranians but not the British gained Acheson only frustration.[40]

The advent of the Razmara government was a significant event in

---

39. Ibid., 4-8, 29-30.
40. Secretary of State to the Embassy in Iran, June 23, 1950, *FRUS*, 5:562-63.

Iranian politics, and one that had great potential for U.S. interests. A detailed evaluation of the situation at this point by two leading specialists on Iranian affairs, Vaughan Ferguson and William Rountree, emphasized the dangers of communist subversion but made a positive appraisal of Razmara's government. "The Cabinet is composed of young, reportedly honest, and professionally competent officials," Ferguson and Rountree wrote, "who represent a refreshing contrast from the traditional Iranian cabinet minister." Razmara's commitment to necessary reforms seemed impressive, but the fate of the reforms and of Razmara's government itself depended upon solving the intractable dispute over oil revenues. "If the Prime Minister insists on Parliamentary action upon the bill in its present form," Ferguson and Rountree wrote of the agreement splitting the revenues 20–80, "he may fall, and if it is rejected either by the Government or the Majlis, the Iranian parliament, there will be needless delays in renegotiation which we consider most undesirable since there can be neither economic nor political stability in Iran until this issue is settled." They continued, "Accordingly, we are again raising the question with the British government in an attempt to convince both the Government and the management of the Company that the present situation cannot be permitted to continue much longer."[41]

This assessment of the situation was realistic, but the hope grasped at in the final sentence was delusional unless Acheson exerted real pressure on the British. The hopefulness may have reflected too roseate thinking about the new government and its ability to navigate between the irreconcilable demands of the British and the Iranian nationalists. "The Razmara cabinet was a phenomenon in Iranian politics," wrote Arthur L. Richards of the embassy staff in the summer of 1950. Never had such a young, educated, and qualified group been in positions of power before. Only two of the new ministers had cabinet experience, but with "strong leadership, competent functionaries, and adequate financing," prospects of their success seemed bright. If the first two of these conditions were in place as Richards wrote, the third was not, and would not be until oil revenues were reallocated and Iran received a sizable loan from the Export-Import Bank, both of which the British were blocking. The Razmara government, Richards concluded, had the necessary attributes to "bring about a more orderly and prosperous situation in Iran provided it has the technical, financial and moral support of the United States and Great Britain."[42]

41. Memorandum prepared by McGhee for Acheson, July 7, 1950, Office Files of George McGhee, box 14, Iran folder, lot 53D468, National Archives.
42. "Recent Political Events in Iran," July 7, 1950, RG 84, Tehran Embassy Records, Confidential File, box 24, folder General 1950, National Archives.

That support was, of course, the hinge on which everything else depended, and Ambassador Grady was prepared to give it but Acheson was not, though Acheson did commit some resources to Grady's efforts. In McGhee's words, Grady had "the assistance of a special economic staff of five officers who have already arrived or will reach Tehran shortly." Also, "the regular complement of the Tehran Embassy and the consulates in Tabriz and Meshed" were expanded, a new consulate was to open in Isfahan, and there were plans to expand the United States Information Agency.[43]

On July 18, 1950, in London, Ambassador Lewis Douglas and Michael R. Wright of the Foreign Office discussed the Iranian situation, including the division of oil revenues. The Iranians like other Middle Easterners had "insatiable appetites . . . in matters of this kind," Wright told Douglas. The AIOC's insistence on a 20–80 split was "quite correct," and any concessions on that ratio would lead only to new demands. The situation "was serious," Wright acknowledged, and London wanted "an early conclusion to the AIOC problem," but he asked for U.S. support, including assurances that the United States had not and would not encourage the Iranians in the dispute over oil revenues. Douglas gave him the assurances he wanted, and agreed to forward Wright's suggestion that the U.S. and the British ambassadors in Tehran make a joint appraisal of the situation and recommend a strategy for dealing with it. Grady rejected the proposal, pointing out that joint action would offend the Iranians.[44]

By the late summer of 1950, Acheson had concluded that the continued stalemate on oil revenues would cause the larger situation in Iran to degenerate. He therefore decided to prod the British into the concessions necessary to make the AIOC agreement acceptable to the Majlis. The British interpreted Acheson's gentle feelers on the subject to mean that Acheson, McGhee, and the State Department were becoming unsympathetic to their needs. Nothing could have been further from the truth. In fact, Acheson was pushing for concessions because he could see that it was the only way to achieve his larger purpose of maintaining the British presence in Iran. Concessions would reduce British revenues but not British control of the oil fields, and leave the British with considerable political influence in Iran. The alternative was for the British to risk losing everything.

To break the stalemate, Grady proposed in late July that the AIOC increase its revenue payments to Iran without regard to the terms of the

43. Ibid.
44. Douglas to Secretary of State, July 18, 1950, *FRUS*, 5:570-71; Grady to State Department, July 20, 1950, Telegram 176, decimal file, 888.2553-AIOC/7-1050, National Archives.

negotiated agreement or the Majlis's failure to ratify that agreement. "This would clear the atmosphere, strengthen the Razmara Government, and avoid the danger of reopening the supplemental agreement for negotiations," Grady suggested, and he made the proposal despite the insistence of AIOC chairman Sir William Fraser that the company had no money to advance to the Iranians. In the aftermath of this exchange, the Iranians insisted that the company was holding back money that belonged to them, and Grady's proposal thus did what the British feared: increase the determination of Iranians for a larger share of oil revenues. By this time, Acheson "was not inclined to disregard" Razmara's threat to cancel the oil concession. That would have a "most direct impact" on British interests, he pointed out to London, and "would have almost total Iranian support." Acheson therefore endorsed Grady's proposal. The State Department, he added in wording that obscured his own disappointment at the British intransigence, "still does not understand [London's] failure [to] exercise control over [the AIOC] at this time."[45]

The root of Acheson's puzzlement lay in his conflation of British and U.S. interests. Following this statement of his failure to understand the British position, Acheson's Anglophile ambassador in London, Lewis Douglas, pointed out some of the differences between the American and British circumstances in dealing with the oil issue. "I regret [the] US and [the] UK Government [are] not completely in accord [on] this question," Douglas cabled Acheson. "Although we feel we have made at least some useful progress in the Foreign Office, there is not yet [an] identity of views between us as to the required action." There were limits to the pressure the British government could exert on the AIOC because of minority stockholders, Douglas added, and in any case for Washington to pressure London to make concessions on oil revenues would "laden the United States with a large degree of moral responsibility" for financial solvency of the AIOC if the company found itself unable to resist "further demands" from the Iranians. The problem, Douglas told Acheson, was not British intransigence but Razmara's unreasonable "demands."[46] "It seems to me," Douglas continued, "that we should give serious consideration to talking as frankly to Razmara on this question as we have to the British and to try to persuade him that it is necessary for him to present to the company an impression of moderation and reasonableness and assurance that present concession by the company will not lead to

45. Secretary of State to the Embassy in the United Kingdom, Aug. 7, 1950, *FRUS*, 5:576-77.

46. About 18 percent of AIOC stock was owned by private individuals. The rest was owned by the British government.

demands for further concessions at a later date." The British believed that
the American handling of the oil revenue issue had favored the Iranians
and "encouraged" Razmara's "intransigence."[47]

Douglas's formulation of the issue exasperated and incensed Grady.
The bottom line for the British, Grady said in effect, was not the AIOC's
responsibility to minority stockholders but the survival of the oil concession itself, and until the British understood that nationalization of the
concession was a genuine possibility, no movement on the issue was
possible. Grady was particularly incensed at charges that his handling
of Razmara had "encouraged his intransigence." "Razmara [is] not our
primary problem here," he told Douglas impatiently. "He is [an] intelligent, reasonable person who realizes [that an] oil settlement must be made
if he is to proceed with his development program. [The] real problem is
[the] irrational, nationalistic Majlis which has [a] stand-off attitude toward
Razmara." Razmara was an asset the United States could and should take
advantage of, whatever the British thought. The imperative need, Grady
said, was to give "Razmara [the] means to make material improvements
(balancing the budget, starting development projects, etc.). . . . Our best
chance is to help Razmara get strength to settle [the oil] matter." Douglas
replied that he was "terribly sorry there has been misunderstanding."
He moderated his argument and asked that the London embassy be kept
more informed about efforts in Tehran to convince the Iranians to be more
conciliatory.[48]

An important issue in the Anglo-American controversy over Iran was
the disagreement over a proposed loan from the Export-Import Bank. Iran
wanted and needed the loan, and the British and American negotiators
had discussed it for some time, but the British opposed the loan, and their
opposition to it came into sharp relief in the fall of 1950. McGhee and
others in the State Department insisted that the loan was essential for
Iran, but Britain blocked it because of the cost to itself of the convertibility
of sterling to dollars. Iran was part of the sterling bloc, and the Export-
Import Bank would advance the loan only if Britain agreed to provide the
dollar conversion necessary to service it. British earnings in Iran would in
effect be collateral for the loan, as McGhee argued, and the British had an
obligation to provide the necessary dollars from those earnings. The oil
company in Iran was Britain's biggest overseas asset and a tremendous

47. Douglas to Acheson, Aug. 10, 1950, in ibid., 578-79.
48. Grady to Douglas, Aug. 15, 1950, in ibid., 581-83; Douglas to Grady, Aug. 18, 1950,
in ibid., 583-85.

earner of dollars. Iran thus "obtained very little" from the oil concession, he noted, whereas Britain obtained a great deal, and "simply had no alternative [but] to provide the Iranians with their dollar requirements."[49]

Representatives of the British Treasury pleaded poverty in response to this argument and expressed fears that the agreement McGhee argued for would become open-ended and lead to further demands in the future. The British may also have held up the loan to pressure the Majlis into approving the agreement on the oil concession. In any case, the British Treasury hoped that the United States would take responsibility for the dollar requirements, "including the question of loan servicing." Britain was, however, willing to consider advancing £2 or £3 million to the Iranians in the form of "half-shares" in the AIOC to relieve the current financial pressures.

McGhee continued to press the issue. Britain already owed Iran £40 million under the pending oil revenue agreement, and conversion for loan servicing was simply a standard part of loans between the dollar and the sterling blocs and could not be avoided. Moreover, the Export-Import Bank would not lend money against assets that could not be used to retire the debt. However, from the British point of view, British assumption of the conversion costs would, in effect, amount to a "gilt-edged loan."[50]

The issue was still hanging when Bevin and Acheson met in New York in early October. There, Bevin conceded that aid to Iran was a joint responsibility, but Britain was unable to pay for the convertibility of the proposed loan beyond a one-year period, a condition the United States had already rejected. Bevin did, however, offer to allow Iran to exchange sterling in the amount of $6 million for British agricultural and other heavy equipment.[51]

Grady was unimpressed with these token concessions. The one-year convertibility guarantee was "no concession at all," he told Acheson, "since repayment does not begin until after three years and, assuming interest [is] due only [on] credit actually used, the first year's interest will amount to not more than one or two hundred thousand dollars." The British were well aware of the importance of the loan to the United States as well as to Iran, Grady continued, and were using the convertibility issue as an indirect way of killing it. One reason for their opposition, Grady believed, was that they would be unable to control the expenditure of the money, which would lessen their leverage over the Shah's government.

49. Record of Informal United States–United Kingdom Discussions, London, Sept. 21, 1950, in ibid., 593-600.

50. Ibid.

51. Douglas to Secretary of State, Oct. 24, 1950, in ibid., 609-10.

"In order to maintain its prestige and economic and political influence in Iran," Grady told Acheson of the British government, "it is apparently attempting to force us, if US aid cannot be stopped to Iran, to admit the UK as an equal partner in our program."[52]

This, to Grady, was the crux of the problem. "It can only be concluded," he advised Acheson from Tehran, "that [Britain is] bent on sabotaging our efforts to strengthen Iran in order to preserve its dubious supremacy and control here. Not only is such [a] course inconsistent with our mutual interest . . . to stem Communist and Soviet aggression, but it jeopardizes the global position of the Western democracies" as well. The United States was already making "staggering contributions" to European defense and economic recovery, from which Britain was a major beneficiary, and if London continued its obstructionist tactics in Iran, the United States "must proceed independently." To involve Britain in the U.S. aid program in Iran, Grady warned, "would be a serious liability."[53]

Douglas replied from London that his embassy did not concur "in [the] thesis that [the] UK [is] bent on sabotaging our efforts" in Iran. Rather, the British saw the Iranian economic situation differently from the Americans, and did not appreciate the psychological aspects of aid to the country. They were also disturbed by the "open-endedness" of the proposed commitment.[54]

Grady rejected this assessment. "The highly charitable attitude in the interpretation of British motives by our London conferees though most edifying and inspiring is, in my opinion, possibly somewhat misplaced," he cabled Acheson. "The record is pretty clear." Grady also urged that a report on this situation be given to the Economic Cooperation Administration officials then considering grants to Asia. And he went further. The United States should "seek as soon as practicable the dissolution of the sterling block [*sic*]," Grady told Acheson. "Iran's royalties by every right belong to her to use as she chooses, not to serve the purposes of British economic policy."[55]

Acheson rejected Grady's advice, and acquiesced to British obstructionism. "No useful purpose will be served by further discussion with them on this issue," he told Grady, effectively killing the loan.[56] British behavior on the loan and on oil revenues, Acheson argued, reflected economic

52. Grady to Acheson, Oct. 31, 1950, in ibid., 612-13.
53. Ibid.
54. Douglas to Acheson, Nov. 3, 1950, decimal file, 888.10/11-350, National Archives.
55. Grady to Acheson, Nov. 9, 1950, decimal file, 888.10/11-50, National Archives. See also *FRUS, 1950*, 5:613.
56. Acheson to Grady, Nov. 18, 1950, *FRUS*, 5:614.

weakness rather than the desire to sabotage U.S. objectives or strategic interests.

Acheson thus clung to the Anglo-American partnership and to his effort to preserve British imperial power even at the expense of U.S. interests in Iran. "Our present effort," Acheson wrote Grady in late 1950, "must be [the] difficult twofold task of attempting [to] seek [a] parallel although not identical UK-US approach [to the] Iran problem which will further our aims in Iran without undermining [the] British position and at [the] same time taking every appropriate action [to] disabuse Iran's impression [that a] basic cleavage exists."[57] There is an earnest and unrealistic desire in this "doublespeak" that belies Acheson's realist reputation.

In a warm personal note to Bevin on November 20, Acheson addressed the failure of the British to modify their positions. Instead of pressuring Bevin, Acheson stressed the basic agreement of the two governments on Iran. "The views of our two Governments are, however, to some extent divergent on the exact means of carrying out our aims in Iran"; he then added, "and it is a matter of sincere regret that you have not found it possible to agree to the suggestion relating to conversion of sterling for debt service." Apologetically, Acheson told Bevin he had decided to go forward with the loan without British cooperation; however, in this as in everything else in the Iranian fiasco, the decision was too late to avoid the damage the delay and the attendant controversy had caused. While the AIOC remained deadlocked with the Majlis, the Arabian-American Oil Company, or Aramco, prepared to sign an agreement splitting its revenues with the Saudi Arabian government 50–50. This formula, which Max Thornburg had earlier negotiated on behalf of Venezuela, thus became the industry standard in the Middle East. The Saudi concessions, Acheson warned Bevin with studied understatement, "may, when they become known to the Iranian government, make the position of AIOC in relation to financial terms of the proposed agreement far more difficult."[58]

Acheson understood that the Iranian reaction to the Aramco agreement would be more important than that of the British. He understood too the potential impact of the agreement on the growing anti-Americanism in Iran. Delay of the loan and wrangling over oil revenues, plus U.S. support for the British, combined to spread the long-standing Iranian animus toward the British onto the Americans. When the Shah publicly criticized the Americans for their lack of support against the British, the spread of anti-American sentiment accelerated. When Razmara in turn distanced

---

57. Ibid.
58. Acheson to Bevin, Nov. 20, 1950, in ibid., 616-18.

himself from the Shah's criticisms, the intrigues against his government increased. Arrayed against Razmara were the Shah and the court, the "old guard," and the Majlis, as well as British oil interests, and rumors of his early removal from power circulated.[59]

In an analysis of the Iranian situation, Arthur Richards of the Tehran embassy argued that Razmara had relied upon three things to maintain his hold on power. Two of the three were settling the issue of the oil revenues and increased U.S. aid, neither of which had been forthcoming. Increasingly desperate, Razmara turned to a third potential source of political support, a trade treaty with the Soviet Union. The treaty proved no more useful to him than his hopes of settling the oil revenue question or getting increased American aid. The treaty was never implemented, partly because of apprehensions over the prospect of increased Soviet influence. There was thus little hope for Razmara's government and for protecting U.S. and Western strategic interests unless London and Washington agreed "at the highest levels" to do what was necessary to settle the question of oil revenues equitably and to increase American assistance to the Shah's government.[60]

In Washington, McGhee and William Rountree of the Office of Greek, Turkish, and Iranian Affairs had become equally dismayed over U.S. prospects in Iran. "To me it seems crystal-clear that the traditional British policy in Iran has not changed one iota despite the present world situation," Rountree wrote McGhee at the end of 1950. "They are still determined to let AIOC come first and to permit the Iranian internal situation to remain in a constant state of turmoil," hoping in the end to enable the company and the British to maintain their position in Iran. "It seems to me incredible," Rountree wrote, "that the British would expect us to believe the nonsense put forward" in several of their recent communications on the subject. "I can only suspect that they are taking this attitude in order to discourage our activities there and to keep us from interfering with any political changes they may like to make in Iran."[61]

Rountree rejected Richards's idea of further high-level talks. Such talks "usually result only in assurances of a general nature which are never implemented in actual British operations in Iran." Lower-level talks might

59. Richards to Grady, Dec. 14, 1950, in ibid., 630-32. Grady had returned to Washington in early December 1951 where he met with staff from State and Defense. He stressed Iran's importance in containing the Soviet Union and emphasized the need to provide a substantial aid program. The outbreak of the Korean War, Grady said, made it even more apparent that fast action was needed in Iran. Memorandum of Conversation, by the Officer in Charge of Iranian Affairs, in ibid., 624-26.

60. Ibid., 624-26.

61. Memo by Rountree to McGhee, Dec. 20, 1950, in ibid., 634-35.

be more promising. "If nothing else, we may by this approach," Rountree said, "be able to introduce a note of realism into British thinking regarding Iran which might lead to some control over the activities of the AIOC. At the moment, it seems entirely clear that the AIOC dominates British policy in Iran and anything we can do to induce the British government to escape from its bondage is worth trying."[62]

The situation changed dramatically in November when Razmara withdrew his support from the oil revenue agreement and the Majlis rejected it. Both actions came after the Iranians learned of the Aramco's agreement with the Saudis. The simmering anger against the AIOC, led by the outspoken Mohammed Mossadeq, resulted in calls for nationalization of the company and its concession. Razmara resisted the demands, but three days after he publicly criticized nationalization he was assassinated by a young man on a self-proclaimed "sacred mission" to kill the "British stooge."[63] Supreme Court justice William O. Douglas, who knew Razmara, called his death "a tragic loss both to Iran and to the Western world." Razmara, Douglas said, was "a man devoted to the principles of freedom and who believed in the dignity of man and his right to equal justice under the law." Arguing that relations between Iran and the United States had been good during Razmara's tenure in office, Douglas concluded: "His loss is irreparable. The world has lost a distinguished soldier, a great statesman, a noble character."[64] A dispassionate assessment might be that Razmara had placed his fate and the fate of his government in the hands of the British and the Americans, and they had failed him.

With the death of Razmara, the possibility of a peaceful settlement of the Iranian crisis favorable to American interests was gone. Under Mossadeq, the new prime minister, the situation from the U.S.—and British—perspective went from bad to worse. Instead of the moderate, pro-Western Razmara, the Americans and the British now had to deal with Mossadeq, whose dislike for the British was particularly strong.[65] Grady, however, remained hopeful. "I appeal for your support and the President's in the policy I am trying to follow here," Grady wrote Acheson, "that is a policy of conciliation and an attempt to bring some reasonableness into a most explosive situation." Ever since he had been in Tehran, Grady said, "it was impossible to get the Foreign Office to influence the oil company to

---

62. Ibid.
63. Yergin, *The Prize*, 454-55.
64. Douglas's statement on assassination of Razmara, Grady Papers, box 1, file D.
65. Heiss, *Empire and Nationhood*, 3-5. Heiss has perceptively examined the cultural differences that contributed to misunderstanding Mossadeq.

carry out our strong recommendations with regard to some non-monetary concessions which would enable Razmara to get the supplemental agreements through the Majlis and incidentally to strengthen him to get through various reforms he was seeking." The British "intransigence" continued, as London followed "the old tactics of getting the government out with which it has difficulties." Now, Mossadeq had widespread popular support, and it would be "utter folly to try to push him out. . . . If the British think they can, as some directors have said, bring the Iranians to their senses by having the [Abadan refinery] closed down, they are making a tragic mistake."[66]

Everything Acheson could think of doing in this situation hinged on British cooperation, but trapped in their own wishfulness, the British refused Acheson the lifeline he offered. He therefore failed again. From the new foreign secretary, Herbert Morrison, who had recently replaced the ailing Bevin, he got the same, only blunter, responses. Many "Persians," Morrison told Acheson, believe "there is a difference of opinion between the Americans and the British over the oil question and that America in order to prevent Persia being lost to Russia, will be ready to help Persia out of any difficulties which she may encounter as a result." Acheson's proposal of an American mediator would only encourage that belief, and thus Mossadeq's intransigence. Pointing to a recent ruling by the International Court of Justice that the AIOC should be allowed to operate without hindrance for the time being, Morrison told Acheson, "I feel most strongly that what is wanted from you now is not an offer to mediate, but a firm and categorical statement that it is up to Persia to follow" the court ruling.[67]

Disappointed by Acheson's response to his plea, Grady appealed in late August 1951 to George McGhee. "From the beginning, certainly ever since I arrived, British policy and our policy have been basically different," Grady wrote from Tehran. "We have reached the point now where we must decide to maintain our own policy or accept that of the British." It was Grady's "strong conviction" that British policy "may well lead to disaster," not just for British interests narrowly construed, but for U.S. strategic interests as well. "If we decide to let them call all the plays, we will absorb a large part of [the] present deep antagonism toward [the] British." The objective of U.S. policy should be not to protect British oil but to keep Iran "from slipping behind the Iron Curtain." Unless one of the "great western democracies" maintained close friendship with Iran and

66. Grady to Acheson, July 1, 1951, *FRUS, 1952-1954*, 10:79-82.
67. Morrison to Acheson, July 7, 1951, in ibid., 82-84.

its government, Iran would have nowhere else to look but to the Soviet Union for friendship and assistance.[68]

The plea again fell on deaf ears, though Acheson did reject British suggestions in September that force be used to destabilize Mossadeq's government and safeguard AIOC property. At least some of the credit for that rejection belonged to Robert Lovett, the new secretary of defense, though Acheson never openly advocated force to achieve his objectives in the British imperium.[69] This objection to the use of force was consistent with Acheson's strategic vision. His objective was peaceful preservation of imperial hierarchies under circumstances in which colonial peoples cooperated because they recognized it was in their interest to do so. Grady would certainly have applauded Acheson's rejection of force, but by this time, September 1951, he had concluded that his usefulness in Iran had ended. Grady had always seen himself as a "troubleshooter" whose expertise was in solving problems, and once that was done it was time for him to move on. He had done that in Greece, where he had enjoyed a free hand, and he had now failed in Iran. He therefore resigned in frustration. In Mossadeq's last conversation with Grady, on September 10, the prime minister pleaded again for the export-import loan, and voiced his anger at Washington for "working with" London "to boycott Iran in order to force an oil settlement that was satisfactory to the British."[70]

By this time, the bankruptcy of Acheson's policy was evident, even in the State Department. Back in April, Henry S. Villard of the Policy Planning Staff had noted that "unless the British are willing to modify their attitude they will probably soon find that events have overtaken them." Acheson's endeavor to "steer a middle course between the British and Iranian positions," Villard told Paul Nitze, "is fraught with difficulties." Now, in November, Villard repeated the warning. "I think we should recognize the fact that there is a direct cleavage between the U.S. and the U.K. on this aspect of common policy in Iran," he told Nitze again. "The refusal of the British even to consider our proposals as subject for negotiation shows how far apart we are." Villard recommended unilateral U.S. action to help Iran financially, a recommendation that if followed would have begun the process of disengaging the United States from the self-defeating policy of following the British lead. British hopes of

68. Grady to McGhee, Aug. 27, 1951, in ibid., 149-50.
69. Leffler, *Preponderance of Power*, 424; Heiss, *Empire and Nationhood*, 97; Notes on Cabinet Meeting, Sept. 21, 1951, Matthew J. Connelly Papers, box 2, HSTL; C.M. (51) 60th Conclusions, Sept. 27, 1951, CAB 128/20, PRO. See also Mark J. Gasiorowski, *U.S. Foreign Policy and the Shah: Building a Client State in Iran*.
70. Grady to State Department, Sept. 11, 1951, *FRUS, 1952-1954*, 10:161.

maintaining their position in Iran were "far-fetched and unrealistic," Villard said, apparently resting on nothing more substantial than the belief that if they could hold on long enough someone would come to power in Tehran who would concede what they wanted. However, "Instead of being able to salvage something out of the oil industry, they stand to lose everything no matter what Government is in power in Tehran."[71]

Villard was only one of many who came to criticize Acheson's willingness to risk U.S. strategic interests by binding them to the sinking imperial fortunes of Britain. From Delhi, Ambassador Chester Bowles cabled Acheson in the spring of 1952 that "many millions of ardently non-communist" Indians "are half convinced that the United States has become an imperial power." Citing instances in which the United States had recently stood with the British (and the French, too) against aspiring nationalist movements, including "actions which have seemed to support the British in Iran and Egypt," Bowles cautioned Acheson that his policies were creating "the impression (aided and abetted by persistent and skilful Soviet propaganda) that the United States has forsaken the high principles for which it once stood."[72]

Grady's criticism of Acheson's handling of the Iran situation thus resonated in larger circles, and he continued to speak out long after he and Acheson left office. Indeed, the critique he wrote for the *Washington Post* in 1953 may stand as the epitaph of Acheson's policy: "Despite our longstanding commitment to the principle of self-determination of peoples we are actively supporting British and French colonialism wherever that support is needed, particularly in the Middle East, Egypt and North Africa. This is not traditional American policy. Unless we insist that the British and the French adjust their policies to the realities of today and refuse to support in any way their colonialism, the vital under-developed areas will abandon the West and become, in effect, part of the Soviet empire."[73]

71. Memorandum, Villard to Nitze, "U.S.-U.K. Conversations on Iran," Apr. 24, 1951, Records of the Policy Planning Staff, box 18, Iran file, National Archives; Memorandum, Villard to Nitze, Nov. 9, 1951, in ibid.

72. Bowles to Acheson, May 19, 1952, box 180, Foreign Affairs File, President's Secretary's File, HSTL.

73. *Washington Post*, Mar. 26, 1953.

7

The Egypt Connection

Egypt presented Dean Acheson with special problems. There, as in Ireland, India, and Iran, Acheson shortsightedly locked U.S. foreign policy to that of Britain facing another trauma of imperial decline, symbolized this time by the looming loss of Suez. The result again was disaster for the British and defeat for Acheson, though even Acheson came in his last weeks in office to see the folly of what the British were doing and to what he was acquiescing.[1]

Through all the turmoil in Egypt, Acheson worked to maintain the principle of Anglo-American partnership even as he urged the British to pursue a policy that might enable them to retain Suez. In fact, Ernest Bevin appears to have been moving toward just such a policy before he had to step down as foreign secretary in March 1951 because of failing health. With Herbert Morrison in charge from March through October 1951, British policy reverted to its traditional vision of empire. Acheson's effort never went beyond friendly persuasion in trying to convince the British, in one of his favorite dictums, to accept the world as it was rather than as they wished it to be. His differences with the British were always over how to maintain their position in Egypt, not whether they should try to do so. Here, too, then, Acheson followed the imperial paradigm he imbibed from his Ulster heritage.

Acheson's chief objective in Egypt was to maintain the British imperial presence as a bulwark of Western strategic interests in the cold war, and

---

1. None of the studies on U.S. policy in Egypt adequately focuses on the roots of Truman-Acheson diplomacy. Most studies jump to the Nasser era and Eisenhower-Dulles. There are nevertheless useful works on Egypt and the West. See especially Peter L. Hahn, *The United States, Great Britain, and Egypt, 1945-1956: Strategy and Diplomacy in the Early Cold War.* Hahn's valuable analysis examines strategic objectives of American policy. Three other useful volumes are Peter Mansfield, *The British in Egypt*; M. E. Yapp, *The Near East since the First World War*; and P. J. Vatikiotis, *The History of Modern Egypt: From Muhammad Ali to Mubarak.*

of political order in the colonial world. Toward that end, he urged London to placate Egyptian nationalists with limited concessions, which, he believed, would at a minimum leave the British in military and operational control of Suez. His patience with the British, whose goals were much more ambitious, encouraged and facilitated the British strategy of delay in hopes that changing circumstances would enable them to ride out the storm of Egyptian nationalism that they could not otherwise hope to weather.

As in Iran, Acheson faced growing undercurrents of resistance from subordinates, but his efforts to neutralize the criticism of Ambassador Jefferson Caffery in Cairo, which paralleled that of Henry Grady in Tehran, were less successful. This was in part because of the considerable respect Caffery had in diplomatic circles; it was also due to the greater adroitness of Caffery's handling of Acheson as well as the shortsightedness of Acheson's policies. Another problem for Acheson was that some officials in the State Department, faced with a dire situation in Egypt, began to take pragmatic looks at Anglo-American–Egyptian relations. Even George McGhee, assistant secretary of state for Near Eastern, South Asian, and African affairs, came in 1951 to recognize the limits of British power and that British policy was hastening the loss of Western influence in Egypt and elsewhere in the colonial world. Yet, for the most part, McGhee remained loyal to the premises of the Achesonian worldview and worked to keep U.S. and British policy locked together. It fell to Henry A. Byroade, who succeeded McGhee, to edge American policy down more realistic paths. Byroade's effort made it possible for others at State to start to discuss the obvious: that an American approach not so wedded to Britain's imperial interests was needed in the Middle East.

Historians of U.S. policy toward Egypt in the cold war have concentrated on the years following the rise to power of Gamal Abdel Nasser in 1952 to the relative neglect of the preceding years. Yet, the earlier years were of signal importance because it was then that the Western diplomats—Acheson, chiefly—missed the opportunity to influence Egyptian nationalism in pro-Western directions and to ally to the West those who spawned that nationalism. Instead, Acheson's support of the British against Egyptian nationalists culminated in the Free Officers coup in July 1952 and the pan-Arabist, anti-Western policies of Nasser's government.

When Acheson became secretary of state in January 1949, there was already talk that Britain's days in Egypt were numbered. In that month, the Foreign Office alerted the State Department to the possibility of political revolution in Egypt and consequent threats to British hegemony. Anglo-American efforts to blunt those threats were so insensitive to the concerns of Egyptians that they rankled even King Farouk, whose government the British propped up as a counter to the nationalists. Believing that his government depended in part at least on appearances, Farouk expressed his "discontent" to the American chargé d'affaires in Cairo in 1949 at being left out of discussions about Egypt's role in the event of war between the Western powers and the Soviet Union.[2]

Though the situation in early 1949 involved strategic matters concerning Egypt's orientation in the cold war, its symbol for U.S. and British policy makers alike was Suez. The canal there was a vital international waterway, and the British military forces guarding it were major Western assets in the region. Those forces guaranteed the British presence in Egypt, a presence underwritten in a series of treaties and understandings Britain had imposed on Egypt over the years. In March 1949 the Suez Canal Company, in which the British government was the majority shareholder, "negotiated" a new agreement with the Egyptian government imposing terms contrary to Egyptian law. Under one of these terms, the company gave itself twenty years to comply with the Egyptian law that foreign corporations must have specified proportions of Egyptian employees within three years of their establishment. The agreement also pledged the company to pay the government 7 percent of its gross profits in place of previously specified fixed sums, a rate that ostensibly increased the payment but that the company could recoup through labor concessions specified in the agreement. The agreement further provided that 25 percent of the company's directors would be Egyptian nationals within fifteen to twenty years, despite the requirement in law that 40 percent of the directors of foreign corporations be Egyptians by 1951. (At the time of the agreement, two of thirty-two directors were Egyptians.) British officials used the acquiescence in the new agreement to insist that Cairo accepted the fact that the Suez Canal Company was above the law. They also were certain that the rough handling Egypt had received at the hands of Israel in the Arab-Israeli War in 1948 had made the Egyptians appropriately conciliatory in dealing with Western powers.[3]

The State Department had no hand in negotiating the new canal treaty, and its comments on the negotiations were bromides intended to soothe both sides. "We would regard as outmoded any revision which left Egypt subservient to the UK," a department statement said of the new treaty in

2. Holmes to Secretary of State, Jan. 7, 1949, *FRUS*, 6:187; Satterthwaite to Humelsine, Jan. 25, 1949, in ibid., 188-90.
3. Conover to Howard, Mar. 8, 1949, in ibid., 195-96.

May 1949. "We would not object, however, to an amicable arrangement for continued British military responsibilities in the Canal Zone." What constituted "subservience" the statement failed to specify, a failure that left the department free to accept whatever the British agreed to. Thus, early in Acheson's tenure at State, his commitment to British imperial interests was written into U.S. policy. "Although we reserve entire independence of action with regard to our representations to the Government of Egypt," the statement continued, "we have of late constantly consulted with and advised the British of contemplated action on major issues of vital interest to both countries." This statement thus presented a notable policy shift as a matter of continuity, pointing to earlier pledges of Anglo-American cooperation as precedents. In this, too, the parallel with Iran was exact. Accordingly, the statement concluded, "we should increase our exchange of information and views with the British in Cairo, London, and Washington."[4] This "increase" in "constantly" consulting with the British marked the change in strategy that was the heart of the new Achesonian policy Washington and London would informally agree to in May 1950.

The statement on Egypt, however, was more candid than its counterpart on Iran in recognizing the potential difficulties of dealing with a government faced with a growing nationalist opposition to the British allies. King Farouk signaled his willingness to accommodate the British, the statement noted, but "has so far proposed no definite formula for overcoming the anticipated popular reaction against any revision of the 1936 Treaty of Alliance that did not provide for complete withdrawal of British troops from Egypt and for the unity of Egypt and the Sudan."[5] The other side of this circumstance—that the United States was untainted by the legacy of colonialism—"should be regarded as an encouraging contribution to the attainment of our basic goals." The statement concluded in Achesonian terms: "We think the opportunity remains for us to continue to give friendly advice and counsel, which would serve to temper Egyptian tendencies toward extreme nationalism."

With Acheson's thinking thus pervasive at State, it was the Pentagon that cautioned against too closely identifying U.S. and British interests in Egypt. Less than a week after State agreed to the statement just quoted, the U.S. Joint Chiefs of Staff told their British counterparts they were

4. Policy Statement on Egypt Prepared in the State Department, May 5, 1949, in ibid., 208-17.
5. The treaty of 1936 ended the occupation of Egypt and granted a large measure of self-government. Troops withdrew to the canal zone, but the British retained the right of reoccupation in the event of war. The Royal Air Force maintained its flyover rights. The treaty was to be renegotiated in 1956.

"re-evaluating strategic plans in the light of recent international developments," and suggested "that during the course of Anglo-Egyptian discussions regarding requirements, the British Chiefs of Staff identify the requirements for facilities and installations as those to be used by the 'United Kingdom and her allies' and not mention the 'United States' directly." The Pentagon chiefs suggested that although it might be necessary to disclose to the Egyptians that the chief British base for military operations in the Middle East would be in Egypt, the base should not be identified to them as an Anglo-American base. In fact, the Pentagon hoped that any discussion of military plans with the Egyptians would include no reference to U.S. forces.[6]

These reservations no doubt reflected the understanding in the Pentagon that Britain no longer had the manpower or other military assets necessary to defend its ambitions in the Middle East. To commit U.S. policy to defend those ambitions was thus foolhardy. "To follow the time-honored assumption that the US can rely upon the UK to defend the Middle East is to indulge in wishful thinking," George McGhee of State would himself later acknowledge. Friendly governments in the region were already questioning the ability of the British to defend them. "Most local governments if they had to choose, would prefer to rely on American rather than British aid," McGhee said at the end of 1950. Yet, here, too, McGhee shrank from the implications of his own argument. Any reevaluation of policy, he wrote, should move "away from the concept of primary British responsibility and toward the concept of combined US-UK responsibility and active US-UK cooperation in the development and implementation of plans."[7]

As an omen of things to come, the Anglo-Egyptian talks on the status of British forces in Egypt stalled in 1950. The talks, designed to revise the 1936 Treaty of Alliance between Egypt and Britain, had begun after World War II but because of the lack of progress were broken off by Egypt in 1947. Discussions resumed in early 1950 with the Egyptians insisting on setting a time frame for the evacuation of all British troops from Egypt, including those at Suez, as a precondition for discussing other security matters and the political relationship between the two nations. The Egyptians demanded the evacuation of British forces within a year or two, whereas the British refused to discuss that demand until the Egyptians committed themselves to comprehensive defense arrangements that included a con-

---

6. Memorandum for the Representatives of the British Chiefs of Staff, May 11, 1949, in ibid., 219.
    7. McGhee to Acheson, Dec. 27, 1950, *FRUS, 1951,* 5:4-11.

tinued British military presence at Suez. In return for such a commitment, the British pledged to negotiate troop dispositions and consider a partial withdrawal of forces already at Suez.

The talks also stalemated over the political future of Egypt's southern neighbor, Sudan, another British protectorate. The complicating issue here was King Farouk's claim that Sudan was a part of Egypt and had been since ancient times. Farouk therefore insisted that the British recognize him as King of Egypt and the Sudan, and agree too that once freed from British control the two countries would be united under the Egyptian crown. The British refused to negotiate with the Egyptians over the future of Sudan, insisting that they were bound by prior promises of self-determination to the Sudanese.

Confronted with unacceptable demands, the British stalled the talks, a time-honored tactic for putting off recalcitrant colonials while searching for more accommodating ones. They believed Farouk was self-interested enough to be bought off with money and the symbols of office. As a strategy for dealing with a growing nationalist movement, this set of reactions struck U.S. policy makers as inadequate, even bewildering. From Acheson on down, they pressured the British to do the things necessary to reconcile moderate Egyptians to the continued presence of British forces in Egypt. The British would not or could not do that, and the talks remained stalemated when the Free Officers coup in July 1952 rendered the issues moot.

Jefferson Caffery, a skilled career diplomat, became Acheson's ambassador to Cairo in October 1949. He went quickly to work to strengthen U.S.-Egyptian relations, which were then recently troubled by American support of Israel in the aftermath of the first Arab-Israeli War.[8] Caffery's prestige in diplomatic circles, earned over a career that went back thirty-eight years and included a recent stint as ambassador to France, lent weight to his opinions with Acheson and others at the State Department. Philip Dur, the historian of Caffery's career, has argued that Caffery's affection for foreign countries was "strictly subordinate to his loyalty to the United States." In an unpublished memoir, Caffery himself wrote: "The [American] ambassador must never forget that he is there to serve the U.S.A. and no other race or people. . . . An American ambassador is an American; he is pro-American period." French foreign minister George Bidault said after Caffery's service in France that Caffery may have admired France, but he "was completely intransigent and obstinate

8. Philip Dur, *Ambassador of Revolution: Jefferson Caffery and American Foreign Policy.*

as far as his country's interests were concerned."[9] It is not surprising, therefore, that Caffery was from the outset reluctant to tie U.S. interests to those of the neocolonial British in Egypt. In fact, he raised the issue soon enough after he went to Cairo to have affected the course of events had Acheson heeded his advice.

Shortly after arriving in Cairo, Caffery had a "frank initial exchange of views" with King Farouk that laid "the basis for a new and improved phase of the United States–Egypt relations." While Farouk emphasized to Caffery the damage to Arab-American relations occasioned by the U.S. recognition of Israel, Caffery remained confident that he could work amicably with the Egyptians.[10] Caffery also cultivated a good working relationship with his British counterpart in Cairo, Sir Ralph Stevenson. The two men were soon at ease with each other, sharing confidences. Their relationship was in fact the best of what might have come from the Anglo-American alliance that Acheson hoped to build. That circumstance, however, rested on the fact that Caffery used the relationship to try to bend British policy to strategic realities rather than to further Britain's imperial interests. This earned him the enmity of Anthony Eden, who succeeded Herbert Morrison at the Foreign Office when the Conservatives returned to power in London in October 1951.[11]

That was in the future. In the meantime, the Anglo-Egyptian talks on the future of British military forces in Egypt continued. In March 1950, Prime Minister Mustafa Nahas repeated the Egyptian demand that the British agree to remove their military forces from Egypt and Sudan as a preliminary to talks on the status of Suez. In the face of this demand, as McGhee noted in April, "The British believe there is no great hurry and that the important problem is to choose the right moment for the negotiations." They also believed they could manipulate Farouk to moderate the nationalist demands of the Wafdist government. The Wafdists, led by Nahas, had came to power on January 3, 1950, after a lopsided election victory and were in no mood to compromise. In late January, Bevin discussed the issues with Nahas and Foreign Minister Mohammed Salaheddin, only to learn that both men were adamant that Egypt would not allow itself to be put in a place in which it might become a "victim" of Western strategic

9. Philip Dur, "Jefferson Caffery of Louisiana: Highlights of His Career," pt. 2, p. 252. Quote from George Bidault, *Resistance*, 78.

10. Caffery to Acheson, Oct. 12, 1949, *FRUS*, 6:223-24; Webb to Caffery, Nov. 14, 1949, in ibid., 224-25.

11. Evelyn Shuckburgh, *Descent to Suez: Foreign Office Diaries, 1951-1956*, 165. See also p. 71 for British recognition that Caffery was working against them in Egypt.

concerns.[12] As the impasse in the talks continued, the United States, at Acheson's behest, remained on the sidelines. It gradually became clear to the Egyptians this inaction worked to the British advantage.

The Egyptians endeavored to change this U.S. stance. In July 1950, Egyptian ambassador Mohamed Kamel Bey Abdul Rahim pleaded Egypt's case with McGhee in Washington. Egyptian opinion, Rahim stressed, rejected the continued presence of British troops in the country, and he "wondered whether the U.S. could not give some friendly advice to Great Britain to agree to evacuate its troops." The evacuation might be gradual, over a period of as much as two years, to nearby British bases in Cyrenaica, Cyprus, or Jordan, without damage to Western strategic interests in the region. Rahim did not ask the United States to mediate the dispute, but he "felt strongly that the only way in which [the United States] could preserve friendship with Egypt would be for the Anglo-Egyptian question to be arranged in a manner which would satisfy Egyptian aspirations." McGhee wondered if it was wise to evacuate the troops under present circumstances, and in any case the matter was one between the United Kingdom and Egypt. Nonetheless, in view of Rahim's request, the State Department "would give consideration to this question and see if there was anything we might appropriately do."[13]

No such consideration took place, as McGhee told Michael Wright of the Foreign Office in September. Washington had "supported the British position as far as we were able to do so," McGhee said. "We had turned down all Egyptian efforts to get us to intervene and had emphasized that this is not the time to jeopardize the security of the area." Wright reminded McGhee that it was the Egyptians, not the British, who were intractable and unrealistic in the negotiations; he then asked if Washington had any views on the "program of political development in the Sudan." Samuel Kopper of the Office of Near Eastern Affairs responded that Washington "had little information concerning the Sudan upon which to make an evaluation. As far as we knew things [there] seemed to be going satisfactorily."[14] This lack of independent information about the Sudan remained a problem until 1952 when a special U.S. envoy traveled to the country for firsthand observation.

12. Stabler to Berry, June 1, 1950, *FRUS*, 5:289; McGhee to Webb, Apr. 3, 1950, in ibid., 288; Memorandum of Conversation, Jan. 28, 1950, Records of the Foreign Office, FO 800/457, PRO. See also Hahn, *United States, Great Britain, and Egypt*, 94-98.

13. Memorandum of Conversation, by the officer in charge of Egypt and Anglo-Egyptian Sudan Affairs, Wells Stabler, July 17, 1950, *FRUS*, 5:293-94.

14. Ibid., 300.

In October 1950, as the Anglo-Egyptian impasse continued, Jefferson Caffery sounded a note of alarm. Responding to queries about the British role in the stalled negotiations, Caffery warned Acheson that "the British should not permit their present resentment at the Wafd to rush them into impetuous acts." Fond of pointing out examples of British misunderstandings of Egypt, Caffery noted that the British had helped the Wafd come to power believing the party would compromise on Suez and Sudan. However, the British had been "dead wrong" on that and other Egyptian matters, for the Wafd in power had been "very recalcitrant" on Suez and Sudan and on the issue of British troops in Egypt. Caffery believed the Wafd was determined to avoid even the appearance of cooperating with the British, fearing a repeat of the notorious Abdin Palace tank incident of 1942 in which the British used military force to compel Farouk to accept an earlier Wafd government headed by Nahas.[15]

In October 1950, Egyptian foreign minister Salaheddin met with Acheson to explain the views of the Cairo government. Salaheddin assured Acheson that his government was anxious to do its part in defending the Middle East against the Soviet threat, but could do so only if British forces left the country. Acheson wondered if "Egypt would care to see the British abandon their responsibility" to defend Egypt, and Salaheddin answered, "yes, it would be happy to see this." When Acheson expressed surprise, Salaheddin qualified the reply by stating that "he had offered the U.K. very generous terms by which British troops could defend the area in time of war." The British had rejected the offer "either because they did not trust Egypt or because they wished to keep it weak." As to Sudan, Salaheddin told Acheson that Egypt wanted a plebiscite to decide the country's future, but the British-controlled government there would have to be replaced before an honest vote could take place.

Salaheddin expanded on the Sudan problem in a later meeting with McGhee. It "was the Egyptian view that the British had no intention of withdrawing from the Sudan," he told McGhee, pointing out that they "were making no effort to bring the Sudanese into the administration" of the government there. McGhee responded that "the department understood that the British were pursuing a policy of bringing the Sudanese into the government."[16]

At the end of 1950, as the Anglo-Egyptian stalemate continued, it became increasingly clear in Washington that Britain was incapable of defending Western strategic interests in the Middle East. In November,

---

15. Caffery to Acheson, Oct. 3, 1950, in ibid., 302-3.
16. Memorandum of Conversation, Oct. 17, 1950, in ibid., 310-11.

rioting in Cairo followed a new call by Prime Minister Nahas for the immediate evacuation of British troops and for the union of Egypt and Sudan under the Egyptian crown. Following the riots, Bevin told the British Parliament that the 1936 treaty concerning Suez, the legal basis for the presence of British troops in Egypt, could be annulled or amended only by the agreement of both parties, and Britain had no intention of doing either before 1956, when the treaty expired. In the face of a new wave of demonstrations in Cairo, London did, however, postpone a shipment of tanks to Egypt pending upcoming talks between Bevin and Salaheddin.

As the situation deteriorated, Acheson involved himself in day-to-day policy matters, making certain that the Americans and the British worked in tandem on the issues. Acheson proposed, on November 30, that Caffery and Sir Ralph Stevenson jointly ask the Egyptians if it would be helpful if the Americans joined the stalled talks. Acknowledging the risks involved in the proposal—that the Egyptians might reject it outright, or make acceptance contingent on U.S. commitments to help get the British forces out of Egypt or to defend Egypt after the British left—Acheson nevertheless believed the danger of continued stalemate justified his involvement.

Caffery believed the prospects of three-party talks no better than those of the now stalled two-party talks, even if the Egyptians agreed to them, unless Washington was "prepared to pay the price involved." Given the turmoil in the region, the adamant stands of both the British and the Egyptians on the issues involved, and the pressure on Washington to defend Israel, Caffery considered it hard to know how high that price might be. He assumed the price would include pledges of military assistance to Egypt, "at least a facade of military consultation which would give [the] outside appearance of a full exchange of views on a sovereign basis," and "something on Palestine." In light of the strategic importance of the region, Caffery believed there was no immediate alternative but to continue to aid the British. His reasoning at this point rested on an assumption that the British would presently make realistic proposals to break the stalemate in the negotiations, an assumption he soon saw was incorrect. Before that became clear he told Acheson, "In order to offset [the] overly publicized xenophobic stand [of the] Wafd government, it is essential from practical politics point of view that we offer [an] alternative [the] Wafd can sell its vociferous public."[17]

Caffery came quickly to see that the British were and would remain

---

17. Acheson to Caffery, Nov. 20, 1950, in ibid., 321; Caffery to Acheson, Nov. 22, 1950, in ibid., 322-23.

intransigent, and to salvage American interests the United States would have to act independently of Britain. Three days after his initial response to Acheson's proposal, Caffery assessed the situation again. In Egypt, as elsewhere in the colonial world, the United States was still held in high esteem, he told Acheson, in spite of the opposition to American support for Israel. "From [the Egyptian] public we have received many favorable comments, and [the] press has not contained a real attack against us for [a] long time and on occasion [has made] favorable comment." That could change, however, unless the Egyptian public was convinced that U.S. policy favored Egypt's long-term interests. Caffery was aware of the difficulties this entailed. "What is needed is a new look" at policy toward Egypt, Caffery remarked, "and obviously the British alone cannot create it." But "we can," and the United States could and should begin to do so at once, even if it meant acting independently of the British.[18]

The violence that began in late 1950 continued, and the increased tensions that followed in its wake persuaded some in the State Department to question the idea of a joint Anglo-American response. The demands of the Korean War complicated the reexamination of Egyptian policy, but McGhee and Ambassador-at-Large Philip Jessup set in motion a series of actions that made reexamination easier. They asked the Pentagon for a new assessment of security issues in the region, discussed relevant matters with Roger Allen of the Foreign Office, and circulated a report of their findings and concerns to embassies in the Arab states. Acheson evidently approved the report, but if he did so it was probably only as a basis for discussion. McGhee passed the report on to Acheson while he was preoccupied with British prime minister Clement Attlee, who was then in Washington to mute talk of using nuclear weapons in Korea. On December 6, 1950, the day the report went to the embassies, Acheson was in lengthy meetings with Attlee and Truman.[19] Acheson might have agreed to circulate the report as a way of momentarily easing the growing dissatisfaction over his practice of acting jointly with the British on policies that were obviously failing.

The report reviewed the situation in Egypt, outlined policy options, and asked for comment and recommendations. The first option was to continue the present course of following British initiatives and accepting the continuing stalemate in the Anglo-Egyptian negotiations. "By playing by ear," the dispatch read, the British hoped to keep the stalled talks alive and the 1936 treaty "in full effect" for the foreseeable future. The chances

18. Caffery to Acheson, Nov. 25, 1950, in ibid., 323-24.
19. Acheson, *Present at the Creation*, 483-85.

of that policy succeeding, however, depended on an assumption that the current Egyptian "agitation is transitory emotionalism" that would "wane by itself" or could be "bought off." The report suggested that assumption was doubtful at best and the policies based on it likely to be increasingly counterproductive. Those policies, they suggested, "might add fuel to the Egypt nationalism and might deepen bitter sentiment of [the] kind still plaguing Anglo-Irish relations." An alternative to them might be the kind of thing the British had done in India, Pakistan, and Ceylon, "where equal-to-equal cooperation has produced friendship in unexpected measure." The report made clear that these remarks did not alter the current policy of supporting the British in Egypt. Caffery's response to the report was pessimistic. Because of the rigidities of both parties, particularly the Egyptians, he told Washington, the "prospects for satisfactory solution . . . are frankly nil." Wells Stabler, the desk officer for Egyptian and Sudanese affairs, was less pessimistic, but also realistic. "In the long run both the UK and the U.S. will stand to lose," Stabler told McGhee, "if a compromise solution is not found which will give some satisfaction to Egyptian national aspirations." Without such a compromise, the United States "would face the possibility of a hostile population in Egypt during the time of war." Continued British inflexibility "will exacerbate passionate Egyptian sentiments and in the long run create an Anglo-Irish type of situation to the detriment of US-UK interests."[20]

Two months later, in February 1951, Caffery no longer supported the British stance in the negotiations, and Stevenson too was worried that it was shortsighted. Stevenson, Caffery told Washington, "cannot hold off the Egyptians much longer." The issues in the negotiations were political as well as military; the status of Sudan as well as of British forces in Egypt must be part of a comprehensive settlement. Britain and Egypt must agree to "self-government" in the Sudan as soon as practicable, and must guarantee the Sudanese the right to choose their form of government. Since there was no guarantee that the Sudanese would opt for union with Egypt, Caffery believed the proposed plebiscite was "essentially a face-saving device for the Egyptians" and agreeing to it would cost the British little.[21]

However, the British refusal to yield anything was soon evident. The British military insisted that Bevin accept nothing short of what amounted

20. Secretary of State to Certain Diplomatic Offices, Dec. 7, 1950, *FRUS*, 5:328-29; Stabler to McGhee, Dec. 14, 1950, in ibid., 330-32.
21. Caffery to State Department, Feb. 12, 1951, in ibid., 343-44; Caffery to State Department, Feb. 13, 1951, in ibid., 344-45.

to perpetual control of the Suez bases under the existing treaty until 1956 and thereafter under a lease arrangement. That demand worried Stevenson, who, Caffery told Washington, believed the military was naive and that "the Foreign Office may be banking too heavily on the previous success of stalling tactics." Caffery himself considered it "at least a minor miracle that serious disturbances have not already occurred over the long protracted negotiations."[22]

Domestic politics contributed to the British inflexibility. Bevin and Attlee had to worry about parliamentary critics of concessions within their own Labour Party as well as among the Tories. Indeed, Washington understood that parliamentary opinion was "clearly opposed to any further concessions." Despite this understanding, the State Department directed Walter Gifford, now the ambassador in London, to impress on the British the urgency of a solution. "We believe it important [that] agreement be reached with Egypt [at the] soonest possible [time]," the department cabled Gifford; "otherwise [a] dangerous and explosive situation might well be created [the] consequences of which would be difficult [to] counter."[23]

Recalling U.S. rhetoric from as recently as the Franklin D. Roosevelt administration, the Egyptians, like the Iranians, Indians, and Irish, believed they might have an ally in the United States in their struggle for political independence and sought U.S. assistance in dealing with the British. Citing the American heritage of opposition to colonialism, Foreign Minister Mohammed Salaheddin again in the early spring of 1951 asked McGhee for assistance "in this matter which causes us grave concern." Salaheddin welcomed McGhee's assurances of the "increased interest of America in the Middle East," but told McGhee that it was politically necessary that British troops leave Egypt. In agreeing to give them eighteen months to complete the departure, Salaheddin said he was moderating more extreme demands that they leave immediately. Salaheddin complained to McGhee that Herbert Morrison had reneged on concessions to which Ernest Bevin had informally agreed before he left office. McGhee agreed to discuss these matters with the British, but his response to Salaheddin clearly indicated sympathy for the British. Salaheddin left the discussion convinced that U.S. policy would stay wedded to that of the British. "I believe that what is now taking place in Iran," he told McGhee in leaving, "should be regarded as a practical lesson to us, to you, and to the British."[24]

22. Caffery to State Department, Feb. 13, 1951, in ibid., 346.
23. State Department to Gifford, RG 59, 641.7494/3-2151, National Archives; State Department to Gifford, RG 59, 641.7494/3-2351, National Archives.
24. Minutes of Meeting between McGhee and Salaheddin Bey, Mar. 31, 1951, Records of the Policy Planning Staff, RG 59, box 14, lot 64D563, Egypt file, National Archives.

In April 1951, Acheson dispatched McGhee to Cairo and London for further talks only to have him hear the same arguments repeated with the same inflexibility. Salaheddin insisted again that the Sudan and Suez questions could not be separated and that a "new Brit tune" had begun with Morrison, whom he again accused of receding from concessions to which Bevin had earlier agreed. In London, the British were equally adamant that there would be no bargaining with Cairo over Sudan. McGhee warned London that permitting the impasse to continue "could be extremely dangerous and was in fact unthinkable," and he urged the British to be "as flexible as possible and not take any final, irrevocable stand."[25]

By withholding supplies and labor, the Egyptians could, as McGhee noted, make the British position at Suez "very difficult if not untenable." Retaliatory measures against such passive tactics would be hard to justify, and the resort to force "of very doubtful wisdom." "We must ask ourselves quite seriously whether the liability of political unrest throughout the Near East did not outweigh the military value of adhering to British treaty rights," he added pleadingly. "An impasse with Egypt . . . could well nigh be fatal." He had heard from British sources that Britain was prepared to use force if necessary to retain the bases in Suez, and equally prepared to use the forces at those bases to seize control of Cairo if necessary. Both Ambassador Stevenson and R. J. Bowker for the Foreign Office assured McGhee that Britain wanted to avoid the use of force. "On the other hand," Bowker told him, "it was obviously the right and duty of the government [to use force] if the safety of the British citizens was at stake." In the aftermath of McGhee's discussions, perhaps because Herbert Morrison was less flexible than Ernest Bevin had been, the British government moved toward *less* compromising positions, and Egyptian criticism of the British hardened. Presently, Caffery was reporting that the press, the public, and many politicians in Egypt were criticizing the United States for being complicit in British policy.[26]

With the situation deteriorating, the State Department made still another attempt in the spring of 1951 to nudge the British toward compromise. Again the attempt foundered on Acheson's unwillingness to force the issue. The attempt grew out of the growing apprehension over the consequences of continued inaction, but the State Department hoped to

25. Caffery to State Department, Apr. 1, 1951, *FRUS*, 5:352-54; Memorandum of Informal United States–United Kingdom Discussions in London, Apr. 2-3, 1951, in ibid., 352-61.
26. Memorandum of Informal United States–United Kingdom Discussions in Connection with the Visit to London of George McGhee, Apr. 2-3, 1951, in ibid., 356-60; Gordon H. Mattison, Counselor of the Embassy in Cairo, Apr. 14, 1951, in ibid., 361-63.

"carry out in close correlation with the United Kingdom." The problem was the danger of "a further decline in Anglo-Egyptian relations, with attendant disorders and a depreciation of the United Kingdom–United States position." Such a decline, Washington feared, "might prejudice the successful execution of new American initiatives in other parts of the Middle East, might in fact go far to negate them."[27]

This wording was significant, reflecting as it did the growing frustration in Washington over Britain's unwillingness to break the impasse in the negotiations. For the first time, a State Department proposal linked failure in the negotiations with damage to U.S. interests. Making this linkage reflected the growing willingness in Washington to state the obvious fact that American interests in the decolonizing cold war world were hamstrung by British commitments to neocolonial imperatives that had nothing to do with U.S. interests and often ran counter to its strategic needs. "We are . . . concerned by a general restlessness among the Egyptian people and politicians over what they regard as an unsatisfactory state of affairs," Washington now told London, "and by the analogy which is inevitably drawn between nationalization of oil in Iran and 'nationalization' of bases in Egypt." London should therefore do what was necessary to break the impasse, show more flexibility, display a more cooperative attitude, invite the Egyptian foreign minister to London for talks, and perhaps resume arms shipments to the Egyptian government.[28]

The British, in appropriately diplomatic language, refused to budge. They defended their positions in the negotiations, and refused to invite the Egyptian foreign minister to London, saying such an invitation "would inevitably lead the Egyptian government and people to expect an early and favorable resolution of outstanding differences." In responding to Washington, the Foreign Office cited the feeling in Parliament against "any action on the part of the Government which might be called appeasement to Egypt" and the belief in London "that the lack of mutual confidence made a bilateral solution of the problem nigh impossible." This exchange hinted at the growing impatience of London and Washington with each other. Wells Stabler, who was present at some of these talks concerning Washington's proposal, took note of reports that the Foreign Office was skeptical of U.S. pledges of support for a British military presence at Suez after a settlement with Egypt. Stabler assured Dennis Greenhill of the British Embassy of U.S. support on the matter but added: "Our fear was that if the UK maintained an inflexible line, the reaction of the Egyptians

27. State Department to the British Embassy, May 21, 1951, in ibid., 366-67.
28. Ibid.

would be so hostile that the base might become a liability rather than an asset."[29]

The exchanges over the Washington proposal in the spring of 1951 affected the thinking of Acheson's chief lieutenant on Middle Eastern policy, George McGhee. In a meeting with representatives of the Pentagon in early May, McGhee noted that the Egyptians had turned down the most recent British proposal in the Suez negotiations, but he blamed the rejection on the British. "The problem is in large measure the parliamentary situation in the U.K.," he explained, noting that Bevin had made "a reasonable proposal, namely a phased withdrawal by 1956," as the 1936 treaty mandated, but thereafter "the British position stiffened because of the parliamentary reaction." The Egyptians, he added, were also "solid on the Sudan problem. If the British do not accede to their wishes, the Egyptians are prepared for an impasse and for forcing the British out."[30]

Referring to the British position in the negotiations as an effort to defend "a sphere of influence," McGhee told the Joint Chiefs: "There is a rising tide of nationalism throughout the area. We must consider carefully whether we can support British policy in the Middle East. Because Britain is opposed to this nationalist development, the British are increasingly unpopular in the area and are a liability to us. This liability is such that it may exceed the military value of cooperating with them." This startling, realistic assessment had military as well as political implications. "We may as well face the fact that there isn't a complete meeting of the minds between you and [the] British Chiefs regarding the division of responsibility in the area," McGhee told the U.S. military chiefs of the situation in the Middle East. "The Turks do not want to accept the idea of U.K. [strategic] responsibility [in the region]. The Greeks and the Iranians won't even discuss it." Despite this hostility, McGhee pointed out, Washington at present assigned responsibility for the strategic defense of the Middle East to the British.[31]

Despite these anomalies, McGhee was reluctant to challenge Acheson's policy melding British and U.S. interests in the region, or to confront the actual and political consequences of nationalist resentments against the British, including the likelihood of their spilling over onto the United States. If the United States could avoid that spillover, McGhee said, "we would have a plus factor in the Middle East." McGhee's response focused on the practical difficulties of assuming British responsibilities in view

29. Memorandum of Conversation, June 19, 1951, in ibid., 368-69.
30. Draft minute of discussions at the State–Joint Chiefs of Staff meeting, May 2, 1951, in ibid., 113-19.
31. Ibid.

of the drain on the nation's military resources in Korea. However, the military chiefs pressed the point, trying to pin down McGhee on the political as well as the military costs of Acheson's close association with the British. "We've got to recognize that times have changed," the chairman of the Joint Chiefs, Gen. Omar N. Bradley, told McGhee; "it is no longer wise to play power politics in the old way." "We are in a new era," Freeman Matthews of State added, echoing that view, "and the forces of nationalism are such that power politics of the old-fashioned variety will not do the job."[32]

Despite this recognition of the "positive liability" of tying U.S. interests to Britain's, the policy remained unchanged. To bind the Americans to their interests, the British in early 1951 had proposed creation of a unified Middle East Command (MEC) to integrate all allied forces in the region into a single structure. This, they hoped, would remove the onus of "occupation" from their forces in places such as Suez by making them components of a multinational defense force controlled by a unified staff of allied and regional commanders. It would also bind the United States formally to the British military presence in Suez and elsewhere. To McGhee, the proposal was worth exploring because it opened a new possibility of influencing British negotiators in the Egyptian talks, but this reasoning ignored the main point of contention: the refusal of Egyptians to countenance the continued presence of British forces in their country under any guise. It also ignored the fact that the British refused to consider the Egyptians equal partners in any arrangement. The Egyptian government rejected the proposal in October 1951. "If ever there was a political stillbirth," Acheson later wrote of the proposal, "this was it."[33]

The British remained as inflexible as ever. In August 1951, less than two months before Prime Minister Nahas unilaterally abrogated the 1936 Anglo-Egyptian treaty, Herbert Morrison responded to reports that the State Department was faltering in its support of the British by reminding Acheson that the treaty had been "freely negotiated," and Britain exercised its "responsibility" at Suez "on behalf of all freedom-loving nations." Thus, "no question of imperialism exists," Morrison insisted, despite Egyptian resentment at the British presence. Egyptians were "prisoners of their own propaganda," for despite the propaganda they "realize in their hearts that we have to stay in Egypt." In making that statement,

---

32. Ibid.
33. Acheson, *Present at the Creation*, 564. See also Hahn, *United States, Great Britain, and Egypt*, 94.

Morrison was clinging to the rock of domestic political pressure in an effort to avoid the hard place of nationalist agitation. He profoundly misread Egyptian opinion, and he may have underestimated the willingness of British opinion to tolerate the shrinking of the empire. "I can assure you that no British Government of whatever complexion, could offer to [leave Egypt] and hope to remain in office," he told Acheson confidently. Britain was staying in Egypt. "If the Egyptians will recognize that fact, so much the better; but if not, we and they will have to take the consequences of our remaining nonetheless." If the Americans and the British presented a united front, then "the consequences of a refusal to withdraw may not be so very terrible after all." Acheson replied that they could discuss the problem further at their upcoming meeting in September.[34]

As Acheson clung to the British, others at State sought ways to circumvent British intransigence. Among those who did so was Freeman Matthews, a deputy undersecretary, who asked the Joint Chiefs of Staff to reevaluate the importance of the Suez bases for regional defense. Noting that the negotiations seemed hopelessly deadlocked, Matthews pointed out that the Egyptian government might soon unilaterally abrogate the 1936 treaty and in so doing make the continued presence of British forces there untenable, or at least useless as a regional defense base. Would not such a development make the British forces at the Suez bases more a liability than an asset? The chiefs responded, in the hope of avoiding that scenario, that the best option might be for the British to maintain the bases with small garrisons to keep them usable in an emergency. The chiefs steered away from U.S. intervention in Egypt, but said that if world opinion were marshaled under the aegis of the United Nations, they would encourage political support for the British as a "defensive" reaction to Egyptian abrogation of the 1936 treaty.[35]

In late September, the Foreign Office further complicated the negotiations by insisting that the Sudan was in fact two political entities, northern Sudan and southern Sudan, that must be dealt with separately. The Foreign Office would not stand in the way of self-government for either or both of these entities, but "fixing a definite date [is] most difficult." In any case, decisions about the Sudan could be made only in consultation with

34. Morrison to Acheson, Aug. 15, 1951, PREM, 8/1389, PRO. See also *FRUS, 1951*, 5:376 n. 5. Morrison to Acheson, Aug. 15, 1951, PREM 8/1389, PRO; Acheson to Morrison, Aug. 30, 1951, *FRUS*, 5:381.

35. Matthews to Marshall, Aug. 21, 1951, *FRUS*, 5:376-77; Bradley to Marshall, Aug. 29, 1951, in ibid., 378-80.

the Sudanese people, which the proposal offered no means of accomplishing. The State Department dissociated Washington from this proposal. "If [the] present UK proposals should prove unacceptable to Egypt and appear as [a] stumbling block for estab[lishing] MEC," Washington told the London embassy, "we hope UK will have ready second and more liberal set of proposals."[36]

King Farouk acknowledged the U.S. effort to facilitate the negotiations. In discussions with Caffery, Farouk "warmly welcomed our entrance into the ring," as Caffery reported to Washington; without the United States, the king told Caffery, "nothing would or could be done." "You are the only ones who can put it over," the king enthused, hoping no doubt to encourage Caffery as well as to widen the differences between Washington and London. Toward those ends, Farouk warned Caffery that he, Farouk, was losing the battle against the radicals in his government who wanted to abrogate the 1936 treaty. In fact, he told Caffery, they were already preparing papers of abrogation. "If you come up with something that I conscientiously believe my fatherland can accept, the government will accept it too," Farouk continued. "I am wholeheartedly on [the] side of the west and in case of war you can count on me. Having that in mind do not do anything to weaken my position. If I am strong enough I can help you, but if I am weak, I won't be able to help you at all."[37]

Without Acheson's assistance, Caffery could do nothing, and by the time of his conference with Farouk it might already have been too late. On October 8, 1951, little more than a week after the conference, Prime Minister Nahas announced the unilateral abrogation of the 1936 treaty. There was jubilation in the streets of Cairo, Caffery reported. In a parade the next day, demonstrators carried Egyptian flags and banners proclaiming, "Long Live King of Egypt and the Sudan"; "Long Live Nahas, Hero of Independence"; and, more ominously, "Get Out of Our Country" and "Long Live Mossedeq." In the aftermath, Farouk told Stevenson, Britain had waited too long. The Foreign Office kept an outward aplomb, describing Nahas's action as a bargaining tactic in the ongoing negotiations. And Acheson was quick to swing behind the British. In a press release on October 10, Acheson focused on legal technicalities, noting that the treaty had no provisions for unilateral abrogation, suggesting that the Egyptian government lacked "proper respect for international obligations." In his account of this episode in his memoirs, Acheson focused on what he depicted as Egyptian intransigence. He did suggest, however, that

36. State Department to British Embassy, Sept. 22, 1951, in ibid., 387.
37. Caffery to State Department, Sept. 30, 1951, in ibid., 389.

Morrison's confidence that Nahas would do nothing "that might prejudice a settlement" had been "misplaced."[38]

Morrison "deeply" appreciated Acheson's support and pledged to stay the course already set. "We are prepared to talk patiently but I ought to make it clear that we have reached in the agreed proposals the limit of concessions we could make regarding the position of British troops and the base," Morrison told Acheson. It was "out of the question" for Britain to forsake the people of Sudan, and British troops would stay at Suez while the negotiations continued, prepared to respond to whatever pressure the Egyptians might attempt to exert.[39] "Much as we should regret the necessity of using force we would not shrink from our responsibilities if the situation demanded it," Morrison continued.

> I am confident that in this course we should have the full moral support of the United States and other countries to whom as well as to us the freedom of the Middle East region is a vital interest. The consequences of a withdrawal which to us is unthinkable whether from the military, political or moral point of view would be so disastrous not only for this country but for the Western allies as a whole as to leave us all no alternative but to stand firm together. Indeed, if we were to withdraw the whole world would say that Britain had lost not to Egypt but to her Allies.[40]

State Department officials conferred over how to respond to Morrison. Matthews, who wanted reevaluation of U.S. policy, conferred with McGhee and others, including Sir Oliver Franks. He then contacted Acheson by phone at his farm in Maryland, Harewood, outlining to him "our thinking concerning an interim reply." What Matthews said to Acheson was unrecorded, but Acheson evidently disagreed with at least some of it. Acheson told Matthews that he "felt we should take a rather 'stouthearted' attitude," implying that Matthews had advised some other stance toward the Egyptians. He believed the situation in Egypt, involving as it did the unilateral abrogation of treaty rights and the presence of British forces on the ground, was "quite a different one from that in Iran," implying again that Matthews had equated the two in some respects. Acheson instructed Matthews to notify Franks that the United States

---

38. Caffery to State Department, in ibid., 392-94, 397; Gifford to State Department, Oct. 9, 1951, in ibid., 395; *Department of State Bulletin*, Oct. 22, 1951, 647; Acheson, *Present at the Creation*, 563.

39. Morrison to Acheson, Oct. 12, 1951, *FRUS*, 5:398-400.

40. Ibid.

fully supported the British, except regarding military action, about which Acheson's "first impression was not unfavorable." In any case, approval of military action would require consultation with Truman and the Defense Department. In a personal message to Morrison later, Acheson was more supportive, declaring that loss of the Suez bases would have "grave consequences," and offering to support any action the British took to keep the canal open. Though he urged military restraint with this personal message, Acheson moved the United States firmly behind British military defense of the canal and bases at Suez.[41]

The diplomats were no longer in control of the situation, however. The rioting in Egypt increased, and on October 16, British forces fired on demonstrators attacking British dependents at Ismailia, killing five of them. Caffery believed the British soldiers "went beyond what was strictly necessary" in this and other incidents, and urged Stevenson to make sure British forces did "nothing which might worsen the situation." Already, their actions had "considerably increased animosity against the British." Instead of exercising the restraint Caffery urged, the British cut fuel oil supplies to Cairo, which Caffery believed "was going a bit too far." The action, he wrote, "simply does not show a sense of proportion," since the oil was essential for electricity, public utilities, transportation, and industry. Stevenson was "extremely unhappy" but he had no say-so in the decision.[42]

Tensions escalated. Farouk told Caffery that the British were "making it impossible" for his or any Egyptian government to accept a compromise solution to any of the basic issues. By October 27, Caffery was hearing rumors that some in the Egyptian government were talking of declaring war on Britain, and refrained from doing so only because it would give the British reason to invade the country. Despite the mounting tensions, Caffery believed U.S. support had been "of great help" to the British at a time when "they needed help," and had "made our moderating voice more effective with them." It had also "not yet irreparably damaged us with the Egyptians who still have hope that the US can do something to save them from the mess which they are in."[43]

Caffery, then, understood the value of American support to the British,

---

41. Memorandum for the Files by the deputy undersecretary of state, Matthews, Oct. 15, 1951, in ibid., 402-3; Acheson to Morrison, Oct. 17, 1951, in ibid., 404-5.

42. Caffery to State Department, Oct. 18, 1951, in ibid., 406; Caffery to State Department, Oct. 12, 1951, in ibid., 407-8.

43. Caffery to State Department, Oct. 24, 1951, in ibid., 409; Caffery to State Department, Oct. 27, 1951, in ibid., 411-12.

and the potential danger of that support to U.S. interests. This brought him face-to-face with the implications of Achesonian policy. In a carefully crafted message at the end of October, Caffery told Washington it was necessary to face up to the fact that the Egyptians would not accept British presence in Suez unless the British made it worth their while, and Caffery believed substantial concessions on Sudan might accomplish that, and suggested that State lay the groundwork toward that end. That would be difficult, perhaps impossible, if the British took some of the actions they were considering. The "British have in mind [a] number of drastic reprisals in [the canal] zone and I will go along with them as I have gone always in [the] past," Caffery told Washington, "but I can not go along with an action which if carried out will end only in reoccupation and revolution."[44]

This qualification of Caffery's support for British action was significant. Not only was it less than Acheson's policy of unlimited support, but also for the first time the point at which Caffery was willing to consider dissociating U.S. policy and interests from those of the British was put in writing. The shift was (in part) a response to British actions. When Caffery made it, British reprisals against the Cairo protests continued and the protests were escalating. Ambassador Stevenson was in "black despair" over the situation when Caffery met him in November. Events in the canal zone, he told Caffery, "are headed straight for an explosion to be followed by reoccupation of Egypt which inevitably will be followed by the British being thrown out of Egypt forever." The behavior of the military was, in Stevenson's view, self-destructive, but the actions of the new Tory government in London led by Winston Churchill, who had just authorized another partial cutoff of oil supplies to Cairo, were no better. "They have defeated me," Stevenson lamented. Significantly, both Stevenson and Caffery were now urging compromise on the British government as the only hope of maintaining control of the canal. "As I have remarked before," Caffery cabled Washington, "if the military shut off the oil again, let's stop talking about finding a solution." A few days later, he repeated the warning. "If this state of affairs is allowed to continue Egypt will eventually fall in the lap of my Russian colleague like an overripe plum." The only thing that stood in the way was the "still considerable prestige" of the United States. However, if the British were still "playing their game" at the end of another fortnight, "I reluctantly suggest that there is only one

44. Caffery to State Department, Oct. 30, 1951, in ibid., 413-14; Caffery to State Department, Oct. 31, 1951, in ibid., 415.

way left for us to protect ourselves and that is the next time . . . they turn off the tap" to announce publicly "that the US has no responsibility" for the action.[45]

Caffery's alarm led Acheson to raise the matter immediately with Foreign Minister Anthony Eden at the ministerial talks then under way in Rome. His abrasive tone in the discussion, so out of character in Acheson's dealings with the British, reflected not only his frustration at British inflexibility but also his concern over the deteriorating situation in Egypt. Acheson may also have been trying to demonstrate to concerned State Department staffers that he was pushing London in more reasonable directions. He told Eden that the fundamental question was not military but political, that British actions seemed designed to keep the Egyptian government and people in turmoil, and that Eden had yielded to military pressure when diplomatic measures were needed. Both the American and the British ambassadors in Egypt agreed with this assessment, Acheson continued, and though Washington would stand with Britain on whatever was necessary to protect the canal, it would not support such counterproductive provocations as cutting off the fuel supply for Cairo. Acheson concluded by saying that Eden "was wholly wrong and was undermining [the] solidarity of United States and British relations in regard [to] this problem." In the long run, Britain must have at least "passive acceptance" of the Egyptian government to remain in Suez. "Eden [then] asked what [the] US expected of him," and Acheson replied "that we wanted [the] reversal of [the] British decision" to cut off the oil supply.[46]

This discussion signals the failure of Acheson's policy of following the British lead in the colonial world. After three years, the fruits of the policy were too evident for even Acheson to ignore. As he lectured Eden in Rome, Acheson knew that the government of India was growing increasingly difficult in its encouragement of the nonaligned movement, that Kashmir was threatening the stability of South Asia, that Iran was driving out the British and the government there was more nationalistic than ever, and that Ireland remained a thorn in Britain's side. The folly of "one policy for the world" was thus starkly revealed.[47] What was missing from the policy—and the source of its failure—was any meaningful consideration for the wishes and well-being of the peoples the British had exploited to maintain their empire, peoples whose roiling resentments and thwarted

45. Caffery to State Department, Oct. 31, 1951, in ibid., 415; Caffery to State Department, Nov. 24, 1951, in ibid., 424-25; Caffery to State Department, Nov. 26, 1951, in ibid., 426-27.
46. Acheson to State Department, Nov. 26, 1951, in ibid., 427-28.
47. See Chapter 1.

aspirations it was Acheson's misfortune to confront. Caffery had pointed to the problem in Egypt, but his remarks applied equally well to other places in the colonial world where Britain had ruled and Acheson had worked to maintain its rule. "Without reference to the varied causes which have brought Egypt[ians] to the white-heated animosity against the Brit[ish]," Caffery wrote, "it is important in any thinking re [the] current situation [to] bear fully in mind the fact that this animosity is deeply genuine and permeates the entire society." There were no elements of the press or the public in which support could be found for a continued British presence in Egypt.[48]

With events in a downward spiral, the State Department restated U.S. policy, this time incorporating Caffery's view that Egyptian nationalism "is a deeply rooted movement which will neither subside nor alter its course by mere passage of time," and rejecting the British strategy of "drift" and delay. Unless the legitimate concerns of Nahas and the Wafd party were addressed soon, their government would fall and be "replaced by extremist elements which may lead Egypt down the road to chaos and anarchy."[49]

To avoid this, the British must accommodate the Egyptians on Sudan and compromise with them on matters related to the defense of the region. "We are impressed by the conclusion reached by US and UK Embassies in Cairo and concurred in by British Generals [at] Fayid," the department told the London embassy, "that as of now [the] lack of Egyptian cooperation has resulted in [the] Canal base being 'no longer operative.'" If the purpose of British policy was to maintain the base in a usable manner, it was already a failure. The department proposed immediate resumption of the stalled negotiations on the basis of British offers to recognize Farouk as king of the Sudan in return for Egyptian agreement to a plebiscite on Sudanese self-determination, and to compromise on measures necessary for regional defense.[50]

This proposal pleased Caffery, and Stevenson was "delighted" with it and as "convinced" as Caffery that it signaled "the only way out" of the impasse. "I again repeat and emphasize that if [the] Foreign Office continues to adhere to policies set out in London [earlier] we are headed for real trouble," Caffery told Washington. Hussein Sirry Pasha, whom

48. Caffery to State Department, Dec. 6, 1951, in ibid., 430.
49. Secretary of State to Embassy in United Kingdom, Dec. 14, 1951, in ibid., 438. The telegram was drafted by G. Lewis Jones and Wells Stabler. Stabler, State's officer in charge of Egypt and Anglo-Egyptian-Sudan affairs, had become a potent critic of British diplomacy in Egypt.
50. Ibid., 439.

Caffery described as "probably the outstanding political leader here who is basically friendly to the Western World," had recently told Caffery that he could undertake to form a new government only after the British accommodated Egyptian demands.[51]

There was little reason to believe the British would do that. On the contrary, the Foreign Office instructed Stevenson on December 18 to "lecture the King in the Miles Lampson way." The reference was to the one-time British high commissioner in Cairo known for his high-handed dealings with Egyptian leaders and for his references to King Farouk in communications to the Foreign Office as "the boy." "This would have been all right in 1888 or even in 1920," Stevenson told Caffery of these instructions, but now "it would only make the king very angry indeed as it would bring to mind the tanks of 1942."[52]

The immediate stumbling block to resuming negotiations was the political future of Sudan. The British refused to concede the Egyptian demands or to set in motion the machinery necessary for the Sudanese people to express themselves on the subject of self-determination. By November 1951, the State Department was doubting the sincerity of the professed desire of the British to discover the wishes of the Sudanese people concerning their political future. James Webb of State wrote Caffery asking what evidence he had that Britain had spoken with Sudanese leaders about the issues raised in Anglo-Egyptian negotiations. Caffery responded that to his knowledge the British had not consulted the Sudanese, and suggested that they refused to "face facts on the Sudan." Unless they did so, Suez "may . . . explode with a loud bang at no distant date," resulting possibly in communist control.[53]

As this prospect loomed, a series of personnel changes at State facilitated the shift of U.S. policy, already under way, away from close cooperation with Britain. McGhee, Acheson's chief lieutenant on Middle Eastern policy, left the department to become ambassador to Turkey in December 1951. McGhee's temporary successor, Burton Y. Berry, held the post on an interim basis until April 1952, when Henry A. Byroade took over as a permanent replacement. Neither Berry nor Byroade supported Acheson's policy of Anglo-American cooperation to the degree McGhee did, and Acheson's personal involvement in Middle Eastern policy making grew

51. Caffery to State Department, Dec. 19, 1951, decimal file, 641.74/12-1951, National Archives.
52. Peter Mansfield, *A History of the Middle East*, 195. For more on Lampson, see Yapp, *Near East*, 58, 60. Caffery to State Department, Dec. 19, 1951, *FRUS*, 5:440-43.
53. Webb to Caffery, Nov. 21, 1951, *FRUS*, 5:428; Caffery to State Department, Nov. 30, 1951, in ibid., 429.

after McGhee's departure.[54] At the outset of his tenure, Berry went to Egypt for a firsthand look at the situation, and on his return made a pessimistic report of what he had seen. The situation in Egypt was "terrible," he told a joint meeting of policy planners from State and Defense. "The hatred against [the British] is general and intense. It is shared by everyone in the country. The result is that the position we desire in Egypt, the area we want for bases, and the influence of Egypt in the Arab world in support of our interests, are denied to us." The problem was "exceedingly complex" and a solution to it "urgently needed." No solution could be imposed by force. If the British struck at the Egyptians for their harassments in the canal zone, as the military wanted to do, "the Egyptians will retaliate by cleaning the British out of Cairo and Alexandria." Should that occur, "the British will occupy Cairo and Alexandria and that will lead to the eventual loss of Egypt to the British."[55]

At the Churchill-Truman summit in January 1952, Eden and Acheson again discussed Egypt, but Acheson was unwilling to pressure Eden, and Eden offered no concession to restart the negotiations. Incredibly, Eden argued at one point that progress could perhaps be made if the Egyptians returned to the terms of the 1899 treaty.[56] In an effort to clarify matters in Sudan, the State Department dispatched Wells Stabler to the country, and what he found there was not reassuring. "There is a hard core of British officials with 20 or more years of service in the Sudan," Stabler reported on his return, "who look upon the country as a private preserve" and who have no plans for "guiding" the Sudanese toward constitutional development or expressions of their political will. They did, however, hold Egypt in disdain, and hoped to maintain British control of Sudan as long as possible. Should they fail in that hope, Stabler found, many of them would turn the government over to the Sudanese rather than to the Egyptians as a fait accompli. Such a turnover, they expected, would be followed by a continued British presence and de facto domination. Stabler found no agreement among the Sudanese regarding their political future, but little

54. Peter Hahn has also recognized Acheson's growing involvement in making policy toward the Egyptian problem (see *United States, Great Britain, and Egypt*, 136).

55. Discussions of State–Joint Chiefs of Staff Meeting, Dec. 12, 1951, *FRUS*, 5:434-36. Berry praised Caffery's handling of the situation in Egypt. "Our Ambassador is greatly respected. He speaks with a ring of authority. There is no doubt that he is the outstanding foreigner in Egypt."

56. Minutes of third session of the Truman-Churchill talks, Washington, Jan. 8, 1952, *FRUS, 1952-1954*, 9:1744. In later meetings, Acheson and Eden continued to wrangle over legal technicalities, but Acheson did not press Eden nor was any solution found. See Memorandum of Conversation between American and British representatives, Washington, in ibid., 1746.

support for union with Egypt. Britons in Khartoum talked occasionally of "Sudanization" of the country's politics and government, but Stabler found little evidence of the implementation of such a policy. In short, the British in Sudan expected to remain there indefinitely, and British talk of self-determination was a sham. They might, however, accept a symbolic union of Sudan and Egypt at the monarchical level, and Stabler believed there would be little opposition to that from the Sudanese. In any event, British consultation with the Sudanese should no longer be a problem since members of the new legislative assembly were now in Khartoum for a good part of the year.[57]

The situation in Egypt continued to deteriorate. On January 25, a British military force launched "Operation Rodeo," which engaged Egyptian police in Ismailia, killing about fifty policemen. Widespread violence and looting ensued immediately. The next day became known as "Black Saturday," and without reference to the killing of the policemen Acheson in his memoirs described how "mobs swept through the streets of Cairo." In the aftermath of these outbursts, Acheson expressed his sorrow to Eden that the "police action" at Ismailia "had not worked out as Mr. Eden hoped and expected," and told Sir Oliver Franks, "The whole thing looks bad." Acheson said it appeared to him that the operation at Ismailia had not been carried out with "unusual skill." "The 'splutter of musketry,'" he said with some irony, "apparently does not stop things as we had been told from time to time that it would."[58] It seems that in the harsh light of the mid-twentieth century, the stories of imperial fable and adventure lost their luster. No longer could a small contingent of British soldiers scatter the natives (in Ireland, India, or the Middle East) by firing a few shots.

In the aftermath of this violence, Farouk dismissed Nahas and asked Ali Maher to form a government. The change in government encouraged British intransigence. London offered to open discussions without prior commitments from the new government, provided the government halt the violence and withdraw Egyptian threats to sever diplomatic relations with Britain and to expel British subjects. This response, like the change of government itself, was another step toward the precipice, as many in the State Department recognized. G. Lewis Jones, now at the Near Eastern desk at State, told Ambassador Walter Gifford that he hoped London would "take advantage of" the "present opportunity" offered by the appointment of a new government in Cairo, because "Maher may be our

---

57. Philip Jessup Papers, box 4, Egypt file.
58. Acheson, *Present at the Creation*, 565; Memorandum of Telephone Conversation by Battle, Jan. 27, 1952, *FRUS, 1952-1954,* 9:1755.

last chance." Caffery cabled Washington that Maher's government must demonstrate in the "relatively near future its ability to progress towards its disclosed ends," or a more radical and intractable government would take its place. "At this point," he warned, "it is useless and disturbing to contemplate the nature of a future government which would take over if the presently constituted one is allowed to fall."[59]

Progress was impossible until the British showed more flexibility, and the British remained adamant. Pressured by Washington on the Sudan issue, the Foreign Office replied in February that there could be no consultation with the Sudanese, this time until Sudan had a representative parliament, which would not happen until sometime in the summer. In late February, Berry proposed to the British a series of small concessions, including the withdrawal of a token number of troops and movement on Sudan. London refused and a potential window of opportunity closed. On March 1, Maher resigned, and Caffery warned again of the perilous nature of the situation. Noting British misreadings of the situation and proclivities for focusing on peripheral issues to avoid basic ones, Caffery wrote, "If nothing is done soon, we might as well forget any hope we may have for stability and pro-Western orientation in Egypt." The situation was "rapidly getting to the point of no return. If Egypt goes there is serious doubt whether [the] rest of [the] Middle East can stand." If the British remained adamant, he advised, "we must face the realities of the situation and determine how far our commitments elsewhere in the world would permit us to tell the British that we will have to disassociate ourselves from them in the Middle East because we believe they are wrong in what they are doing." Knowing that required a decision from Acheson, Caffery added, "Unless we are prepared to carry through such a threat it would be best not to make it. It would do us no good to have a bluff called."[60]

Knowing that Acheson would never cut American policy completely free from Britain, Caffery suggested that unilateral U.S. recognition of Farouk as king of Sudan "might set [the] stage to enable us single-handedly to hold Egypt this side of the Iron Curtain." The move would demonstrate U.S. sympathy for Egyptian aspirations as well as American independence of Britain in Egyptian affairs. As concerned other issues in the stalled talks, Caffery recommended continued pressure to encourage the British to "see the light." However, if the British failed to cooperate,

59. Jones to Gifford, Jan. 28, 1952, *FRUS, 1952-1954*, 9:1758; Caffery to State Department, Feb. 1, 1952, in ibid., 1750.
60. State Department to Acheson, Feb. 21, 1952, in ibid., 1769; Berry to Acheson, Feb. 27, 1952, in ibid., 1772; Caffery to State Department, in ibid., 1773-74.

Caffery believed it was time to "pull in our oars" and dissociate the United States from British policies. The significance of Caffery's action is deepened by an understanding of how he viewed the role of an ambassador. The historian of Caffery's diplomacy, Philip F. Dur, argues that Caffery did not consider himself responsible for making policy. The fact that Caffery was now proposing new policy thus illustrates the depth of his concern with continuing to support British initiatives in Egypt.[61]

Acheson was by this time under pressure from within the department to do the kind of thing Caffery was proposing. He had Stabler draft a "personal" message to Eden to make concessions in Egypt. "I fear that unless the situation is changed substantially in the immediate future," Acheson pleaded, "opportunity for negotiations with moderate elements will have been lost and achievement of Western objectives with respect to Egypt thrown into grave doubt." He added to the plea a series of proposals that went substantially further than anything he had suggested before. He proposed that London offer to turn over to Egypt administrative responsibilities for the military bases in Suez, define Egypt's role in regional defense in a manner acceptable to the Egyptians, offer the Egyptian government an aid package large enough to finance that regional defense role, and recognize Farouk as king of Sudan. The only condition Eden should attach to these actions, Acheson advised, related to the last one: in return for the recognition of Farouk as king of Sudan, Egypt must acknowledge the "right of the Sudanese people to full, free, and prompt self-determination." Egypt, Acheson explained, "insists on recognition by the West of the King of Egypt's title as King of the Sudan. The Egyptian claim appears to be valid."[62]

When Ambassador Gifford received these proposals in London, he protested that their timing was inopportune because of parliamentary and cabinet politics, and because Eden had already agreed to some of the proposals. He asked Acheson for permission to delay delivery of the proposals to Eden. "The "British do not accept the Egyptian claim re [the] King's title as valid," he told Acheson, "and I do not think they would take kindly to this statement" that the "claim appears to be valid." In Cairo, Caffery was "fully appreciative" of Gifford's objections, and of the

---

61. Caffery to State Department, in ibid., 1776. For more on Caffery's involvement in Egypt, see Dur, "Jefferson Caffery of Louisiana: Highlights of His Career."

62. Acheson to Eden, Mar. 26, 1952, *FRUS, 1952-1954*, 9:1778. For background, see also "Notes on the Egyptian Situation," prepared by Wells Stabler, Jan. 7, 1952, Records of the Policy Planning Staff, lot 64D563, box 717, "Egypt, 1950-1953" file, National Archives.

"implication" of Acheson's message for "our overall relations with the British," but he advised that the message be delivered "immediately."[63]

Acheson took Caffery's rather than Gifford's advice, though he softened the message by deleting the reference to the validity of Farouk's title as king of Sudan. "I feel Eden ought to read in full [the] views contained [in] my personal [message] as representing my own thinking," he wrote Gifford. "When you see him, I wish you [to] tell him that I have personally spent a great deal of time on [the] problem of Egypt, that I want to share my thoughts with him, and that I want to do [so] in a way that will be most helpful to him. If after reading [the] full text [of] my message he feels it would not be helpful to have it left with him, such procedure is quite satisfactory to me."[64]

Eden's reply was predictable. Emphasizing the things he and Acheson agreed on, Eden could not agree to a change in the status of Sudan without consulting the Sudanese people. To do so would impair the sense of trust toward Britain among "the Sudanese people and indeed among many other peoples on the African continent." There was also "a strong feeling on this point in Parliament." Sudan, it seems, was to be the centerpiece of a "new" British empire west of Suez, now that everything to the east was, or was in the process of being, lost. "The plain truth," wrote Eden in his imperial mode, "remains that unless the Egypt[ians] are prepared to face facts which are admittedly uncomfortable from their point of view, all our efforts to help them may prove in vain. Although we are willing to withdraw our forces from Egypt upon certain terms, the Egyptians cannot drive us out of Egypt." Neither could they "obstruct the progress which the Sudanese are aiming towards self-government and self-determination" nor expect Britain to help them "by recognizing the King of Egypt's claim to the title of King of Sudan against the wishes of the Sudanese."[65]

Acheson made no response to Eden's telegram, and the situation drifted. In May, the State Department for the first time described the Anglo-Egyptian talks as being at an "impasse."[66] Berry and other staffers hoped to use the upcoming foreign ministers meeting in Paris to produce movement. They proposed that unless Eden agree to a resolution of the Sudan issue, the United States should undertake initiatives of its own, over

63. Gifford to State Department, Mar. 28, 1952, *FRUS, 1952-1954*, 9:1783; Caffery to State Department, Mar. 29, 1952, in ibid., 1784 n.

64. Acheson to Gifford, Mar. 28, 1952, in ibid., 1785.

65. Gifford to State Department, Apr. 18, 1952, in ibid., 1790-92.

66. Berry via Matthews to Acheson, May 14, 1952, Jessup Papers, box 4, Egypt file.

British objections if necessary, to resolve the Egyptian problem. To do that would mean the end of Acheson's design for the colonial world as well as an acknowledgment of the shrunken role of Britain in the postcolonial and cold war worlds. "This is a hard thing for the British to do," the staffers told Acheson.

> It can only be done on their own initiative. But the alternative—the drift towards general breakup in Egypt—will be harder. Harder not only for the British but for us too. For, as in Indo-China, these problems always come back to weaken the combined strength we are all trying to create. And they come back also, as in Iran, Tunisia, and Morocco, to weaken an asset, which is not ours alone but belongs to the West—the belief that the interests of the U.S. are broad enough to include those of other people.[67]

Still, nothing happened. Efforts by State Department staffers to push Acheson as well as Eden to break the deadlock produced no more than restatements of old positions. In a memo to Acheson in June 1952, Henry A. Byroade, now assistant secretary for Near Eastern, South Asian, and African affairs, reviewed the situation. "It does not appear that your suggestion regarding British consultation with the Sudanese has been given the attention in London it merits," Byroade began. Indeed, it now appeared that London would not consult the Sudanese at all until prior guarantees were received from the Egyptians about self-determination. The only way to find out if the Sudanese were willing to accept the title of king granted to Farouk was to ask them, "and this the UK is unwilling to do." Describing this as a stalling tactic, Byroade observed dryly that there "seems to be a divergence of opinion" between London and Washington not only about "the urgency of the situation" in Egypt but about the stability of the Egyptian government as well. It was time to clarify matters, and Acheson's upcoming visit to London for ministerial talks was an appropriate occasion.[68]

When he met Eden in late June 1952, Acheson seems to have been imbued with a sense of fatalism by the souring of his foreign policy in the colonial world. "We seem to be in a circle," he told Eden of the Egyptian problem. "We are very disturbed that if the problem continues and talks break down, there will be serious trouble in Egypt which will spread to North Africa and the rest of the Middle East." He also wondered to all those present at the meeting "whether, irrespective of the possibility of

67. Perkins and Berry to Acheson, May 19, 1952, in ibid.
68. Byroade to Acheson, June 17, 1952, *FRUS, 1952-1954,* 9:1810-12.

a blow-up in Egypt, the end of the road is not that the Egyptians lose the Sudan and the British their base at Suez." Ambassador Stevenson responded that "he would not go that far," noting that the Egyptian and British flags still flew side by side in Sudan. "This state of affairs could go on for some time," Stevenson suggested, "and . . . there would not be an abrupt break." Acheson "thought that there was a point beyond which this could not go."[69]

Acheson was resigning himself to the inevitable. On July 2, 1952, the government of Prime Minister Neguib Hilali Pasha fell, increasing the turmoil in Egypt. In the aftermath, Caffery advised Washington to refuse British requests that the "US should involve itself in [the] Egyptian domestic political crisis" to prevent "the elimination of the only sound elements in Egyptian political life." Any such involvement would entangle the United States in the British imbroglio with no control over British actions. In Acheson's absence, Acting Secretary of State David K. E. Bruce put the blame for the turmoil on the British for failing to resolve their differences with the Egyptians through negotiations. Henry Byroade and Caffery agreed. The significance of the change of government in Cairo, Byroade observed, was that it demonstrated that "no Egyptian government can last too long without making progress, real or illusory, with the British."[70]

The looming failure of British—and American—policy in Egypt unleashed pent-up frustrations among State Department staffers responsible for Middle Eastern policy. "Even in fields of action or geographical territories where we do not recognize a predominant British interest and responsibility (as in Greece and Turkey), our policy always implicitly or explicitly provides for support of whatever British position exists or for utilization of British influence as an important adjunct to our own," wrote John Jernegan, the deputy assistant secretary for Near Eastern, South Asian, and African affairs. That might have made sense when Britain was a major imperial power, but Britain's power was "no longer what it was [even] a few years ago." Jernegan provided a laundry list of the places in which Britain had overplayed their hand and generated problems for the United States. "The United States is severely criticized for its alleged support of British imperialism in the Middle East," Jernegan wrote in a typical assessment. It was "no longer safe to assume, automatically, that Britain can and should be considered the principal protector of western

69. United States Minutes of the United States–United Kingdom Ministerial Talks, London, June 24, 1952, in ibid., 1819-23.
70. Bruce to Caffery, July 2, 1952, in ibid., 1826-27; Byroade to Bruce, July 3, 1952, in ibid., 1828-29.

interests in the Middle East." Furthermore, "it is conceivable that the interests of the United States and the western community as a whole would be better served if Britain were relegated to a secondary position." That being the case, Washington must ask itself some fundamental questions. "Are the economic and strategic advantages great enough to offset the political antagonisms generated by the maintenance of British positions in countries hostile to it?" Also, "Does British activity in the Middle East make our own relations with the area easier or more difficult?"[71]

In a separate assessment, Edward A. Plitt of the Near East desk came to similar conclusions. Plitt noted that Britain's power was in obvious decline and with it Britain's ability to influence events in the Middle East and elsewhere. As a result, "The Middle East has awakened to a resentment of the British. If the United States attempts to replace the . . . [British Empire] by following in its footsteps, we will inherit this resentment. Such a mistake must be avoided at all costs." In another paper, Plitt listed as one of the chief failures of recent U.S. foreign policy the fact that the United States was "being associated in the minds of the Middle East people with British and French imperialism." The only way to remove that association was to "take a more positive leadership in the [Middle East] and shape [U.S.] policy with Britain to the extent possible but principally with the people of the area itself."[72]

Whether London was aware of the pervasiveness of these sentiments at State is unclear, but after another of the endless exchanges of position papers, the British declared that if no agreement was forthcoming, they would use force to maintain their position in Egypt. Byroade advised Acheson that the United States could not "accept the use of force as a viable option since it would be contrary to U.S. principles, objectives, and interests." Moreover, "if no deal with Egypt is possible, we may find it more in our long run interest if the British evacuate the base completely."[73]

Acheson was unwilling to accept responsibility for the looming failure. He reacted strongly to a message from Eden that the United States would bear responsibility for the loss of Egypt unless it persuaded Farouk to dismiss the new government and put his claim to Sudan "into cold storage." If Washington failed to do these things, Eden argued, "the full consequences of [the] lack of success would fall on the U.S." The "U.S. does not accept these implications," Acheson responded. "We are not willing

71. Office Files of Harry N. Howard, undated, "British position in the Middle East" file, box 58, National Archives. The document is unsigned, but other documents in the file point to Jernegan being the author.
72. Plitt to Byroade and Jernegan, July 14, 1952, in ibid.
73. Byroade to Acheson, July 14, 1952, *FRUS, 1952-1954*, 9:1832-33.

to be put into such a situation." The Foreign Office had assured him that all was well with the Egyptian government, yet when the government resigned, the "UK rushes to [the] US with [the] idea that either [the] US persuade Egypt to accept [a] UK-proposed settlement or force must be used to maintain the position. U.S. cannot take responsibility for these alternatives."[74]

This was blunt enough but not altogether candid. Acheson had subordinated U.S. interests in the Middle East and elsewhere in the colonial world to British imperatives to a degree that encouraged the kind of intransigence and assertiveness Eden was now displaying. Acheson must therefore bear some responsibility for behavior that his own policies not only tolerated but also encouraged for so long.

On July 21, 1952, the eve of the Free Officers coup, Byroade for the first time proposed to Acheson a unilateral approach to Egypt. Not only had friendly persuasion failed, he told Acheson, but the British "have endeavored to exploit [U.S. sympathy] for the purpose of supporting whatever position they believe correct" as well. "The time has come when we ought to make greater use of our position in Egypt to see whether we can evolve a deal which would be acceptable both to the United Kingdom and Egypt," Byroade concluded. "Perhaps the United States should now try to work out directly with the Egyptians a settlement of the Anglo-American problem."[75]

By this time, the situation was so hopeless that Byroade was concerned that the written record of it would not absolve Acheson and the State Department from responsibility for the loss of Egypt. "From the point of view of US interests, we should not lose sight of the necessity for building up a 'record' for ourselves in attempting to find a reasonable avenue to solution," he told Acheson. "The 'record' might be most useful if a stalemate, with all that implies, is reached. We may well need this record for the maintenance of our position with other Near Eastern states." Byroade then went on to outline a detailed proposal that included the recognition by the United States of Farouk's title as "King of the Sudan."[76] Byroade feared what the actual record to this point would show. In the aftermath of the political fallout over the "loss" of China, that fear was not misplaced.

Acheson must have winced at this. However, he was saved from having

---

74. Acheson to Caffery, in ibid., 1833-35.
75. Byroade to Acheson, July 21, 1952, Records of the Policy Planning Staff, 1947-1953, box 14, National Archives. See also *FRUS, 1952-1954*, 9:1838-41.
76. Byroade to Acheson, July 21, 1952, Records of the Policy Planning Staff, 1947-1953, box 14, National Archives.

to deal further with the problem—at least in the old ways—by yet another change of government in Egypt, this one caused by the Free Officers coup. It must have been with some relief after learning of the coup that Acheson scrawled across Byroade's memo: "This has to be reconsidered now. DA." The reconsideration would have to accommodate the entirely new situation created by the coup and the rise to power of Col. Gamal Abdel Nasser. On July 22, the Free Officers seized Cairo, and in coming days spread their control across Egypt. Nasser resisted demands that Farouk be executed, allowing him instead to abdicate and leave the country. It took London and Washington a while to read Nasser's intentions correctly. Both first viewed the change of government as positive because the Free Officers had little interest in the title of king of Sudan. They were, however, interested in separating Egypt from the British, whose presence was immediately restricted to the military enclave at Suez, and removing Egypt from the Western orbit in the cold war. Nasser was soon a leader in the nonaligned movement, in which capacity he became a thorn in the sides of Acheson, Eden, and their successors.[77]

In his memoirs, Acheson deals with Egypt after July 22, 1952, in half a page. The Suez crisis of 1956 was the product of "colossal blunders by everyone involved," he wrote, but of his own involvement in Egyptian affairs he was less critical. "It is difficult now to see how the United States in the earlier years," he wrote, "could have done more than it did to ameliorate Anglo-Egyptian problems."[78] He might easily have listened to his own staff to tell him what more could have been done.

77. For more on Nasser, see Joel Gordon, *Nasser's Blessed Movement: Egypt's Free Officers and the July Revolution.*
78. Acheson, *Present at the Creation,* 566-67.

8

Epilogue

Dean Acheson's commitment to an imperial-style world order did not end when he left office. In private life, he became a vigorous critic of John Foster Dulles, his successor in the Eisenhower administration. Dulles, in Acheson's estimation, let cold war concerns blind him to the advantages of preserving what he could of the old imperial order. Acheson's extraordinary hostility to Dulles was due ostensibly to Dulles's proclivity to mix morality—or moralizing—with policy. Nevertheless, there was more to the hostility than that. "[O]ne cannot help but believe that it was not so much moralism in foreign-policy making that Acheson objected to," a historian generally sympathetic to Acheson has written, "as moralism as practiced by that 'psalm-singing Presbyterian Wall Street lawyer' John Foster Dulles."[1]

The reference to Dulles's Presbyterianism is helpful; it points to one tip of the iceberg of values Acheson's criticism of Dulles reflected. In the hierarchy of social prejudices nurtured among the Anglican Ulstermen from whom Acheson descended, the largely working-class Scottish Presbyterians of Ulster ranked only marginally above the generally lower-class Irish Catholics. In Acheson's case, the disdain this nurturing encouraged had been reinforced by wealth and high status. Dulles thus represented a religious and social group Acheson had little cause to admire. In addition, Acheson believed that Dulles, as secretary of state in the Eisenhower administration, not only worked to dismantle major aspects of Acheson's foreign policy, but also committed the cardinal sin of disloyalty to the British and French allies at Suez in 1956.

Acheson's objections to Eisenhower-Dulles foreign policy crystallized over the handling of the crisis generated by Egypt's seizure of the Suez Canal in 1956, and the consequent invasion of British, French, and Israeli

---

1. Brinkley, *Dean Acheson*, 26. The Acheson quote is from an interview by Gaddis Smith.

forces to take the canal back. Eisenhower ordered the allied invaders out of Suez, and that symbol of British imperialism was lost forever. All this occurred during the 1956 presidential campaign, and Acheson's criticism of it was partly political. He blamed the Egyptians' seizure of the canal on the decision of the Eisenhower administration to cancel support for building the Aswan Dam across the Upper Nile. Had the dam project gone forward, Acheson believed, Egyptian president "Nasser might have gone on thinking idly of seizing the canal company for another two years but doing nothing about it; and by that time many things would have happened to change the course of events in the Middle East," Acheson wrote, reflecting the traditional imperial policy of waiting for new leaders to arise with whom a deal could be struck.[2] The conviction that "natives" reacted and imperialists acted was one of the staples of Acheson's belief system.

Acheson's most systematic criticism of the Eisenhower-Dulles foreign policy, including the Suez episode, is in his book *Power and Diplomacy*. There he criticized British and U.S. policy makers for violating a key tenet of the special relationship—close, candid communication—prior to the Anglo-French-Israeli intervention. Had such communication occurred— had the Americans been kept fully informed of the allies' thinking and planning—U.S. participation might have been possible, which would have guaranteed an effort sufficiently large and well equipped to have taken the canal quickly with such a show of force as to have overawed the Egyptians. Such an operation might have had a "salutary" effect. Acheson clearly seems to be alluding to the "whiff of grapeshot" school of diplomacy. When imperialists act, in other words, they must act imperially. This "sorry episode" at Suez, however, had had an "ominous antecedent" in Eisenhower's decision in 1954 not to assist the French at Dien Bien Phu.[3] Acheson in both of these instances, and with the benefit of hindsight, was still willing to risk U.S. resources and lives to preserve what he believed was the proper order of things, in striking evidence of his imperial paradigm.

That order applied not just to the British and the French imperiums. Long after he left office, Acheson was still expressing regret that the Truman administration had pressured the Dutch to leave Indonesia in 1949. "We did press the Dutch. As one looks back on it, we may have pressed too hard," Acheson wrote in 1959. Dirk Stikker, who had been the

---

2. Acheson, "The Middle East," Sept. 1956, Acheson Papers, series 3, box 48, folder 26.
3. Acheson, *Power and Diplomacy*, 111-15, 110 n.

Dutch foreign minister in 1949, said in 1970 that Acheson had told him not long before that the United States may have been wrong to press the Dutch to leave Indonesia. The pressure was a policy he inherited from George Marshall, he intimated to Stikker, and Acheson believed he was obliged to follow that course early in his secretaryship, a course that was neither of his own creation nor to his taste.[4] In 1949, in an exchange with Stikker, Acheson clearly pushed the Dutch hard to abandon Indonesia. He drew a dubious distinction between the Dutch and the British, saying the British were less shortsighted on colonial affairs. Acheson also contended that Congress would never indirectly subsidize colonial ventures through the European Recovery Program, something soon proved wrong with France and Indochina. These inconsistencies provide evidence that Acheson was fulfilling his predecessor's policy toward empire, a policy he was soon to take in a new direction.

Acheson's policies toward China have probably garnered more attention than any other issue outside of Europe. There is a rich historiography on the issue, and much of it focuses on the "Cohen-Tucker thesis." Historians Warren Cohen and Barbara Bernkopf Tucker have argued that Acheson was willing to recognize the People's Republic of China, but the Korean War intervened to make the move impossible. Acheson, they argue, had little respect for the Nationalists led by Chiang Kai-shek, believing them to be corrupt and untrustworthy. They argue further that Acheson was an Atlanticist who believed there was little in Asia worth fighting for. The result was that he quickly and easily abandoned any effort to prop up the Nationalist cause.[5]

Acheson's attitudes about China can be more fully illuminated with an understanding of his imperial vision. Without an imperial power directly involved in China, Acheson would have felt contempt for both nationalist movements. He was thus free to choose the one that was clearly going to win by the time he took office: the Communists. Helping Britain maintain control of Hong Kong was an additional prime consideration. Acheson let it be known that any assault on Hong Kong would be a matter for the United Nations Security Council to deal with and that the United States would support the council. Further, in testimony to the Senate after the

4. Acheson to Louis Fischer, Feb. 2, 1959, Acheson Papers, box 10, folder 135; Stikker, Oral History, 15-20.

5. For more on the "Cohen-Tucker thesis," see Warren I. Cohen, "Acheson, His Advisers, and China, 1949-1950," in his *America's Response to China: A History of Sino-American Relations*, as well as Nancy B. Tucker's *Patterns in the Dust: Chinese-American Relations and the Recognition Controversy*.

Korean War broke out, he maintained his position that "to have Hong Kong fall . . . into the hands of the Chinese Communists, would I think, have a very adverse influence on the United Nations interests and on ours in the Far East."[6] In addition, Acheson's public comments should be seen in the light of the May 1950 London conference discussed earlier where Acheson strongly supported an enhanced arrangement between the United States and Britain to coordinate policy around the world, despite the resistance of his closest advisers. Acheson's movement toward recognition depended on a combination of different factors, including an attempt to draw the Chinese away from the Soviet Union. However, among the factors influencing Acheson's views is certainly his concern for helping Britain defend one of its most prized imperial assets. This is further evidence of the movement from the time of Franklin Roosevelt's comments to the British that they should turn over Hong Kong to the Chinese as a goodwill gesture to Acheson's tenure as secretary when he worked to support imperial interests.[7]

In December 1962, Acheson visited West Point where in a public address he presented his perspective on the current state of world affairs. Like his talk in 1950 to the National Press Club, which often has been erroneously claimed to have been the reason for the North Korean invasion of the South, the West Point speech was controversial. Because Acheson was publicly critical of the postimperial British role in the world, some have found this as solid evidence that Acheson was never pro-British and thereby imply his foreign policy was based on realism and not on a romantic attachment to the British. "Great Britain has lost an empire and has not yet found a role," Acheson said in the key passage in the address.

> The attempt to play a separate power role—that is, a role apart from Europe, a role based on a "special relationship" with the United States, a role based on being the head of a "commonwealth" which has no political structure, or unity, or strength, and enjoys a fragile and precarious economic relationship by means of the Sterling area and preferences in the British market—this role is about played out. Great Britain, attempting to work alone and to be a broker between the

6. Harold B. Hinton, "Acheson Denied Hong Kong Pledge: Says Help Will Depend on Events," *New York Times*, Aug. 13, 1949, 1; *New York Times*, June 3, 1951. Nancy Tucker drew my attention to these statements in her valuable study *Taiwan, Hong Kong, and the United States, 1945-1992: Uncertain Friendships*, 200-201.

7. Chiu Hungdah, "The Hong Kong Agreement and American Foreign Policy," *Issues and Studies* 22 (June 1986).

United States and Russia, has seemed to conduct policy as weak as its military.[8]

To take that passage as a general criticism of Britain or of British imperialism is to miss its meaning and significance. In the conventional sense, Acheson was neither more pro- nor more anti-British than other diplomats of his day. However, he was unmatched outside the Foreign Office in his commitment to the British imperium and to what he regarded as its stabilizing effects on the world order. By 1962, Acheson recognized that events had overtaken the empire, and with it the stabilizing role Britain could play in the world. Whenever Acheson was critical of British policy, as he was at West Point, it was because he believed the British had been unequal to their imperial mission. The criticism he made at West Point must have been difficult for him because it signaled the failure of his own earlier efforts as secretary of state to shore up British imperialism. Acheson had done what was possible to provide Britain (to paraphrase Acheson here) with a role based on the special relationship, a role based on being the head of the "Commonwealth" (which Acheson hoped would replace the empire), and a role that would help Britain enjoy an economic relationship with the sterling area.

The recognition of that fact did not, however, end Acheson's support for the remnants of Europe's once powerful and extensive empires, reduced by the 1960s largely to Africa. In 1967, Harry T. Andrews of the South African Foundation in Johannesburg invited Acheson to visit South Africa, which if no longer part of the British Empire was an outpost of white supremacy in the dark continent. The invitation prompted musings of his personal ties to the country. "I am sure that it would be most interesting and enjoyable," Acheson wrote Andrews of the proposed visit. "I have relatives there, only a few of whom I have met. About the turn of the century, my father's sister married a Blackburn and settled near Durban. Her daughter and the daughter's husband, a Mr. and Mrs. Lincoln, I met in Paris fifteen years ago. A grandchild of theirs, a Frank Gregory of Johannesburg, I correspond with from time to time. All of this makes my interest present and real."[9] Acheson's extended family's imperial lineage thus included members who had migrated to South Africa and whose descendants were still there. As in other parts of the former colonial world, Acheson's interest was indeed "present and real."

8. Acheson, "Our Atlantic Alliance: The Political and Economic Strands" (speech delivered at the United States Military Academy, West Point, N.Y., Dec. 5, 1962). Reprinted in *Vital Speeches of the Day* 29:6 (Jan. 1, 1963): 162-66.
9. Acheson to Andrews, Jan. 2, 1967, Acheson Papers, box 1, folder 10.

This personal connection to South Africa may have contributed to Acheson's interest in preserving Portuguese control of nearby Angola. Acheson's sympathy for the Portuguese imperium is inexplicable without awareness of his larger commitment to imperialism. While he was secretary of state, NATO leased air and naval facilities from Portugal in the Azores, and "correct" behavior toward that country and its longtime dictator, Antonio Salazar, had been a necessary aspect of cold war diplomacy. Salazar became a friend, a man whom Acheson in fact admired. In *Present at the Creation,* Acheson included a vignette of Salazar in Lisbon in 1952, and a photograph of the dictator as well. Describing Salazar's demeanor as easy and relaxed, Acheson wrote, "I felt drawn to him as rarely on first meeting." The feeling persisted despite "Dr. Salazar's" authoritarianism, which Acheson also acknowledged. "Indisputably," Acheson wrote, "political liberty, in the modern British and American sense, does not exist in Portugal and, judging from past experience, would probably be incompatible with the economic stability and growth that over forty years Dr. Salazar created."[10]

Whatever it was that drew Acheson to Salazar, a part of it was surely the Portuguese dictator's ardent defense of empire. "To Salazar, the importance of the empire was not as much economic as nationalistic and even spiritual," Thomas Noer has written on this subject. "Continued control was necessary for the morale of the people, the international status of the state, and the legitimacy of the government. . . . Salazar never abandoned his conviction that the end of the empire would lead directly to the collapse of the Portuguese nation."[11] Salazar was a self-proclaimed "nineteenth-century man" and like Acheson shared an admiration for the Victorian age of empire. In much the same language that could be used to describe Acheson's worldview, Noer asserts that "Salazar's belief in the crucial importance of empire and his mystical defense of his policies locked Portugal into a view of the colonies that was unfathomable" to many other nations and was repugnant to black Africans.

Such views resonated with Acheson. "One of the great errors that our government has made in its policy I think has been the enthusiasm with which it has looked forward to the despoliation of our allies," Acheson told a National War College audience in 1963, deploring a recent U.S. vote in the UN critical of the Portuguese control of Angola. "Our vote against Portugal in the United Nations did not solve any problem." On the contrary,

10. Acheson, *Present at the Creation,* 627-28.
11. Noer, *Cold War and Black Liberation: The United States and White Rule in Africa, 1948-1968,* 5-6.

It just made the problem worse, but it made us feel we were on the side of virtue. To make self-determination a benefit to its people, more of them need to read and write. They need an economic system which will enable Angola and Portugal to part. They are like two very weak people who stand up only because they lean against one another. If they are separated, they will both fall down. What is needed is to increase the productivity and strength of Portugal, and the productivity and strength of Angola and Mozambique. Over time this can be done.[12]

Thus, Acheson universalized principles he learned about empire as a youth. He no more questioned the purposes or consequences of Portuguese imperialism than he had earlier questioned those of Britain in India or France in Indochina. As he had for the British in their dealings with Iran and Egypt, he pleaded for time for the Portuguese, whose imperialism may have been even less benevolent than that of the British. Africa for Africans was something that Acheson viewed through his understanding of Ireland for the Irish. Black control of Africa, in Acheson's eyes, meant unleashing uncivilized chaos.

Despite his support for Portuguese colonialism, Acheson's chief African interest seems to have been British Rhodesia. As the British presence in Africa shrank after Ghana became independent in 1957, London accommodated itself to the loss of the remnants of the African empire. As that occurred, the whites-only government in Rhodesia resisted British pressure to admit black Africans to the political process, which would mean a rapid transition to African control of the government in a state in which 95 percent of the population were black Africans. The government responded by declaring Rhodesia independent of the United Kingdom in November 1965. Led by Prime Minister Ian Smith, Rhodesia defied international sanctions. In response, British prime minister Harold Wilson denounced the actions as illegal and treasonable, and supported international sanctions against the country and its government.

Acheson, on the other hand, saw the whites-only government, in the words of a sympathetic biographer, as "a beacon of European light in a dark continent being overrun by anarchy, Marxism, and demonic black-

---

12. Lecture, National War College, Apr. 23, 1963, Acheson Papers, box 51, folder 57. At the 1999 Society of Historians of American Foreign Relations Conference at Princeton University, Dr. Fernando Andresen Guimaraes of the Permanent Mission of Portugal to the United Nations presented a paper regarding Acheson's relationship with Lisbon. Guimaraes praised Acheson's wisdom in supporting Portugal, in part because of the complexities of the Angolan independence movement, but admitted that it was not a realistic possibility that Portugal would deny the Azores to NATO.

power propaganda." He denounced the UN for the sanctions, but saved his special ire for the British government that, he believed, was abandoning its imperial responsibilities. In 1968, Acheson was still criticizing those who objected to white rule in Rhodesia or, as he regarded it, Rhodesians solving their own problems. The constitution written by the whites-only government, he noted, provided for progressive extensions of voting rights to Africans but not majority rule, which was all it could responsibly do at present. "For a time that cannot be measured by clock or calendar, Europeans would exercise the more authoritative voice at national government level, and Africans would have a voice that must be allowed increasing, but not limitless, power," he wrote of the new constitution. "This was not everyone's cup of tea; neither was it everyone's business; nor was it apartheid. . . . How fortunate were the American colonies to have no United Nations to confront in 1776."[13]

Acheson testified before a congressional panel about "our mistaken course in supporting the British-UN embargo" against the all-white government of Rhodesia, and he sent a copy of his testimony to former British prime minister Anthony Eden. "I can think of nothing more ill-advised than for the new [British] Government to let this quarrel drag on," he told Eden. Expressing his sympathy for the leader of Rhodesian independence, he added, "I can conceive of no result except to drive Ian Smith further and further to the right." The end would be the loss "of our investment in Rhodesian chrome mines and paying twice what we did before to the Russians for our chrome." The idea that the West could maintain access to the resources of Africa without imperial domination was an alien concept to Acheson.[14]

One of the last things Acheson did was plan a trip to South Africa. "We are to have a look at the Portuguese areas, Rhodesia, and South Africa," he wrote an Australian friend. "This is mostly a voyage of discovery, which I hope will, when I come back, give some added credibility to my constant assertions that we are following foolish, sentimental, and harmful courses in our policies toward this whole area." Two years later, Acheson was still planning that trip, postponed because of health problems, when he died of a stroke at his desk on October 12, 1971, shortly after he had written a letter to Anthony Eden that was full of details and enthusiasm about the trip.[15]

13. Brinkley, *Dean Acheson*, 316; Acheson, *Fragments of My Fleece*, 160-61.
14. Acheson to Eden, June 30, 1970, box 9, folder 119, Acheson Papers; Eden to Acheson, July 14, 1970, in ibid.
15. Acheson to Howard Beale, Aug. 27, 1969, box 3, folder 28, in ibid.; Acheson to Eden, Oct. 12, 1971, box 9, folder 119, in ibid.

A major objective of this study has been to examine Acheson's claims to be a realist in foreign policy. The result is to reveal Acheson as more a romantic imperialist, a torchbearer for neoimperialism even after many imperialists had accommodated themselves to a postcolonial world. Acheson was proud of his self-proclaimed identity as a traditionalist of the Old World sort, though he would never have openly called himself an imperialist. In his introduction to Louis Halle's *Nature of Power: Civilization and Foreign Policy,* Acheson acknowledged the continuities as well as the ideals he hoped his foreign policy had exemplified. "We are part of something; not something apart," he wrote. "Not Gods without but ganglions within. The means and methods we use, the ends we seek, the kind of people we must forever strive to be are all part of the same thing and are inseparable."[16] Foreign policy was not a thing, or an end, in itself, but part of a larger whole, something much bigger than an individual policy maker, even a secretary of state. If that something is not altogether clear—Acheson guarded his ideals and his words as he did his imperial purposes—it had to do with civilization and social propriety, as he understood those things, more than with the calculating realities of an imperfect world.

One of the essential tenets of realism, one that Acheson frequently voiced, is to "accept the world as it is." Whether Acheson did that on other matters, he did not do so on those relating to preserving imperial influence and power in the colonial world, or in addressing matters relating to indigenous nationalisms in that world. Here, Acheson insisted on seeing the world as he wished it to be, not as it was. The consequences of this failure were compounded by Acheson's violation of another tenet of realism: flexibility in the face of changing circumstances. Acheson's attachment to "one world" united by imperial prosperity and order resulted in unnecessary problems for the Western allies as well as for the emerging nations. He encouraged the British and others to believe that the alliance with the United States enabled them to live beyond their military as well as their economic means, and to hold on to their colonies and spheres of influence past their own abilities to do so. Far from reconciling them to the world as it was and was becoming, Acheson permitted the allies to dream of sustaining empires after the shocks of World Wars I and II had turned that dream into a nightmare. Britain, for example, during this post–World War II period began making ambitious plans for a continued and expanded presence in its African colonies. France, meanwhile, with Acheson's support and hence U.S. financing, set about putting down the colonial uprising in Indochina with vast and tragic significance for the

16. Acheson, introduction to Halle, *Nature of Power,* xxi.

future. Without Acheson's involvement, the limits of American support for colonial adventures would become clear to the French at Dien Bien Phu in 1954 and the British at Suez in 1956. Further, encouraging or enabling the colonial powers to maintain their imperial holdings beyond their means actually exacerbated the financial problems the European allies were facing.

By that time a great deal of damage had been done, to the allies as well as the colonial world, where nationalist leaders had had their expectations of U.S. support dashed. The power of American ideology and the American example, too, were everywhere compelling, and potentially enormous assets in dealing with the decolonizing world. The disillusionment that Acheson's policies helped fuel turned to resentment, as in India, and sometimes to hostility and violence, as in Iran. The resulting damage has yet to be fully undone.

Acheson was a man out of his time, a latter-day Cecil Rhodes more than the twentieth-century Metternich to whom he aspired. "I find [Acheson's] views unrealistic and quite unfortunate," Averell Harriman, who knew him well, told an interviewer in 1970. "His policies on South Africa and Rhodesia—that they are our best friends—I find atrocious. He [is] entirely a European man. A great statesman for a certain period of time in history, [he] has long since been of another era. He is not what you call a universal statesman, he is one of those men who has transcended time."[17]

The transcendence was backward, however, rather than forward. His Victorian imperial worldview was out of place in the middle of the twentieth century. The tragedy was that he never realized that fact, and his friends in Washington and London were slower to do so than were those who confronted his policies in the colonial world. It behooves us to examine this era carefully as the United States confronts a new chapter in international relations and strives to identify, protect, and promote its interests in the post–cold war world of the twenty-first century.

17. Harriman interview, June 28, 1970, box 874, MSS, W. Averell Harriman Papers.

Bibliography

Manuscript Collections and Oral Histories

Acheson, Dean. Oral History. Harry S. Truman Library, Independence, Mo.

———. Papers. Harry S. Truman Library.

———. Papers. Sterling Memorial Library, Yale University, New Haven, Conn.

Barrett, Edward. Oral History. Harry S. Truman Library.

Barrows, Leland. Oral History. Harry S. Truman Library.

Bevin, Ernest. Papers. Public Record Office, Kew, England.

Bowles, Chester. Papers. Sterling Memorial Library, Yale University.

Bruce, David. Oral History. Harry S. Truman Library.

Byroade, Henry. Oral History. Harry S. Truman Library.

Cady, John F. Oral History. Harry S. Truman Library.

Connelly, Matthew J. Papers. Harry S. Truman Library.

Coppock, Joseph D. Oral History. Harry S. Truman Library.

Edwards, William. Oral History. Harry S. Truman Library.

Elsey, George M. Oral History. Harry S. Truman Library.

Engert, Cornelius Van H. Papers. Georgetown University, Lauinger Library Special Collections, Washington, D.C.

Franks, Lord Oliver. Oral History. Harry S. Truman Library.

Garrett, George A. Papers. State Historical Society of Wisconsin, Madison.

Grady, Henry F. Papers. Harry S. Truman Library.

Harriman, W. Averell. Papers. Library of Congress, Washington, D.C.

Henderson, Loy W. Oral History. Harry S. Truman Library.

Hickerson, John D. Oral History. Harry S. Truman Library.

Howard, Harry N. Papers. Harry S. Truman Library.

Jessup, Philip. Papers. National Archives.

Kennan, George F. Seeley Mudd Library, Princeton University, Princeton, N.J.

203

Lippmann, Walter. Papers. Sterling Memorial Library, Yale University.
Locke, Edwin A. Oral History. Harry S. Truman Library.
Makins, Sir Roger. Oral History. Harry S. Truman Library.
Marjolin, Robert. Oral History. Harry S. Truman Library.
Matthews, Francis P. Papers. Harry S. Truman Library.
McGhee, George C. Papers. Harry S. Truman Library.
Murphy, Charles, et al. Joint Oral History. Harry S. Truman Library.
Snyder, John. Oral History. Harry S. Truman Library.
————. Papers. Harry S. Truman Library.
Stikker, Dirk. Oral History. Harry S. Truman Library.
Stinebower, Leroy. Oral History. Harry S. Truman Library.
Sullivan, John L. Oral History. Harry S. Truman Library.
Trezise, Philip. Oral History. Harry S. Truman Library.
Truman, Harry S. Papers. Harry S. Truman Library.
Wood, C. Tyler. Oral History. Harry S. Truman Library.
White, Ivan B. Oral History. Harry S. Truman Library.

Government Archives

National Archives of the United States, Washington, D.C.
    Records of the State Department.
    Records of the Defense Department.
    Records of the Department of the Treasury.
    Records of Foreign Service Posts of the Department of State.
    Records of International Conferences, Commissions, and Expositions.
    Records of the Policy Planning Staff.
    Records of the Psychological Strategy Board.
Public Record Office at Kew, England.
    Records of the Foreign Office.
    Records of the Colonial Office.
    Records of the Prime Minister.
    Records of the Cabinet.

Published Government Documents

Foreign Relations of the United States, 1948. 9 vols. Washington, D.C.: U.S.
    Government Printing Office, 1972–1976.
Foreign Relations of the United States, 1949. 9 vols. Washington, D.C.: U.S.
    Government Printing Office, 1974–1978.

Foreign Relations of the United States, 1950. 7 vols. Washington, D.C.: U.S. Government Printing Office, 1977–1980.

Foreign Relations of the United States, 1951. 7 vols. Washington, D.C.: U.S. Government Printing Office, 1977–1985.

Foreign Relations of the United States, 1952–1954. 26 vols. Washington, D.C.: U.S. Government Printing Office, 1979–1989.

Policy Planning Staff Papers. Ed. Anna Kasten Nelson. 3 vols. New York: Garland, 1983.

Works by Dean Acheson

"The Responsibility for Decision in Foreign Policy." *Yale Review* 44:1 (autumn 1954): 1–12.

A Democrat Looks at His Party. New York: Harper and Brothers, 1955.

A Citizen Looks at Congress. New York: Harper and Brothers, 1957.

Power and Diplomacy. Cambridge: Harvard University Press, 1958.

"Fifty Years After." *Yale Review* 51:1 (Oct. 1961): 1–10.

Sketches from Life of Men I Have Known. New York: Harper and Brothers, 1961.

"Isolationists Are Stupid." *Esquire* (Aug. 1965).

Morning and Noon. Boston: Houghton Mifflin, 1965.

Present at the Creation: My Years in the State Department. New York: W. W. Norton, 1969.

Fragments of My Fleece. New York: W. W. Norton, 1971.

Grapes from Thorns. New York: W. W. Norton, 1972.

This Vast External Realm. New York: W. W. Norton, 1973.

Secondary Sources

Abramson, Rudy. *Spanning the Century: The Life of W. Averell Harriman, 1891–1986.* New York: Morrow, 1992.

Acheson, David C. *Acheson Country: A Memoir.* New York: W. W. Norton, 1993.

Aichele, Gary J. *Oliver Wendell Holmes Jr.: Soldier, Scholar, Judge.* Boston: Twayne, 1989.

Arstein, Walter L. *Britain Yesterday and Today.* Lexington, Ky.: D. C. Heath, 1988.

Bagwell, Richard. *Ireland under the Tudors.* London: Holland Press, 1963.

Baltzell, E. Digby. *The Protestant Establishment: Aristocracy and Caste in America*. New York: Random House, 1964.

Bardon, Jonathan. *A History of Ulster*. Belfast: Blackstaff Press, 1992.

Beisner, Robert L. "Dean Acheson Joins the Cold Warriors." *Diplomatic History* 20:3 (1996): 321–55.

Best, Richard A. *"Co-operation with Like-Minded Peoples": British Influences on American Security Policy, 1945–1949*. Westport, Conn.: Greenwood Press, 1986.

Bidault, George. *Resistance*. Trans. Marianne Sinclair. New York: Frederick A. Praeger, 1967.

Bill, James A. *The Eagle and the Lion: The Tragedy of American-Iranian Relations*. New Haven: Yale University Press, 1988.

Bishop, Donald G. *The Administration of British Foreign Relations*. Syracuse: Syracuse University Press, 1961.

Borg, Dorothy, and Waldo Heinrichs, eds. *Uncertain Years: Chinese-American Relations, 1947–1950*. New York: Columbia University Press, 1980.

Bottigheimer, Karl S. *Ireland and the Irish*. New York: Columbia University Press, 1982.

Brands, Henry W. *India and the United States: The Cold Peace*. Boston: Twayne, 1990.

———. *Inside the Cold War: Loy Henderson and the Rise of the American Empire, 1918–1961*. Boston: Twayne, 1992.

———. *The Specter of Neutralism: The United States and the Emergence of the Third World, 1947–1960*. New York: Columbia University Press, 1990.

Brecher, Michael. *Nehru: A Political Biography*. London: Oxford University Press, 1959.

———. *The Struggle for Kashmir*. New York: Oxford University Press, 1959.

Brinkley, Douglas. *Dean Acheson: The Cold War Years, 1953–1971*. New Haven: Yale University Press, 1992.

———, ed. *Dean Acheson and the Making of U.S. Foreign Policy*. New York: St. Martin's Press, 1993.

Buckland, Patrick. *A History of Northern Ireland*. London: Gill and Macmillan, 1981.

Bullock, Alan. *Ernest Bevin: Foreign Secretary, 1945–51*. New York: W. W. Norton, 1983.

Burke, S. M., and Salim al-Din Quraishi. *The British Raj in India: An Historical Review*. Karachi: Oxford University Press, 1995.

Cairncross, A. K. *Home and Foreign Investment, 1870–1913*. Cambridge: Cambridge University Press, 1953.

Chace, James. *Acheson: The Secretary of State Who Created the American World.* New York: Simon and Schuster, 1998.

Cohen, Warren I. *America's Response to China: A History of Sino-American Relations.* New York: Columbia University Press, 2000.

Cottam, Richard. *Iran and the United States: A Cold War Case Study.* Pittsburgh: Carnegie-Mellon Press, 1988.

Crabb, Cecil, and Kevin Mulcahy. *Presidents and Foreign Policy Making from FDR to Reagan.* Baton Rouge: Louisiana State University Press, 1986.

Cronin, Sean. *Washington's Irish Policy, 1916–1986.* Dublin: Anvil Books, 1987.

Dallek, Robert. *Franklin D. Roosevelt and American Foreign Policy.* New York: Oxford University Press, 1979.

Davis, Troy D. *Dublin's American Policy: Irish American Diplomatic Relations, 1945–1952.* Washington, D.C.: Catholic University of America Press, 1998.

DeConde, Alexander. *Ethnicity, Race, and American Foreign Policy: A History.* Boston: Northeastern University Press, 1992.

De Santis, Vincent. "Eisenhower Revisionism." *Review of Politics* 38 (April 1976): 190–207.

Dimbleby, David, and David Reynolds. *An Ocean Apart: The Relationship between Britain and America in the Twentieth Century.* New York: Vintage Books, 1988.

Donovan, Robert J. *Conflict and Crisis: The Presidency of Harry S. Truman, 1945–1948.* New York: W. W. Norton, 1977.

———. *Tumultuous Years: The Presidency of Harry S. Truman, 1949–1953.* New York: W. W. Norton, 1977.

Dunar, Andrew J. *The Truman Scandals and the Politics of Morality.* Columbia: University of Missouri Press, 1984.

Dur, Philip. *Jefferson Caffery of Louisiana: Ambassador of Revolutions.* Lafayette: University of Southwestern Louisiana Libraries, 1982.

———. "Jefferson Caffery of Louisiana: Highlights of His Career." Parts 1 and 2. *Louisiana History* 15 (1974); 16 (1975).

Edmonds, Robin. *Setting the Mould: The United States and Britain, 1945–1950.* New York: Oxford University Press, 1986.

Edwards, Owen Dudley. *Macaulay.* New York: St. Martin's Press, 1988.

Fanning, Ronan. "The United States and Irish Participation in NATO: The Debate of 1950." *Irish Studies in International Affairs* 1:1 (1979): 38–48.

Farwell, Byron. *Queen Victoria's Little Wars.* New York: W. W. Norton, 1972.

Ferrell, Robert H. *Choosing Truman: The Democratic Convention of 1944.* Columbia: University of Missouri Press, 2000.

————. *Harry S. Truman: A Life.* Columbia: University of Missouri Press, 1994.

Foreman-Peck, James. *A History of the World Economy: International Economic Relations since 1850.* New York: Harvester-Wheatsheaf, 1995.

Fossedal, Gregory A. *Our Finest Hour: Will Clayton, the Marshall Plan, and the Triumph of Democracy.* Stanford: Hoover Institution Press, 1993.

Foster, R. F. *Modern Ireland, 1600–1972.* London: Penguin Books, 1982.

Gaddis, John Lewis. "The Cold War, the Long Peace, and the Future." In *The End of the Cold War: Its Meaning and Implications,* ed. Michael J. Hogan, 21–38. New York: Cambridge University Press, 1992.

————. "The Long Peace: Elements of Stability in the Postwar International System." In *The Cold War and After: Prospects for Peace,* ed. Sean Lynn-Jones. Cambridge: MIT Press, 1991.

————. *The Long Peace: Inquiries into the History of the Cold War.* New York: Oxford University Press, 1982.

————. *Strategies of Containment: A Critical Appraisal of Postwar American National Security Policy.* New York: Oxford University Press, 1982.

————. *The United States and the Origins of the Cold War, 1941–1947.* New York: Columbia University Press, 1972.

————. "Was the Truman Doctrine a Real Turning Point?" *Foreign Affairs* 52 (Jan. 1974): 386–402.

————. *We Now Know: Rethinking Cold War History.* New York: Oxford University Press, 1997.

Gallagher, Thomas M. *Paddy's Lament: Ireland, 1846–1847, Prelude to Hatred.* New York: Harcourt Brace Jovanovich, 1982.

Gallicchio, Marc S. *The Cold War Begins in Asia: American East Asian Policy and the Fall of the Japanese Empire.* New York: Columbia University Press, 1988.

Gardner, Lloyd. *Architects of Illusion: Men and Ideas in American Foreign Policy, 1941–1949.* Chicago: Quadrangle Books, 1970.

Gasiorowski, Mark J. "The 1953 Coup d'Etat in Iran." *International Journal of Middle East Studies* 19 (Aug. 1987): 261–86.

————. *U.S. Foreign Policy and the Shah: Building a Client State in Iran.* Ithaca: Cornell University Press, 1991.

Gellman, Irwin. *Secret Affairs: Franklin Roosevelt, Cordell Hull, Sumner Welles.* Baltimore: Johns Hopkins University Press, 1995.

Goldworthy, David. *Colonial Issues in British Politics, 1945–1961: From "Colonial Development" to "Wind of Change."* Oxford: Clarendon Press, 1971.

Goode, James F. *The United States and Iran, 1946–1951: The Diplomacy of Neglect.* New York: St. Martin's Press, 1989.

Gopal, Sarvepalli. *Jawaharlal Nehru: A Biography.* New Delhi: Oxford University Press, 1989.

Gordon, Joel. *Nasser's Blessed Movement: Egypt's Free Officers and the July Revolution.* New York: Oxford University Press, 1992.

Graebner, Norman A. "Dean Acheson." In his *An Uncertain Tradition: American Secretaries of State in the Twentieth Century,* 267–88. New York: McGraw-Hill, 1961.

Graff, Frank. *Strategy of Involvement: A Diplomatic Biography of Sumner Welles, 1933–1943.* Ann Arbor: University of Michigan Press, 1971.

Greenstein, Fred I. "Can Personality and Politics Be Studied Systematically?" *Political Psychology* 13:1 (March 1992): 105–28.

Greenstein, Fred I., and Richard H. Immerman. "What Did Eisenhower Tell Kennedy about Indochina? The Politics of Misperception." *Journal of American History* 79 (Sept. 1992): 568–87.

Gupta, Sisir. *Kashmir: A Study in India-Pakistan Relations.* Bombay: Asia Publishing House, 1966.

Hahn, Peter L. *The United States, Great Britain, and Egypt, 1945–1956: Strategy and Diplomacy in the Early Cold War.* Chapel Hill: University of North Carolina Press, 1991.

Hahn, Peter L., and Mary Ann Heiss, eds. *Empire and Revolution: The United States and the Third World since 1945.* Columbus: Ohio State University Press, 2001.

Halle, Louis J. *The Nature of Power: Civilization and Foreign Policy.* New York: Columbia University Press, 1955.

Hamburger, Philip. "Mr. Secretary." Parts 1 and 2. *New Yorker* (Nov. 12, 1949): 39–42; (Nov. 19, 1949): 40–42.

Hamby, Alonzo. *Man of the People: A Life of Harry S. Truman.* New York: Oxford University Press, 1995.

Harbutt, Fraser. *The Iron Curtain.* New York: Oxford University Press, 1986.

Harper, John Lamberton. *American Visions of Europe: Franklin D. Roosevelt, George F. Kennan, and Dean G. Acheson.* New York: Cambridge University Press, 1994.

Harris, Kenneth. *Attlee.* London: Weidenfeld and Nicolson, 1982.

Hathaway, Robert. *Ambiguous Partnership.* New York: Columbia University Press, 1981.

———. *Great Britain and the United States: Special Relations since World War II.* Boston: Twayne, 1990.

Heimsath, Charles H., and Surjit Mansingh. *A Diplomatic History of Modern India.* Calcutta: Allied Publishers, 1971.

Heiss, Mary Ann. *Empire and Nationhood: The United States, Great Britain, and Iranian Oil, 1950–1954.* New York: Columbia University Press, 1997.

Hennessy, Peter. *Never Again: Britain, 1945–1951.* New York: Pantheon Books, 1993.

Hess, Gary. *America Encounters India, 1941–1947.* Baltimore: Johns Hopkins University Press, 1971.

———. "Franklin Roosevelt and Indochina." *Journal of American History* 59 (Sept. 1982): 359–68.

———. *The United States Emergence as a Southeast Asian Power, 1945–1950.* New York: Columbia University Press, 1987.

Hogan, Michael J., ed. *The End of the Cold War: Its Meaning and Implications.* New York: Cambridge University Press, 1992.

Hull, Roger. *The Irish Triangle: Conflict in Northern Ireland.* Princeton: Princeton University Press, 1976.

Hutton, Patrick. *History as an Art of Memory.* Burlington: University of Vermont Press, 1993.

Immerman, Richard. "Confessions of an Eisenhower Revisionist: 'An Agonizing Reappraisal.'" *Diplomatic History* 14 (summer 1990): 319–42.

———. *John Foster Dulles: Piety, Pragmatism, and Power in U.S. Foreign Policy.* Wilmington, Del.: Scholarly Resources, 1999.

———. "Psychology." In *Explaining the History of American Foreign Relations,* ed. Michael J. Hogan and Thomas G. Paterson, 151–64. Cambridge: Cambridge University Press, 1991.

———, ed. *John Foster Dulles and the Diplomacy of the Cold War.* Princeton: Princeton University Press, 1990.

Immerman, Richard, and Robert Bowie. *Waging Peace: How Eisenhower Shaped an Enduring Cold War Strategy.* New York: Oxford University Press, 1998.

Isaacson, Walter, and Evan Thomas. *The Wise Men: Six Friends and the World They Made: Acheson, Bohlen, Harriman, Kennan, Lovett, McCloy.* New York: Simon and Schuster, 1986.

James, Lawrence. *The Rise and Fall of the British Empire.* New York: St. Martin's Press, 1997.

Jervis, Robert. *Perceptions and Misperceptions in International Relations.* Princeton: Princeton University Press, 1976.

Jones, Joseph M. *The Fifteen Weeks.* New York: Viking Press, 1955.

Jordan, Anthony J. *Sean MacBride: A Biography.* Dublin: Blackwater Press, 1993.

Kammen, Michael. *In the Past Lane: Historical Perspectives on American Culture.* New York: Oxford University Press, 1997.

———. *The Mystic Chords of Memory: The Transformation of Tradition in American Culture.* New York: Vintage, 1993.

Kaufman, Victor S. *Confronting Communism: U.S. and British Policies toward China.* Columbia: University of Missouri Press, 2001.

Kennan, George F. *American Diplomacy, 1900–1950.* Chicago: University of Chicago Press, 1950.

———. *Memoirs, 1925–1950.* New York: Bantam, 1967.

———. *Memoirs, 1950–1963.* New York: Bantam, 1972.

———. *On Dealing with the Communist World.* New York: Harper and Row, for the Council on Foreign Relations, 1964.

———. *Russia and the West under Lenin and Stalin.* Boston: Little, Brown, 1961.

Keogh, Dermot. *Twentieth-Century Ireland: Nation and State.* New York: St. Martin's, 1994.

Kimball, Warren. *The Juggler: Franklin Roosevelt as Wartime Statesman.* Princeton: Princeton University Press, 1991.

Kissinger, Henry. *Diplomacy.* New York: Simon and Schuster, 1994.

———. *A World Restored: Metternich, Castlereagh, and the Problems of Peace, 1812–1822.* Boston: Houghton Mifflin, 1957.

Kuniholm, Bruce. *The Origins of the Cold War in the Near East: Great Power Conflict and Diplomacy in Iran, Turkey, and Greece.* Princeton: Princeton University Press, 1984.

Kunz, Diane B. *Butter and Guns: America's Cold War Economic Diplomacy.* New York: Free Press, 1997.

Kux, Dennis. *Estranged Democracies: India and the United States, 1941–1991.* Thousand Oaks, Calif.: Sage Publications, 1994.

Lacey, Michael J., ed. *The Truman Presidency.* Cambridge: Cambridge University Press, 1989.

LeFeber, Walter. "Kissinger and Acheson." *Political Science Quarterly* 92 (summer 1977): 189–97.

Larson, Deborah Welch. *Origins of Containment: A Psychological Explanation.* Princeton: Princeton University Press, 1985.

Lee, J. J. *Ireland, 1912–1985: Politics and Society.* New York: Cambridge University Press, 1989.

Lee, Steven Hugh. *Outposts of Empire: Korea, Vietnam, and the Origins of the Cold War in Asia, 1949–1954.* Montreal and Kingston: McGill-Queen's University Press, 1995.

Leffler, Melvyn. *A Preponderance of Power: National Security, the Truman Administration, and the Cold War.* Stanford: Stanford University Press, 1992.

Leyburn, James G. *The Scotch-Irish: A Social History.* Chapel Hill: University of North Carolina Press, 1962.

Lieberson, Godard. *The Irish Uprising, 1916–1922.* New York: Macmillan, 1966.

Louis, Wm. Roger. *The British Empire in the Middle East, 1945–1951: Arab Nationalism, the United States, and Postwar Imperialism.* Oxford: Clarendon Press, 1984.

———. *Imperialism at Bay: The United States and the Decolonization of the British Empire, 1941–1945.* New York: Oxford University Press, 1978.

Louis, Wm. Roger, and Hedley Bull, eds. *The "Special Relationship": Anglo-American Relations since 1945.* Oxford: Clarendon Press, 1986.

Lytle, Mark H. *The Origins of the Iranian-American Alliance, 1941–1953.* New York: Holmes and Meyer, 1987.

Mansfield, Peter. *The British in Egypt.* New York: Holt, Rinehart, and Winston, 1972.

———. *A History of the Middle East.* New York: Viking Press, 1991.

McAuliffe, Mary. "Commentary: Eisenhower, the President." *Journal of American History* 68 (Dec. 1981): 625–32.

McCormick, Thomas J. *America's Half-Century: United States Foreign Policy in the Cold War.* Baltimore: Johns Hopkins University Press, 1989.

McCoy, Donald R. *The Presidency of Harry S. Truman.* Lawrence: University Press of Kansas, 1984.

McCullough, David. *Truman.* New York: Simon and Schuster, 1992.

McDowell, Robert B. *Ireland in the Age of Imperialism and Revolution, 1760–1801.* New York: Oxford University Press, 1979.

McGarry, John, and Brendan O'Leary. *Explaining Northern Ireland: Broken Images.* Oxford: Blackwell Publishers, 1995.

McGhee, George C. *Envoy to the Middle World: Adventures in Diplomacy.* New York: Harper and Row, 1983.

———. *On the Frontline of the Cold War: An Ambassador Reports.* Westport, Conn.: Praeger, 1997.

McGlone, Robert E. "John Brown's Family and Harper's Ferry." In *Memory and American History,* ed. David Thelen. Bloomington: Indiana University Press, 1990.

McGlothen, Ronald. *Controlling the Waves: Dean Acheson and U.S. Foreign Policy in Asia.* New York: W. W. Norton, 1993.

McLellan, David. *Dean Acheson: The State Department Years.* New York: Dodd-Mead, 1976.

McMahon, Robert J. *The Cold War on the Periphery: The United States, India, and Pakistan.* New York: Columbia University Press, 1994.

————. *Colonialism and the Cold War: The United States and the Struggle for Indonesian Independence, 1945–1949.* Ithaca: Cornell University Press, 1981.

————. "Eisenhower and Third World Nationalism: A Critique of the Revisionists." *Political Science Quarterly* 101 (1986): 453–73.

————. *The Limits of Empire: The United States and Southeast Asia since World War II.* New York: Columbia University Press, 1999.

————. "United States Cold War Strategy in South Asia: Making a Military Commitment to Pakistan, 1947–1954." *Journal of American History* (Dec. 1988): 812–40.

Melanson, Richard A., and David Mayers, eds. *Reevaluating Eisenhower: American Foreign Policy in the Fifties.* Urbana: University of Illinois Press, 1987.

Merrill, Dennis. *Bread and the Ballot: The United States and Indian Economic Development.* Chapel Hill: University of North Carolina Press, 1990.

Messer, Robert. *The End of an Alliance: James F. Byrnes, Roosevelt, Truman, and the Origins of the Cold War.* Chapel Hill: University of North Carolina Press, 1982.

Millgate, Jane. *Macaulay.* London: Routledge and Kegan Paul, 1973.

Moorehead, Alan. *The White Nile.* New York: Harper and Brothers, 1960.

Morgenthau, Hans J. *In Defense of the National Interest: A Critical Examination of American Foreign Policy.* New York: Knopf, 1951.

————. *Politics among Nations: The Struggle for Power and Peace.* 6th ed. New York: Knopf, 1985.

————. *Vietnam and the United States.* Washington, D.C.: Public Affairs Press, 1965.

Morris, James. *Heaven's Command: An Imperial Progress.* New York: Harcourt Brace Jovanovich, 1973.

Mulvaney, C. P. *The History of the Northwest Rebellion of 1883.* Toronto: A. H. Hovey, 1885.

Nanda, B. R., ed. *Indian Foreign Policy: The Nehru Years.* Delhi: Vikas Publishing House, 1976.

Nitze, Paul H. *From Hiroshima to Glasnost.* New York: Grove Weidenfeld, 1989.

Noer, Thomas J. *Cold War and Black Liberation: The United States and White Rule in Africa, 1948–1968.* Columbia: University of Missouri Press, 1985.

Novick, Peter. *That Noble Dream: The "Objectivity Question" and the American Historical Profession.* New York: Cambridge University Press, 1988.

O'Clery, Conor. *Daring Diplomacy: Clinton's Secret Search for Peace in Ireland.* Boulder: Roberts Rinehart, 1997.

O'Malley, Padraig. *The Uncivil Wars.* Boston: Houghton Mifflin, 1983.

Orpen, Goddard. *Ireland under the Normans.* Oxford: Clarendon Press, 1968.

Orwell, George. *Burmese Days.* London: Secker and Warburg, 1949.

Pandey, B. N. *Nehru.* New York: Stein and Day, 1976.

Paterson, Thomas G., and Robert J. McMahon, eds. *The Origins of the Cold War.* Lexington, Ky.: D. C. Heath, 1991.

Pearson, Drew. *Diaries, 1949–1959.* New York: Holt, Rinehart, and Winston, 1974.

Pemberton, William E. *Harry S. Truman: Fair Dealer and Cold Warrior.* Boston: Twayne, 1989.

Phillips, Cabell. *The Truman Presidency: The History of a Triumphant Succession.* New York: Macmillan, 1966.

Pogue, Forrest. *George C. Marshall: Statesman, 1945–1949.* New York: Viking Press, 1987.

Porter, Bernard. *The Lion's Share: A Short History of British Imperialism, 1850–1983.* London: Longman, 1989.

Potter, G. R. *Macaulay.* London: Longman, 1959.

Qaimmaqami, Linda Wills. "The Catalyst of Nationalization: Max Thornburg and the Failure of Private Sector Developmentalism in Iran, 1947–1951." *Diplomatic History* (winter 1995): 1–31.

Rahman, Mushtaqur. *Divided Kashmir: Old Problems, New Opportunities for India, Pakistan, and the Kashmiri People.* Boulder: Lynne Rienner Publishers, 1976.

Ranelagh, John. *A Short History of Ireland.* Cambridge: Cambridge University Press, 1983.

Reynolds, David. *Britannia Overruled: British Policy and World Power in the Twentieth Century.* London: Longman, 1991.

———. *Rich Relations: The American Occupation of Britain, 1942–1945.* New York: Random House, 1995.

Roberts, Richard, and David Kynaston, eds. *The Bank of England: Money, Power, and Influence, 1694–1994.* Oxford: Clarendon Press, 1995.

Rosenthal, Joel. *The Righteous Realists.* Baton Rouge: Louisiana State University Press, 1991.

Rubin, Barry. *Paved with Good Intentions: The American Experience and Iran.* New York: Oxford University Press, 1980.

Ruddy, T. Michael. *The Cautious Diplomat: Charles E. Bohlen and the Soviet Union, 1929–1969.* Kent, Ohio: Kent State University Press, 1986.

Sherwood, Elizabeth D. *Allies in Crisis*. New Haven: Yale University Press, 1990.

Shuckburgh, Evelyn. *Descent to Suez: Foreign Office Diaries, 1951–1956*. New York: W. W. Norton, 1986.

Shwadran, Benjamin. *The Middle East, Oil, and the Great Powers*. Rev. ed. New York: John Wiley and Sons, 1973.

Singh, Anita Inder. *The Limits of British Influence: South Asia and the Anglo-America Relationship, 1947–1956*. New York: St. Martin's Press, 1993.

Smith, Gaddis. *Dean Acheson*. New York: Cooper Square, 1972.

Smith, Michael Joseph. *Realist Thought from Weber to Kissinger*. Baton Rouge: Louisiana State University Press, 1987.

Smith, Tony. *America's Mission: The United States and the Worldwide Struggle for Democracy in the Twentieth Century*. Princeton: Princeton University Press, 1994.

Steel, Ronald. *Pax Americana*. New York: Viking Press, 1967.

Stone, I. F. *The Truman Era*. New York: Random House, 1972.

Tahmankar, D. V. *Sardar Patel*. London: George Allen and Unwin, 1970.

Thelen, David, ed. *Memory and American History*. Bloomington: Indiana University Press, 1990.

Thomas, Raju G. C., ed. *Perspectives on Kashmir: The Roots of Conflict in South Asia*. Boulder: Westview Press, 1992.

Thompson, Kenneth W. *Political Realism and the Crisis of World Politics*. Princeton: Princeton University Press, 1960.

Thompson, Kenneth W., and Henry J. Morgenthau, eds. *Principles and Problems of International Politics: Selected Readings*. New York: Knopf, 1950.

Thomson, David. *England in the Twentieth Century*. Baltimore: Penguin Books, 1965.

Truman, Harry S. *Memoirs: 1945, Year of Decisions*. New York: Signet, 1955.

———. *Memoirs: Years of Trial and Hope, 1946–1952*. New York: Signet, 1956.

Tucker, Nancy B. *Patterns in the Dust: Chinese-American Relations and the Recognition Controversy*. New York: Columbia University Press, 1983.

———. *Taiwan, Hong Kong, and the United States, 1945–1992: Uncertain Friendships*. New York: Twayne, 1994.

Vatikiotis, P. J. *The History of Modern Egypt: From Muhammad Ali to Mubarak*. Baltimore: Johns Hopkins University Press, 1991.

Watt, D. C. *Succeeding John Bull: America in Britain's Place*. New York: Cambridge University Press, 1984.

Wedgwood, C. V. *Richelieu and the French Monarchy*. London: English Universities Press, 1958.

Weil, Martin. *A Pretty Good Club: The Founding Fathers of the U.S. Foreign Service.* New York: W. W. Norton, 1978.

Welles, Benjamin. *Sumner Welles: FDR's Global Strategist.* New York: St. Martin's Press, 1997.

Wicker, Elmus. "Roosevelt's 1933 Monetary Experiment." *Journal of American History* 57:4 (March 1971): 864–79.

Williams, Desmond. *The Irish Struggle, 1916–1926.* Toronto: University of Toronto Press, 1966.

Wirsing, Robert G. *India, Pakistan, and the Kashmir Dispute: On Regional Conflict and Its Resolution.* New York: St. Martin's Press, 1994.

Wolpert, Stanley. *Nehru: A Tryst with Destiny.* New York: Oxford University Press, 1996.

———. *A New History of India.* New York: Oxford University Press, 1982.

Woods, Randall Bennet, and Howard Jones. *Dawning of the Cold War: The United States' Quest for Order.* Athens: University of Georgia Press, 1991.

Yapp, M. E. *The Near East since the First World War.* New York: Longman, 1991.

Yergin, Daniel. *The Prize: The Epic Quest for Oil, Money, and Power.* New York: Simon and Schuster, 1992.

———. *Shattered Peace.* Boston: Houghton Mifflin, 1977.

Index